Dismantling Racism, One Relationship at a Time

CONTEMPORARY ISSUES IN INTERPERSONAL COMMUNICATION AND HUMAN RELATIONSHIPS

Series Editor

Pamela Kalbfleisch, University of North Dakota

This scholarly book series focuses on interpersonal communication as the driving force in human relationships. The books in this series consider contemporary issues using interpersonal communication and human relationships research.

Titles in the Series

Mentoring, Sponsoring, and Coaching: Building Empowerment through Interpersonal Communication Theory by Pamela Kalbfleisch
Dismantling Racism, One Relationship at a Time by Tina M. Harris

Dismantling Racism, One Relationship at a Time

Tina M. Harris

ROWMAN & LITTLEFIELD
Lanham • Boulder • New York • London

Published by Rowman & Littlefield
An imprint of The Rowman & Littlefield Publishing Group, Inc.
4501 Forbes Boulevard, Suite 200, Lanham, Maryland 20706
www.rowman.com

86-90 Paul Street, London EC2A 4NE

Copyright © 2023 by The Rowman & Littlefield Publishing Group, Inc.

All rights reserved. No part of this book may be reproduced in any form or by any electronic or mechanical means, including information storage and retrieval systems, without written permission from the publisher, except by a reviewer who may quote passages in a review.

British Library Cataloguing in Publication Information Available

Library of Congress Cataloging-in-Publication Data

Names: Harris, Tina M., author.
Title: Dismantling racism, one relationship at a time / Tina M. Harris.
Description: Lanham : Rowman & Littlefield, [2023] | Series: Contemporary issues in interpersonal communication and human relationships | Includes bibliographical references and index.
Identifiers: LCCN 2023032098 (print) | LCCN 2023032099 (ebook) | ISBN 9781538152560 (cloth ; alk. paper) | ISBN 9781538186909 (paperback ; alk. paper) | ISBN 9781538152577 (ebook)
Subjects: LCSH: Racism--United States. | Intercultural communication--United States. | Interpersonal communication--United States. | Interpersonal relations--United States. | United States--Race relations. | United States--Ethnic relations.
Classification: LCC E184.A1 H3356 2023 (print) | LCC E184.A1 (ebook) | DDC 305.800973–dc23/eng/20230718
LC record available at https://lccn.loc.gov/2023032098
LC ebook record available at https://lccn.loc.gov/2023032099

Contents

Acknowledgments	vii
Foreword	ix
Preface	xv
Chapter 1: The Critical Need for Interracial Communication in a State of Racial Unrest	1
Chapter 2: Establishing an Essential Vocabulary	25
Chapter 3: Interracial Communication within the Family	41
Chapter 4: Interracial Friendships beyond the "One Friend Rule"	59
Chapter 5: Interracial Romantic Relationships and the Trickle-Down Theory	81
Chapter 6: Making Interracial Communication Possible in the Workplace	101
Chapter 7: Intentionality and the Fight against Racism	119
References	139
Index	159
About the Author	165

Acknowledgments

Writing this book would not have been possible were it not for so many people who stood by me in body and spirit throughout the process. I must acknowledge God as my Lord and Savior for giving me the strength, wisdom, and temerity to write a book about race during such tenuous times in the United States regarding race relations. He has guided me throughout this process in a way that has brought much joy and affirmation concerning my purpose. I stayed the course because this was a task I was more than willing to undertake; I wanted to create a resource accessible to both scholars and society that has the potential to bring about racial healing and reconciliation.

Thank you to Dr. Pamela Kalbfleisch for creating this opportunity for me to further realize the work I have been pursuing since my dissertation. Thank you for seeing my vision for this book and helping it manifest. I would be remiss if I did not extend a special thanks to Drs. Roxanne Parrott, Celeste Condit, Don Rubin, and Tom Huebner for the very instrumental role each has played in me being where I am today. Thank you for seeing things in me that I did not know were there. I must also recognize the support and love that esteemed giants in the field, Drs. Dorothy Pennington, Orlando Taylor, and Marsha Houston, continue to provide. I am indebted to you for all each of you has done for me.

I thank my mother, Pastor Mamie Harris, and my father, the late Reverend Joseph, for their guidance, unconditional love, and support throughout my life. I am eternally grateful that you laid a solid foundation of faith for me and had confidence in my potential and future that has undoubtedly gotten me where I am today. Thank you, Dwayne Smith (Mom's husband), for entertaining my many discussions about race; they are always appreciated. Thank you to Aunt Joann Delaney and Aunt Berdie Ann McCune for always being there for me, too. I love you both.

Thank you, my siblings—Greg (Theresa), Ken, and Sonya Harris—for your support and love even when none of this made sense. To my sisters Andrea Jones Black, Lauren Stripling, Dr. Jennifer F. Wood, Donna Lowry

Reid, and Tracy Lott, thank you for your unwavering belief in and support of me every step of the way. I extend a special thanks to Andrea, Lauren, Ken, and Jennifer for being my sounding boards, informal reviewers reading bits and pieces along the way, and cheerleaders when I needed a push and the encouragement to press on. I appreciate you more than you know. Also, thank you to my sisters Reva Moore, Shaun Hicks (and the girls), Elanda Pellicia, and Dr. Tammy Sanders Henderson; I love and appreciate you.

Thank you to my sisters from our Sister Circle early in our careers: Drs. Marsha Houston, Katherine Hendrix, Olga Davis, and Janice Hamlet. I am eternally grateful for the bond we developed so many years ago when we were trying to learn how to navigate the crazy world of academe. I value your unwavering love, friendship, and the many laughs along the way.

Thank you to my Louisiana State University–Manship sister–doctor–colleagues Drs. Meghan Sanders, Jinx Broussard, Asha Winfield, and Sherella Cupid. I so appreciate the Zoom sessions (thanks, Meghan!), friendship, and the space that you each provided me to be me. I am eternally grateful to you and am blessed to call each of you my sister, friend, and colleague.

Thank you to my academic siblings Drs. Ron Jackson, Jennifer Samp, Shinsuke Eguchi, Robin Means Coleman, Kimberly Moffitt, David Oh, Marcus Coleman, Loren Saxton Coleman, Kathleen Glenister Roberts, Gina Castle Bell, Cerise Glenn Manigault, Karla Scott, Trina Wright Dixon, and Travis Dixon. You have been my constant cheerleaders, supporters, and confidantes through too much to retell. If I have forgotten anyone, then I ask you to charge it to my head and not my heart.

I thank my advisees and graduate assistants—both past and present—for your understanding as I balanced mentoring, writing, and so much more over the last few years. I appreciate your support and flexibility. Special thanks to Aarum Youn-Heil, Rockia Harris, Sarah Carpenter, Nick Ashton, Doria Martingayle, Akie F. Wenk, and Malcolm Evans. Geaux Tigers!

Lastly, I thank every single student I have taught or encountered in any way at every university I have taught at, given a lecture at, or visited for other reasons. I have been blessed to walk the journey with you through engaging, difficult, emotional, volatile, enlightening, and heartfelt discussions. I am a better person because of each of you. Thank you, thank you, thank you.

Foreword

BEFOREHAND THOUGHTS (A PRELUDE TO THE FOREWORD)

As I reflected on the privilege afforded me to write the foreword for this book, it occurred to me that its release would likely coincide with the seventieth anniversary of the historic 1954 *Brown v. Board of Education of Topeka, Kansas* court decision, whose anniversary events are already being planned a year in advance, and it is perspicuous that the communication discipline should play a role in those race-based conversations and critical perspectives. The landmark case centered on race and its role in determining the outcome of the quality of education for Black and white pupils in the American system of racially segregated schools and facilities. The court ruled that the then racially segregated schools were inherently unequal and that Black students were greatly disadvantaged, a situation in need of rectifying. The ruling implied the need for a racial power balance through desegregating a system whose unequal education was but one of many imbalances of power and discrimination across racial lines. Given the current racial debates and contestations about critical race theory and diversity, equity, inclusion, and belonging, this book could not have been more timely.

As a "prelude" to the foreword, I find a reading of this book's contents shows strong work that offers outstanding critical perspectives through the lens of communication theory, scholarly research, and critical observations and visions; what I think is unique about this book is that it integratively informs the reader of the historical and sociological contexts of the problems, the theory, and the practical implications given in the contents, and it builds in ways for participants to examine their own identity in the process. In communication literature, this is sometimes referred to as critical reflexivity (my labeling). This is quite important because some readers may understand a book's contents in terms of theory, commentary, analysis, and prescriptions for improvement, but do not grasp the historical background and context that surround an author's perspective or examine their own identity in the process. Because Dr. Harris gives a brief overview of the book's chapters in her chapter 1, I need not repeat the overview. Instead, in the foreword, I choose to highlight certain chapters to illustrate this book's contents: specifically, chapters 1, 3, 6, and 7.

Chapter 1 begins with a report and poetic rendering of the impact and implications of the George Floyd murder case of 2020, with which most readers are familiar the world over. The George Floyd murder and, to a lesser extent, the murder of Breonna Taylor serve as a portent and historical contextualization that runs throughout the Harris book as reminders of the precipitous role of racism and racist events in the United States. Chapter 3, on the effects of race on family orientations toward racial realities in America, shows the role of the history of race relations as a key socializer of family attitudes toward race and Black survival, with, for example, the inscribing of racial cautions on the ways Black families socialize their children, especially boys, to practice safe behaviors around law enforcement officials. Similarly, chapter 6 discusses the reinscribing of racist ideologies in large interracial contexts, such in the workplace and penal institutions. These chapters, among others, point to the sociology and social context of the ways racial power is inscribed and reinscribed in the United States, based on racial identity, which is the dominant marker is U.S. race relations and interracial communication. Chapter 7 is the culmination of the author's thoughts and her way to clinch the text and present a model that is both descriptive and prescriptive. This book is powerful and unique!

FOREWORD

Scholar, author, poet Dr. Tina M. Harris begins chapter 1 of this book with a captivating poem she wrote on the murder of George Floyd, a poem filled with imagery, pathos, metaphor, alliteration, enjambment, meter, and repetition and that touches the reader's sensibilities. The George Floyd murder of 2020 precipitates an assessment and examination of race relations. And readers can wonder if it is coincidental that George Floyd's dying words, "I can't breathe," are coincidental to the dying words, "I can't breathe," uttered by Eric Garner, the forty-three-year-old Black male murdered in 2014 in New York by police officers who had put him in a choke hold on the street after confronting him.

While this book can basically be described as a blend of theory, practice, prescriptions, and commentary on interracial communication in various contexts, it is much more. The author's "voice" comes through in her discussion modality, with portions of her text written as a dynamic, dialogical interaction with other portions of the text, creating something of a thesis-antithesis-synthesis mix. Make no mistake, though, the author's perspective shines through in the textual engagement of readers. In an interracial communication book that I coauthored many years ago, I introduced *power* as a dominant variable in interracial communication. I still hold the view that power is a dominant variable in interracial communication and in race relations in general. Dr. Harris's book calls into question whether a power balance has been achieved in all facets of American race relations and whether there is even not only a widespread conscious awareness of the need to rectify the long-standing, inherited power imbalance but also a will to create true racial equality. She describes how race plays a role in determining how white Americans have both an ascribed and an inherited societal power due to structures designed for the purpose of directly benefiting them. As a result, they have historically been beneficiaries of these systems (chapter 1), and she states perspicuously that "systemic changes are essential," a prescription she foregrounds by the stark facts of the unceasing killings of unarmed Black men and women by police officers, precipitating racially integrated protests and rallies read as a common outcry against the incivility and brutal attacks against Black bodies under suspicious motivation. By using racial unrest and civil disturbances as an undeniable clarion call for action, Harris's introductory section foregrounds a necessary prescription for change, for rallying those of goodwill to engage in communication in such a way as to create an egalitarian relationship among cohorts in promoting effective change. Early on in the book, Harris uses the label "global citizen(s)" for white people with power and goodwill who make a positive difference in race relations—those sensitive to the ways they can make a positive difference across racial lines, often through their own initiatives.

Becoming global citizens has its challenges, though, according to Harris, and requires a conscious state of "wokeness," given the current state of race relations in the United States, and Harris situates our own field of communication as being the key component, agent, agency, and generational arbiter to drive America to racial equality by "addressing the different forms of systemic oppression plaguing the United States and the world."

This comes at a time when many systems in America are pushing back against "woke" policies such as the teaching of critical race theory in educational systems or using diversity, equity, inclusion, and belonging as considerations in the hiring of faculty and staff at their institutions; because these policies are a threat, Harris's book carefully constructs the bases and assumptions necessary for promoting enduring change in attitudes, behaviors, and sentiments across racial lines, prescribing that participants (remember her "global citizens" concept) must be self-reflexive, recognize the power of language, accept the reality of racism and its implications, engage in honest communication with self and others, adopt perspective taking, and commit to being vulnerable, even when it hurts in interpersonal, family, friendship, romance, and workplace settings.

One of the many strengths of Harris's book is her recognition that adhering to simplistic, linear prescriptions for improving interracial communication may be misleading, one-dimensional, and overly simplistic, which could undermine the integrity of what should be a more complex calculus, involving outcomes that derive from preexisting attitudes, misperceptions, and suspicions of intent among interracial communicators. Her ability to problematize the calculus involved in meaningful interracial communication precludes readers' perceiving interracial communication as simplistic, one-dimensional, and formulaic. In quoting Herda (2017, p. 144), Harris informs, "Optimal conditions are not guaranteed in real-world settings," leading her to recognize that interracial communication is "simultaneously beautiful and complex." The need for mutual trust, vulnerability, respect, honesty, risk taking, and goodwill in interracial communication is a prerequisite for positive outcomes.

Shifting to chapter 3, Harris calls attention to the varying degrees to which race and conversations about race are centered within family units, the family being the primary socializing agent for many of us. For Black socialization for survival in America, Black parents see a need to have "the talk" about racial protection and safety, especially for male children, in terms of prescriptions and proscriptions for survival, such as how to behave in nonsuspicious ways when encountered by law enforcement officers, since Black males (and females) have been subjected to harmful attacks when making suspicious verbal and nonverbal moves when encountered or stopped by law enforcement officers, especially in high-context, volatile interactions, such as while driving. Because the family is the social unit responsible for teaching values, social and interpersonal norms, and expectations for attitudes and behaviors, Harris calls attention to differences in how race matters when children are socialized. Studies show that Black families tend to have more discussions about race than white families, especially in times of racial crisis or unrest provoked by violence against Blacks in public spaces. On the other hand, while white families reportedly talk less about race, and the many who do adopt a colorblind mentality or see race/racism as inconsequential, Harris sees this as a privilege not being afforded to Black families and sees a colorblind view of society as problematic because it rejects the reality of systemic oppression and its impact on everyone, including those the system benefits. In readers' minds, this presents something of a dilemma for white nonprejudiced families, which begs the question of how should they talk about race to their children. Nevertheless, Harris presents the view that nondiscussion of race/racism is not an option. This reminds me of a strategy used by activists during civil rights era. Noncommittal to the cause of equality for Black people was criticized by civil rights activists through a strategy called "polarization," which reasons that you cannot be neutral; you are either a part of the problem or a part of the solution. Neutrality is a poor choice, Harris believes, because of "the material consequences racism has on everyone, especially people of color."

One of the challenges of discussing race/racism and family relations that Harris intimates is the different ways families are composed, with various biological and adoptive forms giving different senses of community. Nevertheless, race and racism are topics that people of color in the United States cannot escape, regardless of their family structure and composition. By the way, another group composition about which I read recently in another publication that can be added is the interaction that occurs in racially integrated group homes for youth. A discussion there on race proved interesting. A white female in a group held the view that she thought it best to keep quiet and not say anything about race. She remarked, "Just don't respond to people and turn the other cheek. It just makes everything easier." She continued, "You are creating more of a problem and you will get yourself in trouble by reacting to racism. If you just ignore it and don't say anything, this will end racism" (Ruffin & Lamar, 2022). In the meantime, a Black girl in the group, watching and listening, showed an expression of disbelief at the white girl's comments. My question for readers: Rather than running the perceived risk of offending someone of another race, is it better to keep quiet during discussions about race? Why or why not? This issue can be discussed in interracial classes, using some of the theory that Harris presents in her book.

Harris begins her chapter 6, on workplace communication, by asserting that although racial identities are born into, but professional/workplace identities are chosen, it is important to realize or remember that society is driven by a racial hierarchy that significantly influences a person's quality of life. In this chapter, Harris reinvokes the George Floyd case and social justice initiatives again to set the context for how these prompted some corporate organizations to take a public stand on the atrocities, which became a referendum (my term) for actions toward creating racial equality in the United States. Harris offers specific prescriptions for changing the racist status quo and power imbalance while acknowledging that "race and gender privilege are threatened by changes in the status quo, . . . and create a dilemma for people of color to navigate these institutions and spaces."

Harris uses chapter 6 as an appropriate site for generating prescriptions for racial changes needed to bring about racial equality, especially in the corporate world regarding equal wealth and capital for Black people. Here she creates a point-counterpoint calculus, showing the breadth and depth of the interactive, dynamic calculus, again intimating the view she stated earlier that improving race relations is simultaneously beautiful and complex. A part of the calculus that stymies the progress of Black people in race relations, according to Harris, is that of the threat posed to whites' ascribed status, causing institutions and people to be "on the wrong side of history" and exacerbating the many existing racial disparities ingrained in our national DNA. In views such as these, Harris demonstrates the importance of establishing sociological and historical contexts for race relations, and she highlights the prescriptions she offers throughout her book. The workplace is the largest of the interracial contexts Harris covers and often mirrors the racism found in larger American society, and so she appropriately enumerates the many barriers to interracial communication that exist in the workplace and institutions.

In her closing chapter 7, Harris demonstrates the importance of *intentionality* as the core for dismantling racism, and she presents a pictorial model called the Racial Intentionality Roadmap and describes its operation. This book offers a remedy for improving interracial communication and race relations, and Harris speaks from extensive scholarship, scholarly honors in many circles (such as being designated a Distinguished Scholar by the National Communication Association), and experience on the topic.

It is my hope that everyone who reads this book will become a participant in, and change agent for, racial equality and goodwill in the United States and globally.

Dorthy L. Pennington
University of Kansas

Preface

The offer to write this book came out of the blue, but I believe Pamela Kalbfleisch of the University of North Dakota might say otherwise. We bumped into each other and had a spontaneous breakfast at the tail end of the National Communication Association's annual conference in 2019, which was in Baltimore, Maryland. While catching up since our advisor/advisee days, Pam invited me to write a book in the interpersonal series she was editing for Rowman and Littlefield. I immediately agreed, excited by the invitation and what I envisioned was an excellent opportunity to say some things I had not been able to comprehensively state in my past (and future) research. I wasn't 100 percent sure of what ideas I was going to specifically articulate, but I knew there was something within me that I needed to "get out." I wanted to use this as a means to express the many thoughts I have had about race and communication throughout my career.

In early 2020, I signed the contract, and for various reasons, drafting the proposal itself seemed to come at the wrong time. I was acclimating to my new role as an endowed chair at a new university with new faculty while learning a new school (i.e., unit) and university culture, and to complicate matters, this was all happening in the midst of a perfect storm of two pandemics, the first being the coronavirus and shortly thereafter the racial unrest following the murder of George Floyd. I pressed pause on the proposal because it paled in comparison to the bigger things going on in the world. Every time I sat down to put pen to paper, per se, I was overwhelmed with sadness, fear, and frustration as the world seemed to be falling apart all around me. Those feelings were compounded as the police brutality against Black Americans seemed to be increasing exponentially. Racial tensions were also fueled by the historic upsurge in Asian American and Pacific Islander (AAPI) hate triggered by the Trump administration's xenophobia against Chinese and Chinese Americans, who were blamed for the coronavirus. While I was trying to process everything along with the rest of the world, I couldn't help but notice how people were using social media platforms as a type of coping mechanism. Whether it was to vent, express allyship, educate, argue, or redefine relationships, Facebook, TikTok, Instagram, and Twitter, among others, were allowing many of us to make sense of the unfathomable state of affairs of the world.

Sometime in July or August 2020, I came to the realization that there was a greater purpose (hopefully) for my book than I originally thought. I had struggled many times when I would sit down to write. The ideas and words wouldn't flow; they were stuck. Eventually, they became unplugged and periodically began to flow in waves over the next two years as I methodically determined the overall purpose of the book and the focus of each prospective chapter. The book was evolving into what I believed was an homage to my long-held belief that our interpersonal relationships are the gateway to dismantling racism. Because racism is structural and race is a human construct, it is abundantly clear that communication is fundamental to changing the status quo when it comes to our increasingly diverse society. More importantly, I believe there is a moral imperative to (re)claim the respectability that should be an inherent part of our humanity. Rather than "tolerate" (I loathe that phrase), I believe we should "appreciate" and "respect" each other as we have been created and commit to reversing the course of history that is presently unfolding before us—hence my title, *Dismantling Racism*.

As I wrote every word of this book, I reflected on the extensive amount of research I had gathered (along with the help of my then graduate assistants Dr. Rockia Harris, Kyle Stanley, Renee Lucas, and Diamond Butler), my own personal and professional experiences, and anecdotal evidence from friends, colleagues, students, and society to process my theory about race relations and how things can and should be. Collectively, everything pushed—and continues to push—me to do my part in eradicating racism, racial prejudice, discrimination, racial biases, and everything else that continues to drive us apart as people. It's a small part, but this book and all the fruit that I hope it bears is an extension of my life's work as someone whose path has been to inspire dialogue and facilitate racial healing.

The process of writing this book—from the invitation to contribute to this series to the final print copy—has been a journey unlike any other I have ever taken. It was written during a dual pandemic and was a daunting yet exciting opportunity for me to articulate my conception of and ideologies regarding race, racial differences, and interracial communication as a Black cisgender heterosexual Christian woman. I have dedicated my professional career and a great deal of my personal life, among many others, to addressing the issue of racism as a form of systemic oppression that has had a profound impact on everyone, whether people want to realize it or not. We live in a world driven by a racial hierarchy that dictates the value we are expected to place on different racial groups, such that lighter, whiter-skinned people are deemed more valuable than darker-skinned people. While racist ideologies are fallacious to their core, they remain an integral part of society in so many ways. I have always been disturbed by such thinking and tried to identify the ways I can do my part in unraveling these systems that are engrained in our core as a society and among people groups.

Many tears of alternating pain and joy were shed as I wrote every word in every chapter on every page of what I believe is the culmination of decades of thinking, contemplating, and processing how to rid the world of one of its many diseases. To be honest, my naïve way of thinking about people was birthed through my parents, Pastor Mamie Harris and the late Reverend Joseph Harris, who were champions for justice in their own right. We lived in Rota, Spain, for four and a half years from when I was two and a half to seven years old, and through this cultural immersion at such a young age, I developed a simple way of thinking about human diversity: Just let people be. Let's love and celebrate each other. Let's commit to creating a society where we can engage in healthy, open, and honest dialogue about race. But this will happen only if we put in the effort. We need to expend the time, energy, and resources necessary for creating racial justice, which in this case is through difficult conversations on an individual and collective level. Ultimately, these conversations will lead to strategic and impactful ways to *dismantle racism, one relationship at a time.*

Chapter 1

The Critical Need for Interracial Communication in a State of Racial Unrest

"I Can't Breathe"

Some stand by idly watching my life leave my body.
Others gasp in horror at the pain I am enduring.
Some assume I did something horrific, tragic
To warrant your knee on my neck for 9 minutes and 29 seconds.
You had time to rethink your plan.
But you did not.
You should have felt remorse.
But you did not.
You stayed on my neck as the cameras rolled.
Unflinching.
Unmoved
Even when I moved no more.
You chose to stay with your knee on my neck
Until I breathed my last breath.
"I can't breathe. I can't breathe,"
I cried. I cried. Until I had no more breath to give.

T. M. Harris (June 3, 2021)

On May 25, 2020, "I can't breathe" were the infamous and tragic last words George Floyd spoke and wailed as police officer Derek Chauvin boldly and coldly knelt on Mr. Floyd's neck as he lay prostrate with his hands cuffed behind his back on the street. He no longer posed a threat, and according to video footage, Mr. Floyd was *never* a physical threat to the officers or others milling around the neighborhood Cubs grocery store. Panicked and scared bystanders valiantly stood by and recorded this tragic incident unfolding before their very eyes in real time. Helpless and unable to do anything, then seventeen-year-old Darnella Frazier recorded the now viral video that literally set the world ablaze. Darnella was innocently walking her nine-year-old cousin near the convenience store Cubs when she was subjected to an all too familiar image of a Black man being violently abused by a police officer. She immediately pulled out her camera to record the incident, unaware of the international protest that would ensue opposing to police brutality against African American men, boys, women, and girls. Were it not for her boldness in recording this tragedy, prosecutors would have no evidence with which to charge Chauvin with murder (Cohen, 2021). Were it not for her, many would remain shrouded in ignorance—willfully and otherwise—regarding the ever-brewing racism that has been woven into the fabric of the United States. There was mounting evidence that Black people of all ages and genders continue to be murdered at a higher rate than other racial groups. But here was visual evidence of an act of police-involved murder that was going unchecked (Cohen, 2021). There was ample time for the other officers who were present to intervene, but they willfully stood there and did nothing to "protect and serve" the very community they were supposed to shield from crime and danger. Many people believed they were complicit in bringing crime and danger *into* the neighborhood.

As the world became engrossed in the video, the atrocity of the murder itself, a real-time recording of a seemingly police-sanctioned murder, and rising racial tensions across the country, there was a clarion call for social justice for African Americans, who remain susceptible to police brutality. The summer of 2020 marked a historic moment when millions of people in the United States and around the world, fueled by anger, outrage, grief, sadness, and emotional fatigue, took to the streets to protest the latest atrocity against Black[1] bodies. They were responding to yet another, but more profound, injustice and the ever-growing evidence that police brutality against Black and Brown people is very real and can potentially end in death. National data support this reality, showing what many already knew: "People of color face a higher likelihood of being killed by police than do white men and women," "that risk peaks in young adulthood," and "men of color face a nontrivial lifetime risk of being killed by police" (Edwards et al., 2019, p. 16793). Not surprisingly, police-involved deaths are the biggest threat to the lives of African Americans, constituting but one type of "health inequality" contributing to the "early mortality for people of color" (Edwards et al., 2019, 16793).

Darnella gave one of a few interviews to discuss how the murder itself and her filming it left an indelible imprint on her mind and soul. Having witnessed a murder, she shared that, although she had seen other Black men be murdered at the hands of police, this was the first time she had seen it in person. She explained, "I knew that he was in pain. I knew that he was another Black man in danger with no power." In her youthful wisdom, Darnella captured, in the following quote, the heaviness that weighs down the hearts of many and feeds an all-consuming fear stemming from police brutality:

> We shouldn't have to walk on eggshells around police officers, the same people that are supposed to protect and serve. We are looked at as thugs, animals, and criminals, all because of the color of our skin. Why are Black people the only ones viewed this way when every race has some type of wrongdoing? None of us are to judge. We are all human. (Cohen, 2021, para. 15)

Darnella prefaced this statement by stressing how her role in capturing vital digital criminal evidence in this historic case caused her life to take an unexpected, dramatic turn. What she anticipated to be a normal day was anything but. Her life and the lives of her family members were forever changed. President Joe Biden called her a "brave young woman" for capturing the video, and actor and social activist Kerry Washington stressed how her bravery shown at that moment "must never be forgotten" (Cohen, 2021, para. 10). Without this documentation, it is likely there would never have been evidence to convict the involved officers or to bring justice to Mr. Floyd. Darnella explained that, as a then-seventeen-year-old, she was unprepared for the horrific incident that would come to have critical meaning in her life. She also stated that she carries a lot of weight from it and does not consider herself a hero: "I was just in the right place at the right time. . . . Behind this smile, behind these awards, behind the publicity, I'm a girl trying to heal from something I am reminded of every day" (Cohen, 2021, paras. 12–13).

To varying degrees, Darnella's words are a window into the souls of millions of Black people, Brown people, and white people who grew increasingly dissatisfied with and frustrated by the U.S. criminal justice system and its long-standing history of racial injustice. The months-long national and international protests attested to the frustration and growing expectation that things must change, especially regarding Black-citizen/white-police relations. Attention was also brought to the overwhelming fear of being killed by police, which has become a normal part of life for many African Americans. The issue of police brutality revealed the ever-growing racial division overtaking the country. On one side were Black (and Brown) people and their allies, who were exasperated by the perceived inaction of local and federal governments in preventing what they believed were race-based assaults and murders by law enforcement. On the other side were mostly whites and some self-labeled racists who either believed in colorblind justice, held allegiances to law enforcement, or perceived such fears of police brutality and unwarranted deaths as speculative and meritless. These resistant positionalities rejected the fact that many other murders were driven by racism and believed instead that victims such as Breonna Taylor, Sandra Bland, Tamir Rice, Daunte

Wright, Rayshard Brooks, Atatiana Jones, Daniel Prude, and countless others were partially responsible for their own murders. The list goes on. Those are but a few of the names of the all-too-many victims who lost their lives at the (literal and virtual) hands of police. Each victim was murdered either while sleeping in their own home, being stopped by police for a baseless or minor traffic violation, falling asleep in their car in a drive-thru, walking home from the store with snacks in hand, or having a mental health crisis. Regardless of the circumstance, their deaths were an extreme and unnecessary price to pay for the institutional racism that continues to define our realities.

In addition to being forced to deal with the racial pandemic, the United States and the world were simultaneously subjected to the health pandemic triggered by the coronavirus, which disrupted reality as we knew it in late 2019. This global pandemic rapidly spread to nearly all countries in the world, debilitating and killing people from nearly all walks of life. What became most evident through this ongoing tragedy was that racial and economic disparities were growing and widening at a deadly rate. According to the American Medical Association (AMA) (n.d.), the populations "the hardest hit have been traditionally minoritized and marginalized people—in particular Black, Brown and Indigenous communities—where health inequities were already present." These disparities became undeniable as television stations, newspapers, social media platforms, and other mass media provided real-time reports on the skyrocketing number of positive tests and deaths related to the coronavirus. The most vulnerable populations were Black, Indigenous, and People of Color (BIPOC), essential workers (i.e., blue-color workers), and individuals with preexisting conditions (AMA, n.d.). The Center for Disease Control (2021) echoed the AMA's conclusions and stated that "the COVID-19 pandemic has brought social and racial injustice and inequity to the forefront of public health."

These dual pandemics were inevitable because appropriate measures were not taken in advance to curb them. Granted, vaccines for viruses like COVID-19 would typically undergo extensive testing prior to distribution; however, the urgency of the pandemic prompted scientists to accelerate the process. The severity and intensity of the pandemics could have been mitigated (to some extent) if we, as a society, were willing to engage in difficult yet necessary conversations regarding the pervasiveness of systemic oppression and its impact on vulnerable and powerless populations. It is critical that, prior to having these honest and potentially productive conversations, all parties confront the hard facts about the history of multiple, intersecting systemic oppressions (i.e., racism, sexism, classism, heterosexism) and their material consequences for everyone. The dominant and numerical-majority groups (i.e., whites) have the most societal power due to structures designed to directly benefit them. As a result, they have historically been the primary beneficiaries of these systems. To be clear, this does not mean individuals have not worked hard to get where they are. Rather, they are a part of a legacy, members of the lineage of benefactors who created these systems, which means they have had fewer obstacles to overcome and have been judged based on their merit. Unfortunately, numerical-minority groups or BIPOC have not been afforded the same opportunities. They are either consciously or subconsciously held to different standards due to their race, sex, gender, sexual orientation, ethnicity, or culture and, as a result, must work twice as hard to attain the same level of success as their white counterparts. These systems are perpetuating disparities and widening the schisms between racial groups, making it even more difficult for equity to be realized.

Systemic changes are essential, and the first step in that direction is being aware that inequities do in fact exist. Beneficiaries might be unaware of, ignorant about, or resistant to being educated about these disparities because they are not adversely impacted in the same way as BIPOC. By extension, their privileged status may be a difficult truth to accept and could trigger guilt or defensiveness, neither of which is the goal of awareness. Instead, the purpose is to engage in perspective taking in order to become a global citizen who is adept at having authentic and meaningful dialogue and interactions with outgroup members. A global citizen is someone who seeks opportunities to make valuable contributions to society and to become educated about cultures and people groups different from theirs. The not-for-profit international organization Oxfam refers to this process as "global citizenship," which "is all about encouraging young people to develop the knowledge, skills and values they need to engage with the world. And it's about the belief that we can all make a difference" (Jaros-White, 2021, para. 1). Taken further, this definition applies to people across all age groups and backgrounds, making global citizenry a moral imperative for everyone.

The year 2020 is a testament to the acute need for global citizens in *every* sense of the word, especially in light of the Trump administration's four-year-long advocacy of racist, xenophobic, homophobic, sexist, and classist ideologies. Donald Trump was culpable for the growing hatred that pitted family members, political opponents, and strangers against each other, but oppressive ideologies were existent long before Trump was in office. By virtue of holding the most powerful position in the world, many viewed his endorsement of their oppressive ideologies and charges to destroy democracy as a call to action. Assessments of Trump by veteran national security experts midway through his term led them to label him a "terrorist leader" (Hooghe & Dassonneville, 2018). Since then, Trump has continued to abuse his power to legitimize, condone, and encourage abhorrent behavior targeted at Asian American and Pacific Islanders (AAPI), African Americans, and Mexican immigrants, among others, which has resulted in increases in hate crimes (surging nearly 20 percent from years prior) (Villareal, 2020) and domestic terrorism (Follman, 2021) and ultimately in the incitement of an insurrection at the U.S. Capitol on June 6, 2021 (Follman, 2021). The Brookings Institute reported that this was the "second-largest uptick in hate crimes in the 25 years for which data are available, second only to the spike after September 11, 2001" (Villareal, 2020). Data gathered during the 2016 election season and Trump's single term offer compelling evidence of correlations between his hate-filled rhetoric and policies and the racist attitudes and behavior of some of his supporters; however, experts caution against concluding definitively "that one leads to the other" (Williamson & Gelfland, 2019).

We cannot deny the role Trump's presidency played in worsening race relations in the United States. However, we must be truthful with ourselves (and each other) and accept that white supremacy, prejudice, racism, biases, and discrimination are not new phenomena. We must acknowledge that, in different ways, we have all been duped or forced into believing and accepting a purposely imbalanced system established centuries ago through colonialism. The system has served as a blueprint for oppression, subsequently establishing the foundations for businesses, governments, schools, and neighborhoods designed to maintain economic, social, racial, and gender disparities in overt and covert ways. Regardless of the power that one has or lacks, we must *all* commit to listening to and communicating with each other about our racialized realities, doing so with an open mind and an open heart.

THE GREAT "AWOKENING" OF 2020

As the protests and marches remained steady for most of 2020 and into 2021, there was a surge in the number of white Americans who were newly aware of the reality of racism in the United States (Daniels, 2021). Civil rights activist Jesse Jackson commented that "white Americans are finally 'awakening' to the nation's racial crisis" (Cava, 2020). There were some who were already aware and self-identified as allies, and others who were either in shock or denial as they were subjected to firsthand accounts of systemic oppression shared with the world through videos, news outlets, and social media. One overarching reason for the lack of awareness about racial injustices is the pervasiveness of white privilege (McIntosh, 1998), allowing whites not to think about their racial identities. Unlike BIPOC, many whites remain ignorant of their race/ethnicity and privilege, leading to the inability to recognize when they benefit from it. They are also oblivious to the regularity with which BIPOC experience racism in every aspect of their public and private lives. There are certainly white people who are very much aware of racism and its impact on them and BIPOC. They are most likely proactive in trying to better understand how it functions and what they can do to address it, which might involve reading books and having heartfelt conversations with others about these traditionally taboo topics. In either case, 2020 has taught us that racism affects everyone, and it is up to *all of us* to turn the tide and dismantle racism, one relationship at a time.

A critical lesson learned from 2020 by a considerable portion of the U.S. population and the world at large was that racism is at an all-time high. A truth, a material reality for BIPOC, was finally brought to the public consciousness in the harshest way possible: yet another video recording of a Black man being murdered by a police officer. What distinguished this footage from all the others was that the officer had ample time to prevent a tragedy from happening but chose not to. He willfully murdered a citizen, who happened to be Black and male, and was in no way swayed by the gathering crowd pleading for Floyd's life. Bystanders begged for justice but to no avail. As the various media outlets covered this tragedy and the escalating protests, responses from white Americans were disbelief, shock, frustration, and anger. There were also rebuttals to and justifications for the severity of Floyd's treatment, involving criticisms of his actions (i.e., possessing fake currency) and character (i.e., thug, thief, druggie). While these positions are diametrically opposed to each other, the callousness of the officer compelled people from all races, cultures, and ethnicities to take to the streets and demand justice for Mr. Floyd as well as for past, present, and future victims of police brutality.

As the protests were gaining moment, the term *woke* entered mainstream vernacular. *Woke* is a slang term originating in Black culture and "has become a common phrase among young, Black, conscious people. The phrase means to remain aware of what is going on around you and in society, more specifically, to remain politically aware, or conscious" (Richardson & Ragland, 2018, p. 42). It became a buzzword to signal a person's awakening conscience and awareness of the racial injustices that have been plaguing Black and Brown communities for centuries. The word was catapulted into everyday discourse beyond Black culture throughout 2020 as whites were finally recognizing the reality of racism. Not only were they grasping it, but many were also publicly or privately proclaiming their newfound cognizance and, in many instances, committing to becoming a global citizen. Although they might not have used that exact label, the sentiment was that their political awareness would go beyond cognitive change. The shift in their ideologies about racism would ultimately result in individual behavioral changes and changes to the institutions of which they were a part. "The Great Awokening" (Cohn & Quealy, 2020), as it were, reflected the boiling point in the United States at which racial injustice would no longer be tolerated. This social movement united people from diverse racial, ethnic, and cultural backgrounds as they demonstrated in the streets, shared educational resources on social media platforms, and initiated difficult conversations about race and racism in their interpersonal networks.

Many protesters were compelled to become activists because there was a moral imperative to do so; for them, it was the right thing to do. In Indianapolis, one thousand doctors and medical professionals were among the first to "[join] the protest movement in support of black lives" (Bongiovanni, 2020, para. 1). Although they were dealing with the early stages of the health pandemic, these healthcare providers chose to get involved because they were keenly aware that the racial crisis was impacting African Americans in very profound ways compared to other people groups. In an interview, physician and protest organizer Crystal Azu explained that the protest "started with conversations in [Azu's] network of friends about police brutality and George Floyd's death. She said they were tired of seeing the same footage of black men and women dying at the hands of police over and over" (Bongiovanni, 2020, para. 4). These healthcare practitioners felt it necessary to actively do something to address these disparities instead of idly standing by. They were compelled to become global citizens. Azu further noted that, "As physicians, we know firsthand how health care disparities affect our patients, especially during this season of COVID, and we just wanted to take a stand against racism and also in solidarity with peaceful protesters across the U.S." (Bongiovanni, 2020, para. 5). To be clear, this is not to say that other groups were not affected by COVID-19 or police brutality. Rather, the protests and subsequent support for them were public acknowledgments of the history of racism in the United States that the country has yet to reckon with.

Systemic racism could no longer be denied, and if it were, then the people, groups, and institutions doing so were perceived as willingly complicit in perpetuating and preserving institutional racism. According to Azu, "inequities occur when black communities don't have access to healthful food, encounter biases when they seek health care, and don't have safe sidewalks or streets to walk on in their neighborhoods" (Bongiovanni, 2020, para. 6). For these healthcare providers, they willingly accepted their responsibility to address racism through social activism as global citizens (Cohn & Quealy, 2020). Azu also stated that they chose to protest "because systemic racism is a public health crisis, and we want to take a stand against that" (Bongiovanni, 2020, para. 3). Although Azu did not discuss in the interview any potential professional or personal risks the medical protesters took by publicly speaking out against racism, it is clear they were willing to use their privilege and power to draw attention to serious issues in our healthcare system and with public servants, namely police, that were adversely affecting African Americans. The healthcare providers were the true embodiment of global citizenship because they used their knowledge of systemic racism in healthcare and society to encourage others to become more knowledgeable about these racial health disparities and to develop the skills and values necessary for being culturally competent and other-minded in an increasingly diverse yet unjust world (Cohn & Quealy, 2020). They were leading by example in choosing to make a difference in the world through the spaces they occupy, which in this case were hospitals (Bongiovanni, 2020).

WHY COMMUNICATION MATTERS: BARRIERS TO DIALOGUE AND UNDERSTANDING

The Great Awokening of 2020 unveiled deep-seated racial issues that were quite visible to many even if others remained willingly or unknowingly blind to them. The protests and dual pandemics brought to the forefront the critical role communication can play in addressing the different forms of systemic oppression plaguing the United States and the world. The urgency to have these difficult conversations was also underscored by rising hate crimes against AAPI, calls to defund the police (Coleman, 2020), misunderstandings of the Black Lives Matter movement and the Black Lives Matter organizational network, and countless relationships being terminated due to conflicts over race. People and institutions alike seemed entrenched in their respective ideologies, willing the "opposition" to bend. To frame these issues as merely a difference in ideologies or opinions is to ignore how systems work. In a nutshell, they are designed to benefit some while disenfranchising others. From an ethical or moral standpoint, this way of thinking is very troubling because it fails to acknowledge inequities and discourages any efforts to "make things right." In the end, benefactors and their descendants will continue to reap rewards, in perpetuity, from a system designed to work in their favor. This also means that the disenfranchised will remain in an everlasting state of marginalization, never in a position to break the generational curse of oppression.

The trumpet has sounded; the clarion call has been issued (yet again). As a society, we should be compelled to live in spaces and places where we appreciate and value each other. This also requires that we each take the first of many steps in having these difficult conversations and putting our words into action. We will most likely be pushed out of our comfort zone, possibly paralyzed by fear, guilt, anxiety, stress, and countless other emotions. Nevertheless, we should all be compelled to "be the change we want to see," which requires putting aside our egos and prioritizing the realities and worldviews of others. We must be willing to (1) be self-reflexive at all times, (2) recognize the power of language, (3) accept the reality of racism and the implications thereof, (3) engage in honest communication with self and others, (4) adopt perspective taking, and (5) commit to being vulnerable, even when it hurts. These criteria do not mean we abandon our own realities and worldviews. Instead, we should see them as tools that lead to greater knowledge about the world in which we live.

This heightened awareness will ultimately debunk the necessity of a colorblind mentality and other neutralizing views dismissing our racial, ethnic, cultural, and sexual differences. Opening ourselves up to change will assuredly equip us with the resources critical to communicating frankly about race, racism, privilege, and power, among other concepts. Ultimately, we are committing to disrupt the status quo and expend the requisite strength, dedication, and courage necessary for the change that is to come.

Before we can move into action, we must first establish a foundational understanding of the barriers that may prevent us from even considering, let alone engaging in, productive and frank conversations about race. Please keep in mind that this list of barriers is not exhaustive. It is merely a list of exemplars of common misconceptions and missteps that can deter people from having healthy and real interracial relationships. Being able to recognize these potential barriers is especially important when we consider that we are all socialized to interact with and navigate the world in very different ways. Thus, we should use this knowledge to minimize the negative impact these culture clashes might have on interactions and relationships. (Be advised that the barriers are presented in no particular order; they are equally important.)

Intergroup Contact and Relationship Quality

In 1954, social psychologist Gordon Allport hypothesized that prejudice and intergroup conflict can be reduced by intergroup contact. The assumption is that these interactions will presumably challenge stereotypes, biases, and prejudices on an individual level as long as the following factors are present to some degree: (1) equal status, (2) intergroup cooperation, (3) common goals, and (4) support by social and institutional authorities. Shook and Fazio (2008) elaborate further and explain that there is an underlying assumption of this hypothesis, which is that "prejudice stems from a lack of knowledge and exposure," and by having more frequent interactions with outgroup members, "individuals gain information about other groups and [this] should lead to a reduction in hostility and prejudice" (p. 717). While this sounds reasonable and ideal, social situations and conditions are not always conducive to positive intercultural or interracial interactions.

According to Herda (2017), "optimal conditions are not guaranteed in real-world settings" (p. 114). As such, these interactions may have the opposite effect and result in "interpersonal racial discrimination" (i.e., racial microaggressions) and "worsen[ing] racial attitudes." These negative communication experiences are partly the result of how we are socialized to interact with and perceive outgroup members. Thus, it is only logical to assume that our racial perspectives will shape our view of an outgroup member and have a negative or positive influence on the interaction. Herda (2017) refers to these as "attitudinal consequences." If we have stereotypes and biases against outgroup members, then we are likely to perceive them as a threat and have greater affinity for our ingroup. In her study of interracial friendships between whites, Hispanics, and Blacks, Herda found that Blacks who reported no discrimination had more interracial friendships. While the findings might be encouraging, these "friendship[s] [were] not powerful enough to neutralize discrimination's consequences," and because most Black Americans can be described as "discrimination victims," they are very likely "unaffected by friendship contact" (p. 114). Herda also found that, for Hispanics, the fewer interracial friendships they had, the more potent were the consequences of discrimination; however, these consequences declined with more friendships with outgroup members. These findings might seem contradictory, but they speak to the complexity of interracial friendships specifically and of interracial relationships in general. A BIPOC's negative racial experiences can very likely cause them to avoid interracial friendships as a defense mechanism (Lemay & Teneva, 2020).

Another barrier to interracial dialogue is the perception partners have about the quality of intimacy or closeness. There is not much research on this dimension of interracial relationships, but it is a very important one nonetheless, especially since it is foundational to our desire to connect with others regardless of race. Tropp (2007) conducted a study of Black and white friends on this relationship quality and found that the white partner believed that the relationship was much more intimate than did the Black partner. Similar to Herda's (2017) study, Tropp found that Black partners' perceptions were due to their experiences with racial discrimination in contexts outside of the relationship. Other possibilities are racial microaggressions in past interracial relationships, different racialized experiences, and lack of racial sensitivity, to name a few (Holoien et al., 2015). The saliency of race in interracial interactions has been directly tied to feelings of being understood, which was an issue in roommate and stranger interactions. According to Holoien et al. (2015), "[when] Whites are higher in desire to affiliate with racial minorities [they] failed to accurately perceive the extent to which racial minority partners felt understood" (p. 76). The inverse was true for Blacks in that, when they had a higher desire to affiliate with white friends, their perceptions of those friends were accurate. These findings suggest that, in light of other studies, racial differences create different kinds of experiences for friends, with the BIPOC person being less satisfied with and less affirmed in the relationship. Despite increased interracial contact, the quality of the relationship is impacted in ways that neither party intended. Qureshi and Collazos (2011) found this to be true in therapeutic relationships as well.

Regardless of the type of interracial relationship, whether and how the relationship develops can be attributed to cultural and racial factors. This does not mean that interracial relationships are impossible. Instead, there must be an acknowledgment that racial differences might negatively impact the relationship, and this acknowledgment requires both partners being willing to have open communication about those differences and committing to being more understanding of each other.

Distrust and Utilitarianism

Two other factors that are potential barriers to interracial communication about race are distrust (Trail et al., 2009) and utilitarianism (Munn, 2018). Trust is the basis for all relationships, regardless of the partner's race. This factor potentially becomes more salient when the relationship is interracial, as evidenced in Trail et al.'s (2009) study of interracial roommates over the course of a school year. At least one partner was white and the other was either Black, Asian, or Hispanic. From the self-reports, it was learned that white roommates showed a decline in their intimacy-building behaviors, which directly caused the BIPOC roommate's positive emotions about the relationship to decline as well. Trail et al. (2009) propose that the BIPOC roommates made attributions for the white roommate's behavior in order to reduce their own uncertainty about the relationship. In other words, they may attribute the roommate's behavior change to racial prejudice, as other information might not be available. Even though these conclusions are speculative, they are reasonable, especially in light of other research regarding racial microaggressions experienced by students of color (SOC) on campus and in the local community (Harris et al., 2018) and BIPOC in the workplace and other public contexts. Trail et al. (2009) also state that, over time, "Whites may stop trying to put their best foot forward," which means that their "interpersonal behaviors become less positive" (p. 682) and cause the roommate to have even worse experiences with interracial interactions. Interpreting and processing interpersonal experiences through a racialized lens are a part of the socialization process for BIPOC. Because they are "interpersonally more sensitive and attentive to high-status people during interactions" (Trait et al., 2019, p. 683), they are possibly more dissatisfied in the relationship than their white roommates. These findings are also applicable to other relational contexts.

Brown and Grothaus (2019) interviewed Black doctoral students about their interracial mentoring experiences with white faculty advisors. The students shared positive aspects of these interracial relationships, but they also addressed reasons for mistrusting white people. The four themes that emerged were (1) receiving family messages, (2) experiencing overt racism, (3) experiencing tokenism, and (4) experiencing dissonance. Receiving family messages involved overt messages from family members warning them not to trust white people in order to protect them from the realities of racism and how to navigate life as a Black person. Experiencing overt racism involved racist encounters "with neighbors, educators, and police that hindered their willingness to engage in cross-racial trust," in early childhood and throughout their lifetimes (p. 217). Experiencing tokenism referred to concerns white faculty were using them as a token to address racial injustice. This uncertainty caused Black students to question the motives of those faculty members and to feel "commodified" (p. 218). Experiencing dissonance involved "internal conflicts that stemmed from their experience in the predominately White field of counseling" (p. 218). Black students used past interracial interactions as a barometer for how to manage the current interactions they were having with faculty. The Black students in the study did share positive aspects of an interracial mentoring relationship; however, the negative aspects are highlighted to demonstrate that much more work is needed to completely mitigate these barriers that likely exist in most, if not all, interracial relationships.

Utilitarianism is another barrier and speaks to the function or purpose of an interracial relationship. This barrier is of particular significance because of the context within which it occurs. Munn (2018) interviewed Black and white members of an "an intentionally interracial organization in a large Midwestern city" (p. 473) to understand how race influenced social capital. Social capital is "the resources embedded in a social structure accessed or mobilized in purposive actions" (p. 473). In this case, the organization was a church, and the assumption was that intentionally creating an interracial organization would lead to positive interracial relationships among members. The findings revealed that the relationships lacked depth and intimacy and that white members "described their close friends of color in utilitarian terms and [they were] not integrated into daily activities outside of the interracial organization" (p. 473). Simply put, the interracial relationships were solely functional and did not involve social interactions away from the church. These relationships did not involve resource exchange or social interaction, which was different from white members' relationships with other whites.

Even though those members had racially progressive views, they tended to operate according to the "one friend rule." Munn (2018) defines this "as a social mechanism in which whites name a non-intimate, institutionally tied interracial friendship as 'close' to project a generalized value for diversity" (p. 474). When compared to their intraracial or same-race relationships, whites' interracial relationships with Black members were neither meaningful nor reciprocal; "they mobilize the race of their black or biracial friends for its symbolic value primarily within an interracial organization" (p. 474). Consequently, when people value the symbolic meaning of a relational tie over its relational quality, a "close" interracial friendship is categorized as unidirectional or utilitarian, benefiting only one person. From this study, Munn (2018) concluded that "homophilous networks are still the norm" in the United States due to a commitment to intraracial relationships. This pattern suggests that, for some whites, there is a lack of interest in developing true relationships with BIPOC, and BIPOC may avoid or disengage from these relationships for fear of being "stereotyped, objectified, and discriminated against" (p. 476).

Performative Support (and Outrage)

Another barrier to productive dialogue and true interracial relationships is "performative support." This barrier is similar to what Harris and Moffitt (2019) refer to as "performative feminism," which is "feminist-identifying womyn who strategically create contradictory public and private personae" (p. 3). The public persona actively encourages "dismantling patriarchy, fighting racism, and promoting equity and inclusion, and the private persona actively perpetuates these oppressive systems." Performative support is more general and applies to public declarations of support of BIPOC, specifically in 2020 in response to the racial pandemic. Performative outrage is an amplification of this support that involves a very emotional, feigned public response to racial injustices. In both scenarios, the same contradictions (i.e., public vs. private) exist, and they can be applied to an individual, public figure, or organization. This is a barrier to effective interracial communication because the person or entity using this strategy is (un)knowingly sowing seeds of doubt among BIPOC about their trustworthiness. Their disingenuous and false intentions are eventually revealed, possibly over time, calling into question their character and integrity. It is important to note that enacting performative support minimizes the overall significance of productive race relations.

An example of performative support involves several fast-food companies that released public statements speaking out against racism and structural inequity during the pandemic (Crowley, 2020). Burger King, McDonald's, Popeyes, Papa John's, and Taco Bell each used social media platforms to decry the injustices that were playing out during the summer of 2020. Their expressions of support are troubling and ring hollow because, as Crowley notes, "the fast-food industry is built on a foundation of exploitation" (para. 4). Each chain has historically underpaid its employees and exploits them in the process. By releasing these statements, they become complicit in perpetuating a false narrative regarding their support of BIPOC and the fight against racial injustices. Crowley (2020) notes that the contradictions between the different personae became more evident with the passage of time, in that the companies limit their engagement with this serious social issue to empty rhetoric. The (in)actions speak volumes about the lack of ethos and pathos of the company, which also can be said of individuals who publicly express support (i.e., through social media, interpersonal networks) yet do not have follow-through.

Dastagir (2020) uses the term "performative outrage" to describe public figures whose heightened emotions around racial injustices prompt a public expression of anger while also "ignor[ing] how they have contributed to the issues of racism." This was particularly noticeable during the protests when people and celebrities took to social media to express their outrage over the murders of George Floyd and Breonna Taylor and countless other victims of police brutality. According to Dastagir, social media was the easiest and quickest way people could engage in digital activism, and that involved "posting a hashtag, a meme or an empty black square" (para. 6); however, those behaviors are questionable since it is difficult to determine "whether that outrage is genuine or performative." These actions are juxtaposed against true activists and allies who have been fighting systemic oppression for decades through protests and sustained actions that tirelessly confront systemic racism without fail. In an interview, National Press Secretary of the NAACP Marc Banks explains that "we can gauge whether it's performative . . . when we see down the line, months from now, years from now, has there been an ongoing conversation or ongoing willingness for other communities to continue to confront the issues that black communities face" (Dastagir, 2020, para. 8).

Dastagir (2020) further explains that a characteristic of outrage is that it is usually unconscious and originates from a person's position on a moral issue; however, it becomes performative when the person wants to communicate to others that they are moral while engaging in behavior that is in direct contradiction with the outrage. Examples of individual and collective instances of performative outrage include but are not limited to actress Lea Michele's social media post of #BlackLivesMatter and the online campaign "Blackout Tuesday" (Dastagir, 2020) and football coach Kirk Ferentz's plea for inclusivity (Emmert, 2020). Michele and Ferentz were accused of committing "traumatic microaggressions" against colleagues in their respective professions (Dastagir, 2020). The performers' actions are egregious and unethical due to their failure to publicly acknowledge their racist behaviors and demonstrate true change (Emmert, 2020).

Racial Spokesperson

The final barrier to productive interracial dialogue is an expectation that a BIPOC is a racial spokesperson. Whether it is in a social or professional context, the BIPOC is expected to share insights into, experiences with, and opinions about race-related topics or issues as a representative of an entire race. This is an unrealistic, mentally and emotionally draining, and offensive expectation because it places undue pressure on a person to speak on behalf of a collective, an underlying assumption that the community is a monolith. There is also an expectation that the BIPOC will assume the role of race educator in all of their interracial interactions. The racial spokesperson is typically a BIPOC because they are frequently in situations where they are in the numerical minority (i.e., classroom, work) and are asked to contribute to discussions of race to educate white peers or colleagues. This might be attributed to being socialized to be very aware of their racial identities and engaging in conversations about race at an early age (Huguely et al., 2019). Conversely, white racial socialization for most is intentionally colorblind, is not an active process, stresses egalitarianism, or does not occur at all (Bartoli et al., 2016).

Colleagues Ingrid Desormes and Christie Miller are an example of how interracial relationships are sometimes a difficult relational context within which to discuss their intercultural differences and diversity (Desormes & Miller, 2020). They are speech-language pathologists who met in spring 2019 after Desormes was hired by Miller to be part of a hospital's acute care team that Miller manages. Desormes is a first-generation Haitian American from southeast Florida, and Miller is white, from the suburbs, and from northeast Florida. Their professional relationship evolved into a personal relationship after Desormes learned other staff members negatively stereotyped her as "assertive," which is largely due to culturally different communication styles. Desormes felt it important to have very open conversations with Miller, who was unfamiliar with these interracial dialogues. To highlight the intricate nuances of their relationship, Miller interviewed Desormes for the American Speech-Language-Hearing Association to discuss diversity, equity, and inclusion in the workplace and how Desormes manages her identity as a professional.

Through the interview, we can see the mutual benefits of vulnerability and trust when two people choose to invest in the relationship. The relationship is a professional one, and while it is not a prerequisite that we have intimacy with each other, a foundation does need to be established upon which to build an authentic connection across our differences. This applies to both professional and personal relationships. Desormes and Miller (2020) seized the opportunity to learn from each other and recognize benefits of learning about a racial and cultural worldview different from their own. In the interview, Desormes emphasizes how imperative it is that BIPOC feel safe to be their true selves, which requires "protecting themselves from racial discrimination and the bias of others" (Desormes & Miller, 2020, para. 8). She further explains that, "If you do not feel safe to be your true self at work, you cannot fully be engaged in providing patient care in that setting." A lack of safety can have a direct impact on a BIPOC's self-perception and the extent to which they are willing and able to be part of a company or organization. This is true to a certain degree even in optimal circumstances.

The BIPOC is at risk of being exploited, such as through invisible labor demands (i.e., diversity committees, mentoring BIPOC) or serving as a racial spokesperson for all things racial. To avoid both scenarios, organizations must actively (1) encourage members to self-educate about race issues via reliable sources, (2) hire experts who are BIPOC to facilitate long-term diversity workshops and dialogue, (3) abandon the expectation of BIPOC employees to be racial spokespersons and resident experts on race, and (4) fairly (monetarily) compensate BIPOC who choose to be involved with diversity work extending beyond their normal work responsibilities. These suggestions are only a few of many and can be applied to an individual as well. Individuals and organizations must take it on themselves to avoid exploiting their relationships with BIPOC and expecting them to be a racial spokesperson.

Moving Beyond and Through the Barriers

The summer of 2020 was an exceptional summer; it forced the United States to confront its racist past and present. It was a mirror to our soul, revealing the good, the bad, and the very, very ugly. The protests were triggered by the senseless murder of George Floyd at the knee of a police officer who chose a violent response to Mr. Floyd's use of a fake twenty dollar bill to purchase snacks. The unrest was inevitable, evidenced by the increasing number of Black men, women, boys, and girls being murdered by police while engaging in mundane, everyday activities. In addition to unleashing death and illness, COVID-19 revealed the racial, ethnic, and economic disparities that continue to divide people groups in the United States and worldwide. On May 8, 2020, on social media, United Nations Secretary-General Antonio Guterres stated that "the pandemic continues to unleash a tsunami of hate and xenophobia, scapegoating and scare-mongering" (Human Rights Watch, 2020, para. 1). This statement accurately captures the depth and breadth of the hate- and fear-mongering that have been and continue to adversely affect the lives of AAPI people, as evidenced by the rise in hate crimes against them (Villareal, 2020). These heightened racist ideologies gained momentum and validation due to government leaders and senior officials either refusing to sanction or openly encouraging these very troubling behaviors and limited worldviews. The United Kingdom, Italy, Spain, Greece, France, and Germany were unabashedly in lockstep with the United States and its support of anti-other rhetoric in public discourse. Sadly, these countries boldly "advance[d] anti-immigrant, white supremacist, ultra-nationalist, anti-[S]emitic, and xenophobic conspiracy theories that demonize refugees, foreigners, prominent individuals, and political leaders," which have been amplified due to the COVID-19 crisis (Human Rights Watch, 2020, para. 2).

The evidence is irrefutable that we are living in a world where myriad negative and deadly ideologies abound. These oppressive worldviews have been preserved through institutionalized systems (i.e., racism, sexism, classism, heterosexism) committed to perpetuating these long-standing disparities. It is imperative that we acknowledge and address the fact that these systems are maintained by people, people who are either knowingly or unknowingly complicit in maintaining these unfair systems. That knowledge should ultimately translate into activism, which can take many forms. The first and most essential step is to begin your own research on different racial issues and read information from reliable and credible sources. This will allow a person to be self-sufficient in the learning process while also avoiding placing friends, colleagues, or strangers into the exhausting role of racial spokesperson. As they actively work to become informed and knowledgeable about race issues and the structures that perpetuate them, they should also seek opportunities to engage in difficult dialogues with outgroup members with whom they have an intimate relationship. While not everyone will want to engage, be mindful not to expect the other person to be a racial spokesperson. Hopefully, the two people are close enough to discuss and negotiate these nuances. Discussing these issues with colleagues might be difficult to navigate since it is a professional relationship, and such dialogue might unnecessarily complicate the relationship. The BIPOC person might feel exploited or overwhelmed by being asked to assume yet another responsibility, contributing to the already taxing invisible labor they are quietly undertaking. It is best to test the waters by openly sharing interest in and willingness to have difficult conversations with someone they trust. Explicitly articulating openness to being vulnerable is important, as is working together to identify ways to establish mutual understanding and to collaborate on strategies for promoting true equity and inclusion in personal and professional spaces. Relationships are at the core of dismantling systemic oppression.

Throughout the remainder of this book, an emphasis will be placed on the importance of being a global citizen (Cohen & Quealy, 2020; Jaros-White, 2021) within specific relational contexts. Global citizenry is a lifelong process and requires commitment, dedication, and endurance if a person is *truly* ready and willing to have a broader perspective on the diverse world in which we live. The labels *ally*, *accomplice*, and *coconspirator* are used fairly frequently to describe a white person (Carson, 2020) or BIPOC who is eager to offer support to members of historically marginalized groups. While the intention is good, the person runs the risk of being perceived as disingenuous or self-serving. There is considerable debate in activist and intellectual circles about whether the label *ally* should be conferred on someone or self-assigned.

Jamie Utt (2013) of the website Everyday Feminism provides a summation of the work of activist Mia McKenzie and McKenzie's position on what it means to be a true ally. In order to be an ally, a person must practice all of the following 10 essentials: (1) be all about listening; (2) disavow *ally* as a noun (focus on "actions of the present"); (3) do not assume the self-proclaimed identity of being an ally; (4) accept that fighting systemic oppression is a never-ending process; (5) invest in perpetual self-education; (6) recognize that solidarity requires relationship building with BIPOC (it is moot when done in isolation); (7) provide platforms and spaces for BIPOC voices to be centered (avoid being in the spotlight); (8) engage in intraracial (same-race) communication to discuss racism; (9) "listen, apologize, act accountably, and act differently going forward"; and (10) do not monopolize emotional energy "from those to whom we ally ourselves" (Utt, 2013). Individually and collectively, these criteria speak to the level of investment that is required of an ally. The ally is decentered from solidarity-building efforts and must be willing to prioritize the interest and needs of the less powerful person.

These 10 essentials—in addition to others that will be discussed later—are also applicable to interracial friendships and romantic relationships that have more closeness than associates or acquaintances. Both partners must approach the relationship with openness and a willingness to have difficult conversations about race. More pointedly, partners must come to view dialogue as a relational practice whereby diverse perspectives that are shared between partners should ultimately transform social relationships (Norander & Galanes, 2014). It is through these exchanges that partners recognize the importance of having exposure to diverse perspectives "in concrete ways that acknowledge the raced, gendered, and classed nature of communicative action" (p. 347). From this perspective, partners are willing and committed to seeing the totality of each other while also broadening their worldview. Eventually, this newfound knowledge will lead to transformation in private and public spaces that are complicit in perpetuating institutional racism. This will necessitate both partners being more proactive at work in addressing these disparities or initiating these difficult conversations.

The Great Awokening of 2020 pulled many people out of a slumber that they did not know they were in. Their slumbering state made them oblivious to the institutional barriers that have prevented BIPOC friends, colleagues, neighbors, and strangers from having access to opportunities, safety, and experiences that should be fairly afforded to them. For many BIPOC, their Great Awokening very likely occurred early in life as their parents and families socialized them about how to best navigate a world where they are not positioned to succeed. If they do succeed, then they are held to a higher and more stringent standard than their white counterparts. This might sound harsh, but it is a harsh and true reality nonetheless. The lived experiences of all people groups are very different, and for good reason. That is what makes the world so beautiful. In theory, human diversity is something to behold, something to treasure. It is in practice where the problem lies, where humans are forced to fight for the same resources (i.e., homes, careers, humanity, respect), promoting a "crabs in a barrel" mentality. As this book suggests, it is through our interpersonal relationships that we can address the normalized systems of oppression that perpetuate the many inequities plaguing society and the world.

As Norander and Galanes (2014) argue, diverse perspectives are necessary if we are going to transform social relationships, which ideally will translate into the gradual dismantling of systemic oppression. It is through these sustained communicative exchanges that societal change can occur and we can collectively address the pervasive issue of race, particularly as it relates to dismantling racism. The authors underscore the worth of this book by advancing the argument that dialogue is a relational practice. In other words, it is through our connections to and communication with outgroup members that we can create a community context where diversity issues are addressed honestly and productively and lead to societal change (Norander & Galanes, 2014). Thus, relational practice is the pathway to dismantling racism.

The goal of this book is to explore the ways different types of interracial relationships can serve as a site for engaging in difficult conversations about race. There is a total of seven chapters in this book. Chapter 2, "Establishing an Essential Vocabulary," is focused on concepts identified as fundamental to interracial communication. The emphasis is on defining these concepts and addressing how societal understandings or uses of them are oftentimes inaccurate, causing confusion and creating dissonance in interracial relationships. These misinformed definitions also function as barriers to effective interracial communication. As such, the purpose of this vocabulary list is to provide people with the basic knowledge of concepts that can ultimately lead to developing the linguistic repertoire necessary for engaging in informative and healthy interracial interactions. These concepts and other barriers discussed in chapter 2 will also be addressed when appropriate in chapters 3 to 7. Each chapter focuses on a specific interracial context and the challenges and triumphs that arise due to racial differences and societal barriers that hinder relationships.

Chapter 3, "Interracial Communication within the Family," addresses the role families play in preparing or not their members to have productive conversations about race and healthy interracial relationships. Families are initially involuntary due to being born into them; however, they might qualify as voluntary relationships since members can dissolve relational ties despite biology. They are markedly different from nonfamilial relationships because they are typically where members are socialized on how to interact with the world and others. Thus, in this chapter, particular attention is given to how these approaches impact the actual interracial interactions people have and what communication strategies are deemed best practices for families to adopt to prepare members for effective interracial communication.

Chapter 4, "Interracial Friendships beyond the 'One Friend Rule,'" directs our attention to the different barriers and pressures interracial partners use to navigate their relationships in general. The chapter introduces a relationship inventory involving five steps one can follow to work toward diversifying interpersonal networks, specifically friendships, and challenging structural systems opposing the normalization of interracial friendships.

Chapter 5, "Interracial Romantic Relationships and the Trickle-Down Theory," explores interracial communication in nonfamilial relationships. It introduces the Trickle-Down Theory to illustrate the interconnectedness between racist ideologies and interracial romantic relationships, the general premise being that interracial romantic relationships bring to the surface a person's and a society's true attitudes about race, serving as a racial barometer of sorts regarding the racial tensions of the country. These relationships are voluntary and require a different level of commitment and strategies to initiate and maintain them. Both interracial friendships and interracial romantic relationships have different kinds of relational intimacy that are managed and negotiated by and between the partners. Similarly, chapter 5 addresses how interracial romantic partners, both married and unmarried, are able to engage in productive dialogue with each other about the extent to which racial identities, racial differences, and societal racism impact them individually and collectively as a unit. The end goal should be determining best practices for fostering positive race relations and confronting systemic racism.

Chapter 6, "Making Interracial Communication Possible in the Workplace," addresses interracial communication in the workplace and is of particular interest since, within recent years, many organizations have touted that they either have or are striving for diversity, equity, and inclusion (DEI). There is considerable evidence that professional spaces are not always prepared to manifest true DEI due to various barriers and an unwillingness or inability to transform the organization's uninviting culture. As such, the focus is on what organizational members should do to be best equipped to discuss racism.

Chapter 7, "Intentionality and the Fight against Racism," brings home many of the points made in the previous chapters and introduces the necessity of being intentional and putting forth the time, energy, effort, and other resources necessary to change our relationships and societal structures on which racial hierarchies and ideologies are based. The chapter highlights how this process requires a lifelong commitment from everyone since it has taken centuries for systems of oppression to be erected and maintained as they have been. For this final chapter, readers are introduced to the Racial Intentionality

Roadmap (RaIR) as a personal roadmap everyone can follow to do their part to eradicate racism. The three stages are progressive and can be adopted by individuals, communities, and organizations: (1) Racial Past, (2) Racial Present, and (3) Racial Future. Intentionality is the foundation of RaIR and must be present to begin the roadmap. Intentionality means a person is deliberate or purposeful in efforts to fight racism. This chapter addresses the power of collective agency in the face of injustice and encourages frank discussions of what allyship is, the expectations of an ally, and the ways that racially oppressed groups and allies can effectively work together to dismantle systemic racism through relationships and complicity.

This book was born and written out of a heartfelt desire to offer insight into interracial communication, which is simultaneously beautiful and complex, and how our relationships with people whose realities, experiences, and worldviews are different from our own can lead to healing and understanding. These relationships have the potential to teach us life lessons best learned from those closest to us. The disclosures we make in these relationships are made with the assumption and expectation of mutual trust, vulnerability, respect, and honesty. Once those qualities are established, it becomes easier for both partners to be their true selves, paving the way for increased understanding and awareness of the realness of systemic oppression and the racial privileges therein. Initially, these conversations may be difficult, painful even, but that is a part of the process. Growing pains will certainly come. Instead of viewing them as something to be feared, anticipate that they will be integral to one's evolution as a global citizen. It requires that one recognize and pursue opportunities to become educated about cultures and people groups different from their own, the ultimate goal being to intentionally engage with the world to make a fundamental difference in the spaces they occupy (Jaros-White, 2021). Those opportunities can begin in our relationships and extend into all other areas of our lives.

We all should be compelled to move into action due to the societal inequities that continue to plague the United States and the world. The wake-up call that is 2020 birthed undeniable proof of the minimal progress that has been made toward equity and hence our collective need for activism. The Great Awokening created a tremendous platform from which to actively resist perpetuating institutional racism and sanctioning its far-reaching, deadly effect on BIPOC. It exposed the socially unconscious, "unwoke" benefactors of oppressive systems who were (and are) willing to compromise their integrity and character by preserving these social injustices. Attempting to engage in productive dialogue about these issues is for naught if we are trying to reach the unreachable, the ones who willfully choose to remain asleep or turn a blind to racism. Instead, we must direct our time, energy, and efforts toward people in our circles and beyond who earnestly want to create and be the change they want to see. The time is *now* for us to collectively fight the continued normalization of racism, sexism, classism, heterosexism, xenophobia, and all other forms of systemic oppression.

NOTE

1. The terms *Black* and *African American* will be used interchangeably throughout this book. This book uses lowercase *w* for *white* and uppercase *B* for *Black* to challenge past writing conventions that perpetuate a racial hierarchy (see Bauder, 2020).

Chapter 2

Establishing an Essential Vocabulary

In order to have effective communication, it is imperative that people speak the same language and have a shared understanding of the words being used to convey messages to each other. Using a shared language does not guarantee mutual understanding. We have all experienced a time when there was a miscommunication, misunderstanding, or a recognition that you and a friend, for example, had a very different definition of a given word. This certainly happens when people are speaking two different languages, but what happens when they are speaking the same language? What happens when different racial worldviews shape those understandings? Does this lead to conflict or connection? These may sound like very basic or irrelevant questions, but they are integral to interracial communication. Moreover, they help elucidate for us the centrality of communication in dismantling systemic oppression. These systems of severe disenfranchisement were wholly constructed by humans for the sole purpose of subjugating those deemed lesser than. Racist, sexist, classist, and heterosexist ideologies were all crafted by the powerful, who used their personal and professional relationships to spread their messages to the masses.

Systems of oppression were deviously coordinated to set the foundation for socially and institutionally sanctioned inequities that have endured over time. They were designed to be impenetrable to protect the power imbalance and the beneficiaries thereof. To dissuade the oppressed and their allies from overthrowing the systems, governments and the powers that be have thwarted change at nearly every turn. For centuries, the oppressed and their allies have attempted to overthrow these archaic and deadly systems through revolts and protests, but nearly to no avail. While some progress has recently been made toward equity and protection, such as the police reform bill (H. 4860); Executive Order (EO) 13985, condemning xenophobia, racism, and intolerance against the AAPI community; and Title IX of the Educational

Amendments, the recent racial unrest in the United States has shown the world that we are not as progressive of a nation as we have always believed ourselves to be. This is best epitomized by the Trump administration's aggressive efforts initiated in 2020 to ban the teaching of critical race theory (CRT) in K–12 schools and universities throughout the United States. Governors and legislators from states supporting Trump were in lockstep with these initiatives and fiercely embraced the anti-CRT rhetoric, which has largely been an "ill-informed misinformation campaign designed to poke and inflame white fragility through fear mongering" (Espinoza, 2021, para. 6). The public outrage over CRT reflects a very ill-informed position—whether intentional or not—on a theory that has been in existence for several decades. According to Delgado and Stefancic (2001),

> the critical race theory (CRT) movement is a collection of activists and scholars interested in studying and transforming the relationship among race, racism, and power. The movement considers many of the same issues that conventional civil rights and ethnic studies discourses take up, but places them in a broader perspective that includes economics, history, context, group- and self-interest, and even feelings and the unconscious. (pp. 2–3)

CRT is a theoretical lens offering insight into and a critique of power structures that perpetuate racism and shape racial identities. As with any theory, its purpose is to explain phenomena, which in this case pertain to the relationship between racism and power, and for an amalgam of reasons, opponents are driven by unfounded fear that the powerless and disenfranchised and their allies are trying to strip the powerful of everything. This is not the case. Simply put, they want current systems to be deconstructed in order to be fair, equitable, and just for all, rejecting the postulation that the world is a meritocracy as a fallacy.

The roadmap to dismantling racism is a multifaceted and challenging one, to say the least. Metaphorically speaking, there are multiple routes and modes of transportation for getting there, and these require that everyone realize the same goals and necessary changes. It also warrants developing and implementing strategies that address the issue of systemic oppression on both an individual and institutional level. While change at both levels is essential, it can be argued that individual approaches are a precursor to institution-level changes. Relationships between racially different people can lead to mutual understanding and increased awareness of how the disparities in our racialized realities are the direct result of racism. In order for these mutually beneficial exchanges to take place, the partners must be speaking the language, and that goes beyond the actual words being spoken. This requires that we have a clear understanding of the true meaning of concepts related to racism and systemic oppression. Many critical words have entered our everyday vernacular and drastically deviated from their original meaning, which has caused confusion and miscommunication. More importantly, watered-down definitions or public interpretations of these words have ignored the role and influence societal power plays in explaining systemic oppression. Whether intentional or not, people are being miseducated about the fundamentals of race, racism, and social inequities, which is a considerable barrier to dismantling racism.

Addressing this issue of miseducation is essential—hence the focus of this chapter. The list of terms is in no way exhaustive, but it is a good start nonetheless to building a robust vocabulary that is vital to a person's journey toward being a global citizen. Global citizens capitalize on the fact that knowledge is in fact power, and by actively seeking opportunities to become more learned on the subject, they are also becoming better equipped to and more adept at navigating difficult conversations about race. Global citizens are on a perpetual journey of learning and engaging with others and the world. That journey requires a true commitment to the process, which means investing the time, energy, and effort necessary for being an integral part of the broader global community dedicated to equity and justice.

MAKE IT MAKE SENSE

The mere thought of race and racism can elicit myriad emotional and cognitive responses within people. For some, these may be anxiety and fear because they are in foreign terrain and nervous about new and unpredictable experiences. For others, those words may trigger positive or negative emotions depending on their past. In either case, we all are using our experiential knowledge, or knowledge about things gained through our unique experiences, to influence our relationships, ideologies, beliefs, and values. That knowledge is also used to shape responses to different phenomena. When it comes to interracial relationships, it is paramount that we remember that everyone's journey is different, and if we are going to see our connections to each other as organic opportunities for personal growth and societal change, then we must meet people where they are. It also means that people must meet us where we are. Given these realities, an essential vocabulary is something that all parties must recognize as being accurate and grounded in research by scholars trained to mine through data to get at the truths about issues related to race. This also requires reliance on facts grounded in history.

The concepts below have been divided into four general categories to make it somewhat easier to process the complex relationship between race, racism, and power. These categories are new and show people how to best manage the information overload they will experience while learning about interracial communication and systemic racism. More importantly, readers will be able to better manage and reduce stress and anxiety while adopting sensitivity and mindfulness during the process of becoming a global citizen committed to racial justice. The four categories are (1) institutional structures, (2) outgroup consciousness, (3) internal identity reflection, and (4) external identity expression. The categories focus on relational contexts, nonverbal behaviors, verbal behaviors, or internal processes that influence our interracial interactions.

Before discussing the categories, we must first establish a baseline for what qualifies as interracial communication. A common misperception is that interracial communication is when two people from different races are interacting with each other. That is a very simplistic and problematic perception since it suggests racial differences are automatically framing how we communicate and that interracial relationships are qualitatively different from same-race or intraracial relationships. Interracial communication is the "transactional process of message exchange between individuals in a situational context where racial difference is perceived as a salient factor by at least one individual" (Orbe & Harris, 2015, p. 7). This means interracial communication falls along a continuum within interpersonal communication, where there is an exchange of messages between two people who have mutual influence on each other and are interdependent. It does not involve strangers because they are not invested in each other; their interaction is temporary. In the case of interracial communication, the relationship is interpersonal and undergoes a relational shift when either party believes their racial difference or the issue of race is salient in a positive or negative way. Their communication is impacted by these differences. Consider the following example.

Two college friends—one Black and one white—consider themselves close, are comfortable with each other, and share a lot of interests. During a late night of working on a big project, they take a break and are listening to some music when a popular song comes on that happens to be their favorite. They turn the music up, dance, and sing along to the catchy music until the lighthearted mood comes to a screeching halt when the white friend sings the n-word as part of the song lyrics. The Black friend is taken aback and crestfallen that their friend would use that hateful word. They immediately have a conversation about why the word is offensive and really should not be used by the friend, even when they are singing a song. The white friend genuinely thought that it was alright but learned an important lesson about the etymology of the word and how it was originally used to denigrate Black people during slavery. The word has since been reclaimed by some African Americans and is used as a form of ingroup communication and a term of endearment. Because the friends have a trusting relationship, they were able to communicate openly and honestly about the incident. Their interaction afterward was initially a bit uncomfortable, but they were eventually able to move through it, not "past it," by having a heart-to-heart and actually listening to each other. Instead of allowing the conflict to negatively impact their relationship, the friends used it as an opportunity to learn about themselves and each other's racial viewpoints and to be educated about the power of language.

Understanding the accurate definition of interracial communication should hopefully disarm anyone who has anxiety or apprehension about befriending someone from a different race. They should realize that their racial differences have most likely contributed to their identities (in varying degrees) and how they navigate the world; however, those differences are not and should not be immediate barriers to relationship development (Ford, 2012). The relationship is initially interpersonal; they are two people who are interacting and are dependent on each other. It is a mutually beneficial relationship that does not become interracial until their racial differences shift the nature of the interaction. People typically form relationships, both personal and professional, with people of their same race (i.e., intraracial). This is partially due to biases, prejudices, and stereotypes of outgroup members, which is largely true for whites. As the macroculture, whites do not have the pressure of double consciousness or being an outsider within (Meer, 2019). They are the cultural group to whom others must adapt, prompting BIPOC to be socialized at an early age about how to navigate spaces and places where they are the "only one" or one of a few BIPOC. At play is also the strong possibility that whites with limited interracial experience approach BIPOC with prejudices and stereotypes (Bahk & Jandt, 2008; Willow, 2008) and, as a result, have uncertainty and anxiety. That is why partners should approach the relationship as they would any other but with keen awareness that racial differences will, at some point, influence communication and relational dynamics. Instead of perceiving them as a barrier, the differences should be treated as a bridge to understanding and becoming culturally competent.

Institutional Structures

Institutional structures are societal-level phenomena that are seemingly innocuous but reflect the subconscious reinforcement of systemic racism through broader institutions. The concepts that represent this are (1) *critical race theory*, (2) *racism*, (3) *societal privilege*, and (4) *cultural appropriation* and *cultural appreciation*. Each concept has entered public rhetoric and prompted frank and volatile exchanges between friends, family members, colleagues, and strangers about issues related to race. This was particularly evident in the summer of 2020 as social media platforms were increasingly being used to articulate people's positions on racial justice and other related issues.

Critical Race Theory (CRT)

CRT entered the public sphere in May 2020, and it was apparent that it was being used to politicize racial justice through education. The explanation of the theory has been grossly distorted and misrepresented, further complicating public understanding of racism and the benefits of inclusive curricula. The spirit of the theory has intentionally been lost and is now being weaponized against scholars who study and teach about race and against citizens concerned about and supportive of racial justice.

CRT is about the relationship between race, racism, and power and creating parity across all racial/ethnic groups throughout society. People willing to be educated on race as a serious social issue learn that CRT has six tenets: (1) "racism is an integral part of the United States" that "reinforce[s] racial oppression"; (2) "claims of neutrality, objectivity, and color-blindness" in the legal world and society are unfounded; (3) race is not historical or a thing of the past but rather ever present and informs our past, present, and future; (4) experiential knowledge from BIPOC is at the center; (5) CRT is interdisciplinary and eclectic; and (6) CRT "actively works toward the elimination of racial oppression" (Orbe & Harris, 2015, pp. 154–55).

CRT is an applied theory used in disciplines such as communication studies (Harris & Weber, 2010), sociology (Christian et al., 2021), education (Ladson-Billings, 1995), and marketing (Poole et al., 2021) to critique the institutionalization of racism in nearly every facet of society (Pun, 2020). Its interdisciplinary nature is a testament to its claims of racism being an integral part of the United States. Scholars use both quantitative (i.e., survey) and qualitative (i.e., interview, focus group) approaches to show "how CRT and social science cross empirical boundaries in fruitful collaboration to document the reproduction of racism in the 21st century" (Christian et al., 2021, p. 1019). Simply put, "It is an approach or lens through which an educator can help students examine the role of race and racism in American society" (George, 2021). CRT forces us to confront the harsh reality of racism and the inequities it produces and perpetuates, with the end goal being to eradicate racist laws and policies. Legislators voraciously fighting to ban its use in public schools are deliberately whitewashing history and promoting an egregiously inaccurate and false narrative about the country's commitment to racism. Their actions are further widening a racial divide that continues to plague contemporary race relations (Pun, 2020).

Racism and Colorblind Racism

Racism is a word whose true meaning has been diluted. Most people define racism as a strong dislike for some people or a group because of their skin color. That definition is problematic because it ignores societal power, which is the very reason why the man-made construct of race was introduced. French physician Francis Bernier "created a racial categorization scheme that separated groups of people based on two elements: skin color and facial features" (Orbe & Harris, 2015, p. 29). This resulted in four primary racial groups: Europeans, Africans, Orientals, and Lapps. Johann Friedrich Blumenbach is recognized as the creator of five racial categories—White, Brown, Red, Black, and Yellow—and for driving racial divisions between these groups. Instead of being merely descriptors, the categories became value laden, with white being the most valued and most powerful group (as seen in, e.g., colonialism). The true definition of racism is "racial prejudice + societal power = racism" (Orbe & Harris, 2015, p. 10). This definition acknowledges that some racial groups have been systematically subordinated by a more powerful group, which is European Americans in the United States. As such, it is impossible for BIPOC to practice racism because they do not have institutional power; however, they can practice racial prejudice. Racial prejudice is "inaccurate and/or negative beliefs that espouse or support the superiority of one racial group" (p. 10). A negative or stereotypical prejudgment is made about a group or person because of their race. If a person acts on their racial prejudice, then it is *racial discrimination*. To be clear, all people can have racial prejudice and practice racial discrimination. However, the majority group (macroculture) that has the most societal power (i.e., whites) is the only group that can practice racism.

When people say they "don't see color," they are projecting what they believe is a neutral or objective position on racial/ethnic diversity. This colorblind mentality is a belief that race does not matter, which is also a denial of systemic racism (Vincenty, 2020). Colorblind racism is "rhetoric and discourse that eliminates race as a descriptor with the goal of equality through sameness" (Leonard, 2012; see Bonilla-Silva, 2006). In theory, colorblindness appears to be a well-intended way of thinking, but it is a subtle way to deny the existence of structural racism. As van Sterkenburg and Knoppers (2012) note, colorblind racism perpetuates racism "through the continuance of unobtrusive, routine, and everyday practices of racial/ethnic categorizing and stereotyping" (p. 2). The structure remains intact, and no efforts are made within the system to eliminate or address racism. At the center of colorblindness is the "removal of any taint or suggestion of white supremacy or white guilt while legitimating the existing social, political and economic arrangements which privilege whites" (Gallagher, 2003, p. 22).

Some of the public discourse about the victims of police brutality during the summer of 2020 shows how pervasive colorblind racism is for many people. Rather than question the need for or appropriateness of police brute force (i.e., murder) in nonthreatening encounters with Black citizens, some people chose to question the behavior and character of the victim. Others opted to justify the actions of police and reject the idea of institutional racism existing in law enforcement. Colorblind racism is a troubling racial ideology because it is "strategically designed to justify and downplay contemporary racial disparities" (Ellis & Branch-Ellis, 2020, p. 105).

Societal Privilege

Societal privilege is directly related to power and is defined as "a general favored state, one that has been earned or conferred by birth or luck" (Orbe & Harris, 2015, p. 65). This concept is part of an essential vocabulary because it is at the core of racism. Race is a human construct that was designed to create divisions between people groups and to reserve as much power as possible for whites, who achieved this status largely through colonialism and being the numerical majority. Societal privilege in all its forms is a contemporary benefit of racism. "Unlike that which is earned, power from unearned privilege can look like strength, but what it typically represents is an *unearned entitlement*" (Orbe & Harris, 2015, p. 65). Privilege is usually invisible to the beneficiary because it is rarely labeled. Beneficiaries are rarely, if ever, made aware of the benefits they reap due to their race (McIntosh, 1998). White privilege is a type of societal privilege in the United States wherein a person who is born white has automatic advantages because of their racial group membership. These advantages are unearned, so the individual does not have to work for them. This does not mean that a white person has not worked hard for their accomplishments. Rather, they have not had to face the systemic barriers to which BIPOC are regularly subjected.

Four qualities of privilege are that it is (1) a special advantage, (2) granted (not earned), (3) a right or entitlement because of a "preferred status or rank," or (4) "often outside of the awareness" of the beneficiary (Black & Stone, 2005, p. 244). Privilege is structural and perpetuates power imbalances. Other forms of privilege are gender privilege, class privilege, and heterosexual privilege. Most of these privileges are determined by birth and fixed; however, class privilege is a state that can change. A person's socioeconomic status can shift for various reasons, which subsequently affects their privilege or lack thereof. Gender privilege can also change for a transgender person, depending on their new and authentic gender. A transgender man moves from being oppressed as a female to being privileged because he now directly benefits from being a part of a very privileged group. Understanding privilege within the broader context of oppression is important because it illustrates the far-reaching impact racism and disparities have on all members of society (Black & Stone, 2005).

Cultural Appropriation and Cultural Appreciation

Cultural appropriation and cultural appreciation are two concepts that have been part of public discourse and debate for many years. They continue to be important social issues because they reflect racial divisions in the United States and lack of understanding and respect when it comes to historically marginalized groups. According to Jackson (2021), cultural appropriation is when the "powerful group takes aspects of the culture of the subordinated group, making them its own" (p. 88). A more common definition is "the use of one culture's symbols, artifacts, genres, rituals, or technologies by members of another culture—regardless of intent, ethics, function, or outcome" (Rogers, 2006, p. 476). Both definitions are important because they address the relationship between power and behaviors to underscore the gravity of this troubling behavior. Entertainers Kim Kardashian, Ariana Grande, Katy Perry, Miley Cyrus, and Beyoncé have all come under fire for cultural appropriation. Collectively, they are guilty of adopting aspects of a historically marginalized group and showcasing them on a public platform. They specifically exploited Black, Indian, and Japanese cultures by wearing culturally specific hairstyles (e.g., braids), wearing traditional Japanese (i.e., geisha) and Indian clothing and henna, and selling merchandise with incorrectly spelled cultural phrases. Public backlash was swift in condemning each of them for their inappropriateness and insensitivity. Supporters retorted that these were acts of appreciation and celebration of the depicted cultures, while critics argued that they were being disrespectful and mocking the very cultures the women were claiming to admire and respect.

The issue with cultural appropriation is that the act itself is "a source of pain and [creates] feelings of loss or violation" for members of the cultures that are being exploited (Jackson, 2021, p. 88). Ultimately, cultural appropriation does considerably more harm than good and trivializes the cultures that are being mimicked and mocked. The acts are deliberate, but it is difficult to determine whether the person's intentions are malicious or not. The intention is secondary because it does not matter what the goal was of the behavior. Attention and concern should be about the potential offense the cultural group may take to the behavior. Being a true global citizen requires being very sensitive to the thoughts, feelings, and attitudes of other people, especially if they are BIPOC.

Outgroup Consciousness

Outgroup consciousness refers to behaviors a person engages in that potentially contribute to miscommunication, conflict, or racial tensions. Anyone can be guilty of any of these actions; however, it is important to acknowledge that BIPOC are usually on the receiving end of them. They are socialized at a very young age to be aware of their racial and marginalized identities, so it is logical to assume that they might be more conscious of the covert and overt behaviors that will make it difficult to have productive dialogue and healthy interracial relationships. This means that we must be committed and dedicated to being empathic and sensitive to others. Going that extra mile will allow us to reap the benefits of fostering healthy relationships with people from other racial groups and aid us in becoming global citizens.

Intentionality versus Emotionality

The verbal message that we use to communicate to others is a deliberate action in that we are mentally choosing specific words to orally convey that message to the other person. There are times, however, when we misfire and are reminded of the phrase "Think before you speak." Some call it a Freudian slip, while others consider it accidental. In either case, we are sometimes guilty of hurting others with our words. As a receiver of that message, a person has the right to determine how they are going to receive and, if necessary, respond to that message. That is the general premise behind intentionality and emotionality in the context of interracial relationships. Orbe and Harris (2015) identify these as barriers to interracial relationships and highlight how important it is for partners to communicate about offending behaviors that occur in their relationship. These concepts are best understood from the perspective of the party who is receiving the message that was targeted to them. We will use the slur *gypped* to illustrate this point.

Intentionality is "the degree to which a certain behavior is perceived as purposefully causing hurt or harm" (Orbe & Harris, 2015, p. 204). The focus is on whether the receiver believes the message was intended to cause them hurt or harm. Regardless of what the offender says, the receiver is exercising their choice to decide for themselves if their partner's intent was willful or not. In this scenario, your friend used the slur *gypped* to describe a situation where they believed a merchant at a market where bartering or negotiating is the norm shortchanged them or tried to "rip them off." You are surprised that your friend used the slur, which is derived from the word *Gypsy*, a derogatory term for Romani people, and stereotypes them as thieves (Rubel, 2020). You have heard people use this term before and recently did research to better understand why it is offensive. Because you know your friend is a very mindful person, you place a lot of weight on their perceived intention and conclude that they did not purposefully mean to harm anyone. Even though neither of you is of Romani descent, you initiate a conversation to address the offense in the moment (while it is fresh on your minds) and discuss how use of the slur contributes to the perpetuation of racial/ethnic stereotypes that oftentimes go unchallenged, thereby normalizing such behavior. Your friend is surprised and embarrassed to learn this history and vows to never again use the slur.

Emotionality "involves [the] negative emotions or feelings stemming from first- and secondhand observation(s) of offending behavior" (Orbe & Harris, 2015, p. 204). In the same scenario, you are angry after hearing the friend use the racial slur. It was used in a joking manner, and while the slur was not directed at you, you could not ignore the emotions that you felt because of what your friend said. You are in disbelief and cannot ignore your emotional response. In that moment, you are not concerned with whether your friend's behavior was intentional. Instead, you want to address the impact the slur had on you as a receiver of the message. Although you are not Romani, you can only imagine that a person of Romani descent would feel anger and hurt if they were present and heard your friend use the word *gypped*. You have chosen to address the behavior directly so that you and your friend can benefit from this teachable moment. Hopefully, they will be more empathic when they witness the same behavior in future interactions where offensive language about a racial/ethnic group is used in that group's absence as well as in their presence in the event they are uncomfortable about addressing the situation themselves. The motivation for confronting the behavior should be to do what is ethical and moral rather than feeding a person's ego or embodying the "savior complex."

Advocate-Mentorship

The role of advocate-mentor, or the process of advocate-mentorship, is related to professional responsibilities a global citizen has in the workplace; however, there are relationship qualities and individual behaviors that a BIPOC might recognize and consider a priority as they navigate their professional and their personal relationships. Harris and Lee (2019) introduce the term in their article on mentoring and higher education, which can be applied to nearly any context where activism and support are necessary. (This does not seem applicable to a friendship since power is equally shared.) An advocate-mentor is a senior person (e.g., tenured faculty member, administrator) who will "defend SOC's [students of color's] intellectual abilities, validate their research interest, affirm their value to the department, and champion for research and/or teaching opportunities that will enhance the protégé's career advancement" (p. 107). An advocate-mentor actively works to have compassion and respect for their protégé, "which requires exercising racial, professional, and/or intellectual privilege to engage in activism on behalf of their marginalized protégé" (p. 107). In other words, they are using their power and influence to advance the interests and professional development of the less powerful person.

The spirit of the advocate-mentor role is similar to societal understandings of an ally in that there is a concern about systemic oppression and its impact on BIPOC; however, Harris and Lee (2019) argue that the advocate-mentor label, or simply the term *advocate*, should be used instead of ally. Ally has become a self-assigned label that people use to announce their support of BIPOC. This is a dangerous act because it does not account for the actual activism the person has engaged in to dismantle systemic oppression. They are essentially claiming that their expression of support is sufficient, and that is not necessarily the case. The term *ally* is also criticized for being performative or hollow, which is something that should be wholly avoided if true antiracism is to occur. A person can be an advocate in their social circles by directly confronting racism and doing so without fear of the consequences. Their act of defending BIPOC may be well received because they have nothing to personally gain from addressing the offensive behavior. An advocate may also lose some of their benefits, such as networking opportunities or friendships, and accepts the reality that this is a risk they are willing to take. It is important for the advocate or advocate-mentor to privately and publicly engage in an ongoing pattern of activism and resistance (Terry, 2021) that challenges institutional racism on an individual, department, institutional, and societal level.

Racial Macroaggression and Microaggression

Macroaggression and *microaggression* are also two words that have recently entered the public lexicon and are used on a fairly regular basis. Although not directly related to the murder of Mr. George Floyd, people have used the terms to highlight how interpersonal infractions such as these are a precursor for potentially deadly incidents. People now have a heightened general awareness of how covert and overt actions on an individual level contribute to and perpetuate systemic oppression on a societal level. Whether they realize it or not, people are using scholarly research to understand this whole phenomenon.

The concept *racial microaggression* was first introduced by psychiatrist Chester M. Pierce in the 1970s. It was subsequently popularized by Derald Sue, who is noted for "naming, detailing and classifying the actual manifestations of aversive racism" (Harris et al., 2018, p. 72). Sue et al. (2007) define racial microaggressions as "brief and commonplace daily verbal, behavioral, or environmental indignities, whether intentional or unintentional, that communicate hostile, derogatory, or negative racial slights and insults toward people of color" (p. 271). These behaviors are enacted on the individual level and directly impact the individual. *Racial macroaggressions* occur on the broader, societal level and include "systemic and institutional forms of racism . . . manifested in the philosophy, programs, policies, practices and structures of governmental agencies, legal and judicial systems, health care organizations, educational institutions, and business and industry" (Sue et al., 2019, p. 131). Racial macroaggressions are different from racial microaggressions because they directly impact entire groups or classes of people on a systemic level.

Communication via verbal messages is at the heart of racial micro- and macroaggressions (Davis, 2019; Harris et al., 2018), which is why they are included in this essential vocabulary. Understanding microassaults, microinsults, and microinvalidations committed in our relationships is a piece in the bigger puzzle of dismantling racism. Avoiding these behaviors in our own relationships and confronting them when we either witness them or learn about them after an incident can also be instrumental in improving race relations. Racial micro- and macroaggressions occur across a lifetime, and to no one's surprise, these compounded experiences have a long-lasting effect on the targeted BIPOC (Compton-Lily, 2020) (e.g., negative academic outcomes, impostor syndrome, distrust, adverse health outcomes) and on Black adolescents subjected to both racism and sexism (Gadson & Lewis, 2021; Moore & Nash, 2021).

Internal Identity Reflection

Internal identity reflection is a fairly small category in comparison to the others, but it is equally important given its focus. This category contains two interrelated concepts that apply to an outgroup member and the extent to which they have self-awareness regarding their racial identity. The concepts are racial location and racial standpoint. *Racial location* refers to the racial/ethnic group that a person belongs to (Orbe & Harris, 2015). A person's racial membership is determined by birth and is something over which a person does not have control. This aspect of a person's identity will directly influence how they engage with and make sense of the world in which they live. A racial standpoint is something that a person achieves "through critical reflections on power relations and through the creation of a political stance that exists in opposition to dominant cultural systems" (Wood, 2005, p. 61). While everyone has a racial location, only people of color can attain a *racial standpoint*, and that is through working with other people of color. This awareness is also due to the fact that a racial standpoint is achieved as a direct result of oppression experienced within the structure of societal dominance; therefore, since European Americans are the dominant group and have societal power, they are unable to have a racial standpoint (Orbe & Harris, 2015). Nevertheless, they can have a standpoint due to other oppressive systems that can be shaped by their "membership in traditionally marginalized groups defined by sex, sexual orientation, and socioeconomic status" (Wood, 2005, p. 62).

As with racism, racial standpoints are directly tied to systemic oppression, which means that power has a profound impact on how people experience their world and ultimately understand who they are in the process. The fact that European Americans can have a racial location but not a standpoint is due to their social position in society, by no fault of their own. A structure was created centuries ago in which they are most advantaged as the dominant group, and as a result, there are groups that will be placed at a serious disadvantage because of this system. Given this gulf between racial groups, mutual understanding is something that the partners will have to work toward. Because the powerful and the powerless have markedly different perceptions and realities, each group and member takes a different path toward realizing these disparities. This was made abundantly clear throughout the summer of 2020 and beyond when many people became more cognizant of racial standpoints because of the Great Awokening. To have healthy interracial relationships, partners must establish trust and honesty; otherwise their differences will create a gulf that might be impossible to bridge.

External Identity Expression

The final category of external identity expression is all-encompassing and refers to the identity that everyone should strive to embody, especially when it comes to interracial relationships or other relationship types where people come from different cultural groups. The one concept that reflects this ideal is *cultural competence*. Ahmed and Bates (2017) define cultural competence "as a process which promotes understanding, awareness, and acknowledgement of individual differences and differences within and across cultures with the aim to make cultural adaptations" (p. 55). In other words, the partners must put in the effort to be more knowledgeable about each other's race/cultural experiences and identities, with the end goal being becoming more effective communicators within that relational context and others. Cultural competency is a practical and socially relevant area of communication scholarship stressing the importance of communication skills and behaviors in intercultural interactions. Theories such as anxiety/uncertainty management theory (Gudykunst, 1995), personal network approach (Kim, 1995), systems-theory approach (Kim, 2002), and identity negotiation perspective

(Ting-Toomey, 1993) have offered support for assumptions by scholars that racially and culturally different interactants experience myriad emotions and engage in an assortment of strategies to develop and maintain these relationships. These relationships are literally an exercise in cultural competency because the partners expect each other to be aware of, learn about, and adapt to their respective differences.

Agyeman and Erickson (2012) argue that "recognizing, understanding, and engaging difference, diversity, and cultural heterogeneity in creative and productive ways requires cultural competency" (p. 358). Although their study focused on cultural competency in education, they and other scholars recognize that we are living in an increasingly diverse world, which means that people must be prepared through education to have more interactions and close relationships with people from racial and cultural backgrounds different from their own (Gai, 2014; Horner, 2011). Thus, mastering effective communication skills becomes paramount. Not only will partners with this shared relational goal commit to broadening their communication tool kit, but they will expect their partner to exhibit communication competency. This expectation is the heart of external identity expression in that competency behaviors reflect a partner's character and the trust and vulnerability fostered in the relationship. Both partners should prepare for and expect to evaluate each other consciously and subconsciously on how their competency is improving over the course of their relationship.

THE POWER OF LANGUAGE AND INTENTIONAL DIALOGUE

Many lessons were learned from the summer of 2020 regarding racial and social justice, one of which was that communication is a key—not *the* key—to creating the kind of change that is crucial at this juncture in our country's history. People in the United States and throughout the world bore witness to the mounting evidence that racism is thriving and alive and well. Police brutality rapidly became an open secret that BIPOC knew all too well and was leading to the senseless murders of Black men, boys, women, and girls. Others, mostly European Americans, were shocked by the magnitude and callousness of the repeated, senseless murders that were becoming all too common. The Great Awokening literally jolted many out of a slumber and compelled them to be a part of the societal change we need now more than ever.

Part of this change necessitates a commitment to becoming more educated about racism, prejudice, xenophobia, and other forms of oppression that have had profoundly devastating and sometimes deadly consequences for the oppressed. Education involves intentionally unlearning problematic ideologies formally and informally taught through our social networks (i.e., family, friendships) and institutions (i.e., school, work, media). On an individual level, people can initiate intellectual and moral interventions by doing their own research and finding credible books, online resources, interest groups, and local racial/social justice initiatives created, produced, and led by BIPOC. These resources undoubtedly provide one with nuanced perspectives on racial issues that are usually ignored or relegated to the margins by mainstream society. By initiating and maintaining these individual-level efforts, a person is intentionally seeking opportunities for perspective-taking and equipping themselves with the knowledge and communication skills necessary for healthy and productive conversations. This can ultimately lay the groundwork for us to move out of our comfort zones and seek opportunities to organically diversify our social circles and work environments.

This book is written in the hope that we will all refuse to let the Great Awokening of 2020 be in vain. The racial unrest shook many of us to our core, ultimately serving us a needed and deserved wake-up call. As a nation and a people, we have been complicit in allowing systems of oppression to be normalized. While some have been fighting the good fight, others have chosen to idly stand by, ignore the issues, dismiss and minimize, or deny them. Many of us are also tired—mentally, emotionally, and spiritually drained from the cumulative racism and racial trauma to which we have been subjected for a lifetime. Cumulative racism is defined as "an accumulation of racially traumatic experiences over the course of one's life or a specific period of time; the offending party is usually a person(s) with racial and/or societal privilege" (Harris et al., forthcoming). Advocates have stood by us, supporting us and actively doing their part in dismantling racism through honest, heartfelt conversations and creating change in the spaces where it is needed. Regardless of and because of who we are, we must all boldly, confidently, and assertively create opportunities for these intentional conversations to take place. Being intentional requires actively (and authentically) seeking opportunities to have difficult yet necessary conversations about race and racism with people from racial groups different from our own. Avoid performative activism or performative outrage (see chapter 1), as your vain and selfish motives will surely come to light. Seize opportunities for dialogue—initiate them even—and use them as "learnable" moments, moments where we authentically learn from others and become inspired to be the change we want to see. Combined, our knowledge and relationships will assuredly contribute to dismantling racism by seeing our relationships as the perfect landscape for societal transformation. Just as racism, sexism, prejudice, homophobia, and xenophobia are all learned, they can all be unlearned. We simply need to hold ourselves and others accountable for being the change we are desperately in need of.

Chapter 3

Interracial Communication within the Family

The family is the first interpersonal network we are introduced to as humans. Whether it is our biological or adopted family, we all originate from some type of kin network that plays a critical role in shaping how we understand who we are as a family unit, individuals, and, ultimately, members of society. The communication patterns that exist within this very small community have a significant impact on how we also engage with others and the world around us. We learn social norms, cultural traditions, and behavioral expectations that, in some way, prepare us for life outside of that familial net. According to Orbe and Harris (2015), there are two types of people who influence how we perceive and understand ourselves. A *generalized other* is a person who makes up "the collective body from which the individual sees the self," and *orientational others* are those who have direct influence on our identity development (p. 102). Greater value is placed on orientational others because we (typically) trust them and appreciate their perceptions of us, whereas a generalized other does not know us as well; therefore, we might not place as much value on the opinions of generalized others. There is an assumption that the generalized other and orientational other are qualitatively different in their varying degrees of influence on how we understand who we are. Whether this is true or not, it is imperative that we consider the extent to which we are impacted by others with whom we have an intimate connection and by those with whom we do not.

These relationships inevitably influence not only who we understand ourselves to be but also the perceptions we have of others and the way we choose to interact with them. As social beings, we desire a connection to others, and depending on our needs and experiences, we might be in situations where we are conflicted about interacting with people of a different race, for example. Similarly, we may experience discomfort when our ideologies about race (i.e., racism, privilege, prejudice, discrimination) are challenged after being exposed to ideas, thoughts, and beliefs different from our own. This was evident throughout 2020 during the racial unrest triggered by the murders of George Floyd and Breonna Taylor. There were many white people for whom the issue of police brutality was a foreign concept largely due to their whiteness. Others were self-described allies committed to fighting against racial injustices. On the more toxic side, there were those who attacked cries of injustice and faulted African Americans for making things unnecessarily racial. More extreme responses involved suspicions that "outside agitators" disguised as civil rights protestors were being planted in the crowds to perpetuate tropes of violent, unruly, and disruptive looters. These efforts attempted to delegitimize the intent of the movement; however, they revealed how truly divided our society is about the reality of racism (Zhou, 2020). Public discourse demonstrated how a lack of interracial communication is but one factor contributing to our long history of tense race relations. Some racial groups are very entrenched in beliefs preserving the status quo (Jost & Banaji, 1994), and if coupled with an unwillingness or inability to have difficult conversations, these views mean the responsibility for such dialogue falls on communities of color, particularly those most affected by racism. Thus, it is imperative that we individually and collectively consider the role that everyone plays in dismantling racism. By beginning with our families, we are actively working from the ground up to reshape our society into one that is authentically inclusive and celebratory and encourages positive interracial relationships.

THE HEART OF SOCIOPOLITICAL DIVISIONS

The sociopolitical climate of the United States during the 2016 presidential election was a foreshadowing of the fissures that would continue to widen in political affiliations and close relationships. Relationships were being torn apart, and in some instances dissolved, as families, friends, colleagues, and strangers engaged in heated debates about the sexism, racism, classism, and homophobia perpetuated by the Trump campaign and subsequent administration. People drew lines in the proverbial sand, suspending or terminating relationships because of the ideological rifts that had surfaced. The personal became political and the political became personal. This was borne out in a 2016 Reuters/Ipsos poll of 6,426 people conducted between December 27 and January 18 about their conflicts over politics with family and friends (Whitesides, 2017). Participants were from every state in the United States and revealed a pattern of relational conflict, with a 6 percent increase in the number of conflicts and 16 percent reporting they had ceased all communication with a family member or friend. In terms of political affiliation, 22 percent of those who voted for Democrat Hillary Clinton had stopped communication, and 13 percent of participants terminated a relationship with a family member or close friend because of the presidential election, which was a 1 percent increase since October (Whitesides, 2017). Some specific termination strategies included cutting off cousins, blocking phone numbers of family members, and explicitly telling a longtime friend of twenty-five years, for example, the relationship was over (Smith, 2020). Though not reported in this study, some people even took to social media platforms such as TikTok with emotion-filled video stories reporting being kicked out of their families. Sadly, many of those relationships and others remain in disrepair (Pinsker, 2021).

Collectively, these reports speak to the toll that racism has been taking on people and their relationships. Other political issues have been intertwined with the racial injustices driving these tensions, and it is abundantly clear that people do not have the communication skills necessary for discussing race and other difficult topis. It is also clear that the perspectives or opinions are much deeper than what they appear to be; they are fundamentally moral and ethical issues regarding humanity. The divisions are the result of inhumane governmental policies and practices that infringe on basic human rights that should be—but are not—afforded to historically marginalized groups. People refuse to acknowledge the root of these issues because they are either misinformed, in denial, or willfully choosing to blame the victims. In the latter case, there is a belief that we are living in a world where all things are equal, and they are not. There is disbelief that systemic oppression exists, thereby endorsing a "bootstrap mentality." This ideology holds that society is very much a meritocracy, with an assumption that, from birth, everyone is on the same playing field or that equity is something that can be achieved upon reaching financial independence after adolescence (Fox, 2020). This way of thinking is fallacious for three reasons: (1) meeting basic necessities, as per Maslow's hierarchy of needs, is a priority for economically disadvantaged people and prevents them from achieving other needs (i.e., poverty as a cycle); (2) lower access to and quality of education creates limitations to knowledge and opportunities for those "unprioritized by the U.S. education system"; and (3) racial and gender wage gaps have a material impact on raced and gendered people, impacting "their ability to overcome adversities" (Fox, 2020, p. 2). Those reducing current sociopolitical issues to matters of opinion fail to acknowledge and accept that contemporary society was founded on a system inherently designed to perpetuate inequities. There always have been and will continue to be underprivileged and overprivileged people groups coexisting and competing for the same resources and rights. However, we do not have to remain beholden to racial, gender, and economic disparities. Instead, we can commit to having difficult conversations about how we can use our societal privileges and opportunities to "right the ship," as it were, and make all things equal.

WHY "THE (RACE) TALK" IS NECESSARY

The phrase "The Talk" has qualitatively different meanings for racial groups and for seemingly obvious reasons. Whites and people of color are socialized differently when it comes to racial identities and race, which means that the way they talk about these issues, if they talk about them at all, are different as well. For families of color, most members are made keenly aware of their race early in life. Parents will typically do their part and have a frank conversation about race with their children. Black colloquialism refers to "the race talk" simply as "The Talk"; it is understood that a serious conversation is to be or has been had about what it means to be Black in the United States. Parents equip their children as best they can with the knowledge, resources, and emotional support they need to live in a world where racial inequities are real. More importantly, The Talk involves life lessons designed to provide children—regardless of age—with the survival skills they may ultimately need to escape situations that could very well end in death through no fault of their own.

The Talk is taking place more frequently and intently considering the steady surge in cases of police brutality involving Black people. Because "Black men are 2.5 times more likely than white men to be killed by police during their lifetime" and "Black people who were fatally shot by police seemed to be twice as likely as white people to be unarmed" (Peeples, 2020, para. 22), the Black population as a whole is on high alert that their lives are at risk at any given moment. Added to the mix is the adultification bias against Black boys and girls, which increases the likelihood of them being victims of racial profiling. Adultification bias is defined as "the phenomenon where adults perceive Black youth as being older than they actually are" (Asare, 2021). Even though the aforementioned statistics do not account for this bias, it is reasonable to assume that police and society seeing and treating little boys and girls as adults rather than the children they are is yet another aspect of being Black that is covered in The Talk. This probably occurs with other children of color, too, and for parents of these children, there is the incessant worry of their child being mistaken for an adult and killed—the worst manifestation of racism imaginable. Conversely, The Talk for white parents is very different: it is a heart-to-heart conversation they have with their children about sex. Even if it never happens, it is unlikely to involve any discussion of race, as racialized realities for whites are vastly different and are shaped by privilege. To be clear, white privilege does not mean or suggest white people are exempt from life's hardships and have everything handed to them on a silver platter. White privilege happens on a societal level and refers to "an institutional (rather than personal) set of benefits granted to those of us who, by race, resemble the people who dominate the powerful positions in our institutions" (Kendall, 2006, p. 63). This means that, by the very nature of being born into the dominant group (i.e., the numerical majority), white people have greater access to power and resources than do people of color based on the color of their skin. The overall benefit of white privilege is not having to worry about racism in the way that Black families do or, more importantly, being subjected to racial profiling over the course of one's life. Granted, other forms of systemic oppression (e.g., sexism, classism, heteronormativity) are just as important; however, for the purpose of this book, race is being prioritized because it is *still* a taboo topic many people are uncomfortable talking about. There is hesitancy to talk about it within our same-race circles and certainly across or between races. Thus, this book is challenging us to make the uncomfortable comfortable. Normalizing talking about race is a life-and-death situation.

Communication scholars Guerrero and Afifi (1995b) identified four reasons white parents and their children avoid discussing race together. These reasons are (1) self-protection, which is the desire to "avoid judgment, criticism, embarrassment, and vulnerability"; (2) relationship protection, or the desire to avoid conflict, eliciting anger, or to deescalate the relationship; (3) social inappropriateness, or commitment to a pattern of avoiding topics deemed socially inappropriate to discuss; and (4) parent unresponsiveness, or topic avoidance due to the perception of parental unresponsiveness, trivialization of the topic, or "lack of relevant knowledge necessary for handling the problem" (Docan-Morgan, 20, p. 340). Each reason aims to not disrupt the status quo, and while the desire to protect oneself, a child, or the relationship is understandable, there are consequences for choosing this route. It means that a person is complicit in perpetuating racism, even if they are not doing the actual harm themselves. By not choosing an antiracism stance, a person is allowing a system of oppression that causes various forms of harm to people of color to remain intact. There are certainly risks associated with talking about racism and its impact on the underprivileged and overprivileged, but it should be our moral imperative as humans to bring order and balance to humanity by communicating about racism and how we can deconstruct these oppressive ideologies in all areas of our lives. Thus, the following sections of this chapter illustrate how the family can be used to achieve this very important goal. There will be an overview of three family communication theories—systems theory (Mele et al., 2010), system justification theory (van der Toorn & Jost, 2014), and communication privacy management (Petronio, 2002)—used to describe the interconnectedness of family members and how communication functions to maintain the unit. Then there will be a discussion of how the racial socialization process occurs within white, same-race, interracial, and transracial families. Each family type has different ways of engaging its members in conversations about race and racism—some more than others—and how they should see themselves as raced or unraced/nonraced people. These processes either intentionally or unintentionally contribute to interracial conflict, misunderstandings, and willful ignorance. Racial orientations are sometimes framed as being oppositional, and if authentic interracial communication is to occur, we must be willing and committed to doing the good and hard work that is required. By offering reasonable solutions and recommendations for transcending our differences and making things common (Orbe & Harris, 2022), this chapter will hopefully encourage families across the racial/ethnic spectrum to do their part in dismantling racism.

FAMILY COMMUNICATION

General systems theory is multidisciplinary and places specific attention on the interactions of members within a system. A system is an entity that is a coherent whole believed to have a boundary around it that distinguishes internal and external elements from each other and identifies input and output related to the existing and evolving entity. Thus, the theory is "a theoretical perspective that analyzes a phenomenon seen as a whole and not as simply the sum of elementary parts" (Mele et al., 2010, p. 127). Scholars have identified three types of systems: open, closed, and isolated. An open system is one that facilitates "exchanges of energy, matter, people, and information with the external environment," and a closed system is one that has "no exchanges of information and matter, just exchanges of energy" (p. 127). An isolated system is one that allows for no exchange of elements. Families and companies are examples of systems scholars use this theory to understand.

Families are open systems when they are influenced by people, things, and events that exist outside of the family unit. This would include families of color that have ongoing dialogue about racial profiling and police brutality, for example. Rather than ignore these events, such families have open communication about them and are ultimately influenced by them. In other words, the different parts of the system (i.e., family members) recalibrate to define themselves in light of the racism. Closed family systems are those that essentially just exist and are not impacted by external events. Whether it is purposeful or not, this system experiences no change; it remains unimpacted by broader society. In this instance, it might be a white family that believes unknowingly or knowingly that race and racism have nothing to do with them. The members are expected to remain committed to the system and reject anything that might cause change. The isolated system takes resistance a bit further and actively avoids any kind of influence from society. This kind of family might be very wedded to racist ideologies that discourage a multicultural society and expects its members to maintain the status quo.

According to Mele et al. (2010), there are four functions of actions within the system: (1) adaptation, (2) goal attainment, (3) pattern maintenance, and (4) integration. Individually and collectively, these actions are essential to maintaining the existence and effectiveness of a system in addition to establishing equilibrium or balance. Adaptation means parts of the system have open exchanges with the system's environment that lead to a change in or response from the system. Families of color adapt when they are responding to changes in society, such as racial profiling. There will be more race talks that also involve discussion of strategies for managing interracial interactions that avoid placing oneself in harm's way. The family also reaffirms itself as a Black family proud of its racial/ethnic background and its ability to remain intact despite societal factors threatening its overall well-being and functioning. Goal attainment refers to the system (i.e., family) using resources to attain goals related to other systems present in the environment (Mele et al., 2010). In other words, the system will determine how to best reach its goals of being a system or a family unit. This includes the process by which the organization or family institute traditions and roles each person is expected to assume as an organization member (i.e., parent, child, sibling). Lastly, pattern maintenance and integration are concerned with developing and maintaining a system's culture through symbolic frames. Symbolic frames are values, rituals, ceremonies, and stories, for example, that are important to the system. Because of its commitment to cohesion, the family engages in activities that contribute to its members remaining connected to each other.

A second theory that explains familial communication is system justification theory (Jost & Banaji, 1994), which contends that individuals adapt to aspects of society's status quo "by denying or rationalizing injustices and other problems, even when doing so comes at the expense of their personal and group interests" (van der Toorn & Jost, 2014, p. 414). Thus, members will use "avoidance of threatening information and denial" (Cargile & Kahn, 2021, p. 103). This happens because the more a person believes "in the justice of the social system, the more he or she will engage in various types of system justification" (Cargile & Kahn, 2021, p. 103). In other words, the person's beliefs will have a direct impact on what they may or may not do to change the way things are in society. They will engage in system justification (Rosenthal et al., 2011), which comes in different forms. Consider the following example. A white woman's beliefs about racism change after witnessing media coverage of the 2020 racial unrest and, more importantly, her heartfelt conversations with her Korean American colleague about the rising hate crimes against Asian Americans and Pacific Islanders. She and her family are using their white privilege to make things more equal, even on the local level. Their system justification efforts include conducting extensive research for a comprehensive reading list of books and articles by BIPOC on race and racism to become more educated and to help dismantle racism. They also redefine themselves as antiracists and now willingly and directly confront other family members, neighbors, and strangers when racism crops up. This includes intense self-reflection as individuals and a family to reevaluate their own beliefs, divorcing themselves from all types of racism, and admitting they have white privilege. At the heart of their efforts is a willingness and commitment to regularly have difficult familial talks about race and to be a part of the solution for rather than a part of the problem of racism.

A third theory vital to understanding family communication is communication privacy management (CPM) theory. Petronio and Caughlin (2006) explain that "both keeping and telling information in different situations may be either beneficial or detrimental to the individual family members and the family as a whole" (pp. 35–36). CPM theory posits that people learn and develop rules for how information is to be revealed (Docan-Morgan, 2011), and these involve what is be disclosed, to whom, how much, when, and where to disclose information (Petronio, 2002). Socialization to this process is collectively negotiated and involves privacy rules that are typically implicit, rarely explicitly stated, and communicated within the context of the family (Docan-Morgan, 2011). Parents determine for the family what information is considered private, what is to remain within the family, and what is to be shared with others. Race is a topic some transracial families consider private, and as Docan-Morgan (2011) explains, one rule they use is topic avoidance, which is ineffective because they are choosing to be inactive and potentially allowing a problem to fester.

Taken together, these theories can offer a fuller picture of how real families communicate or not about race. Systems theory can be used to explain the influence of the external environment on the family unit and how it defines itself and functions (Mele et al., 2010). Families as open systems are optimal because they recognize racism as a systemic issue affecting them as individuals, a family, and society members. Ideally, they will redefine themselves due to their racial identities and become committed to being antiracists. Closed and isolated family systems are a hindrance to fighting racism because they refuse to be impacted by the external environment (Mele et al., 2010), which effectively means their willful ignorance regarding racism is perpetuating and doing the opposite. Families avoid these difficult conversations about race and racism for various reasons (Docan-Morgan, 2011), many of which are self-serving. From a racial standpoint, it may be a desire to avoid white guilt and other feelings of discomfort, something families of color cannot avoid. Families of color are forced to have race talks in perpetuity because few people with societal power are willing to use their privilege to dismantle racism. Dismantling racism requires that white people, along with BIPOC, confront racial injustices at work, in their social networks, and other public spaces where racism is likely to occur. This can be done if these conversations are primarily or initially occurring with their families since they are a source of strength and stability. According to Jost and Banaji's (1994) system justification theory, families committed to the status quo regarding the family and society will do nothing to disrupt either system. This means difficult conversations will not take place. Because racist ideologies are most likely learned from families (Snyder, 2011), it is in this relational context that we must all discuss race-related issues such as white privilege, racism, prejudice, and discrimination. This will assuredly lead to revelations about how CPM operates in this underexamined area of communication research (Petronio, 2002). It will also have practical implications for real families by encouraging them to redefine who they are in an increasingly multicultural world.

DISPARITIES IN EXPERIENCES WITH RACISM

Family is an important relational context for exploring the ways we can better communicate about race since that is where we learn many of our life skills and how to navigate the world. Naturally, our ties to our families are typically strong, and when we face situations where those ties or beliefs are challenged, it forces us to make difficult decisions. It also has the potential to adversely affect family dynamics and relationships, as previously discussed. This is particularly the case for those families who rarely or never discuss race, which are more often white families. They are less likely to be negatively impacted by systemic racism than people of color (POC) and are beneficiaries of systemic racism (Bartoli et al., 2016; Docan-Morgan, 2011; Sullivan et al., 2021). Conversely, families of color regularly communicate about race because their racial identities are at the core of who they are, and they must interact with the world as racialized beings. These racial differences were evident in the study by Sullivan et al. (2021) of 1,000 Black and white parents shortly before and after George Floyd's murder. Familial discourse about race and racism became more frequent for Black parents, which included conversations designed to prepare their children for experiences with bias. There was no change in white parents' familial discourse about race. In fact, more effort was spent socializing their children to adopt a colorblind mentality and to see race/racism as "inconsequential, a privilege Black parents cannot afford" (Sullivan et al., 2021).

Though well-intended, this socialization strategy might fail because it is "reducing children's ability to identify and combat racial inequality" (Sullivan et al., 2021, p. 13). Sullivan et al. (2021) conclude that white parents' communication strategies were ineffective even when considering the national racial unrest at the time. They also stress how failure to communicate about racism allows it to "remain unaddressed and underrecognized" (p. 10). From this study and others, it is abundantly clear the onus of responsibility for initiating and managing conversations about race primarily resides with Black people and other POC. "Until White parents begin to talk with their children about racial biases, Black parents may have no choice but to continue to prepare their children to experience them" (Sullivan et al., 2021, p. 4). The findings, while not generalizable, offer significant evidence that these familial conversations are necessary for improved race relations and social justice to take place.

Just like parents of color, white parents must also have these difficult conversations with their children and each other if we are going to see true change in how we communicate across racial lines. Children have vastly different worldviews due to their racial identities, and because race is deemed a nonissue for many whites, white families rarely engage in productive discussions about race (Franco et al., 2020). Conversely, children of color are socialized at an early age to be race-conscious because their parents are very aware of the biases, prejudices, and discrimination their children will face (Franco et al., 2020; Snyder, 2012). They want their children to be prepared and on guard when they have these encounters. For decades, parents of color have always had to have The Talk with their children, and in light of the racial unrest perpetually plaguing the United States, the frequency and intensity of those conversations have increased (Franco et al., 2020; Sullivan et al., 2021; Waring & Bardoloi, 2019). There was an urgency for these conversations in 2020 since the number of Black and Brown boys, girls, women, and men being racially profiled and murdered by police continued to significantly rise. It was also fueled by the countless false accusations of illegal acts hurled at Blacks while engaging in everyday activities. Sadly, this is nothing new, as Black people have always been subjected to brutal accusations that have unnecessarily involved the police, sometimes ending in murder. This is why The Talk is critical: *it is a matter of life and death for Black children and adults.*

The Talk for Black families involves equipping Black children with the knowledge and resources necessary for avoiding life-threatening as well as more subtly racist encounters. The talk that should take place within white families must be frank and honest in addressing racial hierarchies grounded in racism, which must include discussing whiteness and white privilege. To be clear, the goal is not to make people feel guilty because of their racial identities (see chapter 2). Rather, it is to (1) to bring awareness to racial disparities dividing groups into the overprivileged and the underprivileged and (2) encourage an antiracist positionality boldly confronting racism on interpersonal, social, and institutional levels.

The race talk is urgent due to the material consequences racism has for everyone, especially people of color. Racism continues to exist because of the messages communicated that preserve it and allow it to remain unchallenged. People of color are certainly talking about racism and all that it entails because that is their reality; however, whites might not be engaging as much or at all because they are beneficiaries of systemic racist or they might be genuinely afraid for various reasons. Nevertheless, the conversations must begin with understanding the origins of race, which is attributed to Johann Friedrich Blumenbach (1865), who extended work by Carl Linnaeus. Linnaeus believed all humans were *Homo sapiens*, and his goal was to use geography and physical differences to categorize people (Orbe & Harris, 2015). Blumenbach subsequently identified five distinct racial groups that were eventually ranked: Europeans (White), Malays (Brown), Americans (Native Americans/Alaskan natives; Red), Africans (Black), and Asians (Yellow). Over time, these racial categories have become a ranking system that is still currently used as we manage our interracial interactions.

Despite being created more than 100 years ago, this racial hierarchy has unfortunately withstood the test of time and continues to unnecessarily problematize race relations, among other phenomena in society. As a society, we continue to place relative value on each other, and in the United States, Blacks and other BIPOC pay a never-ending price for being devalued as a people group. Whites remain beneficiaries of this system and regularly reap the benefits of their privilege. This has been made abundantly clear by the overwhelming number of incidents where white women have involved police with unfounded accusations of illegal behavior against Black adults and children (Ortiz, 2018). The allegations have been so frequent, outrageous, and life-threatening that the hashtag #WhileBlack was created in 2018 to demonstrate how preposterous these accusations are. Black people engaging in fairly mundane activities are suddenly jolted into the reality of racism and confronted by white women accusing them of illegal behavior. Each instance was found not to be illegal; however, the women were certainly guilty of moral and ethical violations against the victims.

Among the notable examples of these egregious incidents are a white woman calling police to arrest a Black man birdwatching in Central Park (Ransom, 2020), a Black man working in his neighborhood garden (Burch, 2018), and a Black woman student napping on a residence hall sofa at Yale University (Griggs, 2018). Each of these acts is an example of the criminalization of Blackness, or being Black, and unfortunately this happens to children as well. White women have called the police to report behavior they wrongly alleged was illegal, including but not limited to selling bottled water (Campisi et al., 2018), selling hot dogs (Beck, 2018), and swimming in a community pool (Wynne, 2020). There was even an unfathomable and patently false accusation from a Brooklyn woman that a nine-year-old Black boy groped her in a deli despite video footage showing the incident never occurred (Lockhart, 2018).

These are but a few incidents from among surely thousands of others, and unfortunately, they are reminiscent of the historic 1955 murder of fourteen-year-old Chicagoan Emmett Till, who was lied about by Caroyln Bryant, a white Mississippi woman, and accused of grabbing and verbally assaulting her in a store (Guardian, 2017). Despite a lack of evidence, Bryant's husband and brother-in-law brutally murdered the teenager and threw his body into the Tallahatchie River. "Till had a bullet hole in the head, an eye gouged out and other wounds," "barbed wire around his neck," and was anchored "with a cotton gin fan" (*Guardian*, 2017, para. 3). The men were cleared by an all-white jury who deliberated for only one hour; the men then publicly admitted guilt and said the gruesome murder was to "warn other blacks" who were coming south and "stirring up trouble." They wanted to remind them of their "place" in society.

In thinking about these recent events, it is important to remember that these ways of thinking originate somewhere, including in the family. Families have to break through many barriers if they are to do their part in changing these potentially deadly ideologies and dismantling racism. One way to do so is to integrate the race talk into the racial identity socialization process. Granted, parents of color are already having these conversations. The onus of responsibility now also lies with white parents, who either choose to avoid or do not know how to have these conversations altogether, or engage in surface-level conversations that offer no real solutions to the problem of racism. People in general have a difficult time talking about race, and for parents, there is a fear that, for Black children, such discussions will cause their children to be angry and bitter or that children will not comprehend racism (Snyder, 2012). There is even fear among some Black parents that "such discussions will inhibit children from fulfilling their potential" (Snyder, 2012, p. 245). As previously noted, white parents have similar concerns as well, demonstrating how parents across all racial groups face barriers to orienting their children to issues of race.

Racial Identity Socialization as a Gateway to the Race Talk

What is important to note is that racial identity socialization is different for whites and people of color. These differences cause racial disparities in parent/child communication that eventually translate into societal disparities since biased thinking and behaviors certainly occur in the occupations and other spaces that people eventually fill. Snyder (2012) defines racial socialization as "the transmission of information, norms, and values about race and ethnicity to children" (p. 230). As previously discussed, Guerrero and Afifi (1995b) explain that white parents and children often avoid talking about race due to self-protection, relationship protection, social inappropriateness, and parent unresponsiveness. Sullivan et al. (2021) offer support for these conclusions and posit that, when white parents do have these conversations, very few could recall the details of them, including the focus and how effective they were in dealing with race. From this study, Sullivan et al. (2021) argue that white parents must be aggressive in initiating discussions about racial biases with their children. Black parents will undoubtedly continue having these conversations in an effort to prepare their children for the racism they will undoubtedly face. Toward that end, families from all races must discuss the strategies and behaviors that prevent productive interracial communication. These are presented below in no particular order.

Topic Avoidance

The strategy of topic avoidance is an obvious problem when it comes to interracial communication. Docan-Morgan (2011) interviewed white parents and their adopted Korean children, and the children reported that they avoid sharing racially derogatory comments they received about their appearance or ethnicity or about physical attacks they received. They explained that this was because their adoptive parents were unresponsive to their race-related concerns or were more concerned with self-protection. In either case, the parents consciously or subconsciously communicated a lack of concern for their child, which was a natural and unfortunate barrier to their discussing race. This can also occur in same-race families. These findings highlight how communication is critical to understanding the nuances of race from all perspectives.

Intentional Colorblindness

Intentional colorblindness (Bartoli et al., 2016, p. 125) is a troubling socialization strategy in which parents teach their children that race matters less. This eventually worsens race matters because "it leaves common racial stereotypes to persist uninterrogated, and makes it impossible for youth to talk about their race-related experiences in nuanced or accurate ways" (p. 133). Children will be at a deficit because they will interact with people of color and racially aware white people and ultimately dismiss their racialized experiences. This erects a barrier and perpetuates mistrust in both professional and personal relationships.

Snyder's (2012) observation of multiracial adoptees was that white mothers who predominately communicated mainstream and colorblind messages ultimately contributed to children not recognizing race as a salient part of their lives. Topic avoidance also adversely affected their children in that the children indicated no interest in exploring their identity and were less likely to identify with Black culture. Many were loath to admit that assertions of colorblindness actually maintain racism and do not hold anyone responsible for racism (Bonilla-Silva, 2006). This silence that occurs among white people is sometimes called "the racial contract," which philosopher Charles Mills defines as "an in-group agreement among the privileged to restrict moral and political equality to themselves, and maintain the subordination as unequals of the out-group (here, people of color)" (City University of New York, 2021, para. 6).

Denial

Another negative strategy was denial, which means that parents not only do not discuss race and racism but also do not discuss the fact that their child is of African descent. In other words, the parent is in denial about their child's ancestry (Snyder, 2012). Such a strategy is troubling because it prevents children from dealing with the inevitable. As a person of color, they will certainly be in a situation where their otherness will be questioned. It is incumbent upon the parent to acknowledge this aspect of their child and find ways to educate both the child and themselves. This ultimately helps everyone realize that race is a salient part of the lives of people of color and assists families in "provid[ing] space and resources for their children to cope with such experiences" (p. 244). While children can then become more knowledgeable, the parent does as well, ultimately becoming more competent in their interracial communication with outgroup members.

Racial Derogation

Docan-Morgan (2011) observed racial derogation in the racial identity socialization process for adoptees. While he defines this according to transracial adoptee experiences, it applies to same-race family contexts as well. Racial derogation references "instances where the adoptee is the victim of malevolent and/or essentializing comments or questions related to his/her race" (p.

339). Parents using this strategy are ultimately contributing to feelings of isolation and lack of self-worth within the adoptive family. It stands to reason parents also extend their negative talk to other outgroup members, which will surely resonate with the child and communicate to them racist ideologies that apply to other racial/ethnic groups.

Modeling

Modeling of communication behaviors by parents socializes children with racial identities (Snyder, 2012). This strategy was used positively with multiracial adoptees with at least one Black parent or guardian. It involved the use of indirect approaches and modeling to teach the children the importance of taking pride in Black history and culture (Bartoli et al., 2016). There was also open communication about racism and how it would impact the children as well as their friends. This finding is not surprising since the race talk is more likely to occur with Black parents than white parents (Sullivan et al., 2021), and in light of the murders of George Floyd and Breonna Taylor, Black parents had those conversations with more frequency than did white parents, whose communication about race remained unchanged. Additionally, white parents were prone to send colorblind messages and rarely discussed what it meant to be white. When children follow this modeling, white children can be left woefully unprepared to have positive interracial interactions, which also socializes Black children and other children of color to anticipate stressful and unproductive communication with white people. As Sullivan et al. (2021) learned, white parents seemed unaffected by the racial unrest and "remained relatively silent and unconcerned about the topic" (p. 1). Mirroring this kind of behavior and attitude will worsen race relations and cause Black parents to increase the frequency of these conversations, widening the gap between the races.

FAMILIES AND FUTURE RACE TALKS

The research findings discussed in this chapter involved actual families who were willing to discuss how they socialize their children to understand racial identities and discuss race (or not). There was also discussion of three theories used to explain how familial ties influence the ways members identify with each other and whether members are willing to take risks to have conversations about race. It is abundantly clear there is a pattern along racial lines, a racial disparity when it comes to interracial communication. Race is not being discussed in all families, which is a problem. Black and other families of color regularly communicate about race while white families avoid such topics, to the detriment of everyone. These divergent approaches to race relations will continue to be a problem if beneficiaries of racism do not become actively involved in efforts to dismantle racism.

Parents across all races bear responsibility for how their children are socialized to the world around them. It is within the family that "parents' attitudes and behaviors transmit worldviews about race and ethnicity to children by way of subtle, overt, deliberate and unintended mechanisms" (Hughes, 2003, p. 15). Just as negative ideologies are learned and passed down from generation to generation, they can also be unlearned and replaced with more inclusive and affirming ideologies that directly challenge racism. That can only be achieved if there is a willingness to be part of an antiracist agenda. However, this requires an acknowledgment of the barriers preventing these conversations from occurring. Guerrero and Afifi (1995b) found that self-protection, relationship protection, social inappropriateness, and parent unresponsiveness or topic avoidance are a few reasons why these conversations do not take place. While this might not be applicable for all white families, there remains a communication deficit when we consider the ways that families from different races communicate about race.

As families determine how they can be active in the fight against racism, below are recommendations to consider as they rethink how they communicate about race. The recommendations are not listed in any particular order; however, they are presented so that people have multiple options for having difficult conversations with family members. If families commit individually and collectively to these recommendations, then there is genuine hope that racism can be—at the very least—partially dismantled for the benefit of all.

1. Encourage regular communication—family members should regularly pursue opportunities to discuss current events and personal experiences with racism.
2. Be slow to speak; just listen—avoid prioritizing and vocalizing your perspectives, opinions, and beliefs over those of a person of color; commit to listening to the realities of others.
3. Let down your defenses—set aside your ego and avoid being defensive; recognize the legacy and origins of racism as a system designed to benefit whites and disenfranchise people of color.
4. Be open to vulnerability—be willing to expose your thoughts and feelings to others.
5. Do your homework—be on a perpetual journey of learning about racism and all that it entails; it is a lifelong journey.
6. Admit what you do not know—recognize that you are not, nor will you become, an expert; this is a lifelong educational process.

7. Thirst after knowledge—always seek opportunities to learn more about all things race related.
8. Allow interracial relationships to organically develop—be open to the possibility of interracial relationships; however, be aware that manipulating these relationships brings their authenticity into question.

Chapter 4

Interracial Friendships beyond the "One Friend Rule"

The 2020 racial protests and pandemic catapulted race relations, public discourse on race, and racial justice onto a global platform, drawing our attention to the importance of conducting a personal inventory of our interracial relationships. Though not a scientific means of measuring or assessing one's racial attitudes or "wokeness," many people were willing to take a hard look at themselves and contemplate the role they might be playing in perpetuating systemic racism through passivity (i.e., doing nothing). People were commenting, debating, and arguing across social platforms such as Facebook, Twitter, TikTok, and Instagram about racism (in its broadest sense), police brutality, the Black Lives Matter (BLM) movement versus the Black Lives Matter organization, resistance to and rejection of BLM via Blue Lives Matter or All Lives Matter, and much more. A noticeable overarching theme in these public exchanges was the metaphorical line in the sand drawn between people threatening to terminate relationships. Romantic partners, friends, associates, neighbors, and colleagues swore to sever all relational ties, a seemingly "invisible" racial divide that matches formal (i.e., Jim Crow laws) and informal (i.e., social taboos) barriers to interracial interactions in our contemporary personal lives, further dispelling the myth of a postracial United States (D'Silva, 2021). These tensions threatened (and continue to threaten) our social networks and for some have forced a reassessment of relationship goals, whether articulated in these terms or not (Harris, 2021b).

Op-eds from Black female authors Christine Pride (2020) and Judy Belk (2020) speak to the impact the racial unrest had on their respective interracial friendships, both stressing that communication is the key to and at the core of how we can dismantle racism. They both advocate for frank conversations about racism with white girlfriends, despite how difficult or uncomfortable they may be. They both also discuss how receiving numerous calls, texts, and DMs from white friends in response to the murders of George Floyd and

Breonna Taylor opened the door for these kinds of conversations. For Pride (2020), these open conversations made her feel validated and affirmed by her white friends; however, she posed two questions that could be catalysts for national (and international) dialogue among interracial friends: "Is a true and close friendship between a black woman and a white woman possible in our racially polarized world?" and "How diverse is our friendship network?"

These two questions force us all to take a hard look at ourselves and face the truths about the lessons we have learned, been taught, or taught others and use as guideposts for interacting with people of a different race. This relational awakening was evident on social media and elsewhere when op-eds, news stories, and other anecdotal evidence surfaced, attesting to the moral dilemma thrust on so many of us regarding the racial makeup of our social networks. In some instances, interracial friends began openly communicating with each other about police brutality and expressing their commitment to or need for allyship. Belk (2020) describes being inundated with emails, texts, and phone calls from white friends and self-identified allies "checking in on me, wishing me a Happy Juneteenth, apologizing, sharing their outrage and genuinely asking me what they can do to be supportive." She stresses how these conversations are necessary but should not have an expectation that the friend of color will be a race expert and educator to the friend, particularly when the relationship is with a white person. Belk shares how, after taking a relational inventory, she "need[s] to have more Black friends, so I don't have to carry the full load of their angst. It's been exhausting." Belk wants to alleviate the emotional and invisible labor expended in her relationships with her friends who have limited racial awareness. Relationships provide emotional intimacy and connection between partners, and those and other qualities are compromised when, among other things, the partner of color expends time, effort, and energy teaching the other partner about race. Mutual learning is definitely a part of all relationships in that both partners become more knowledgeable about themselves, their partner, and the world they live in. That dimension of the relationship can be stressful and evolve into a burdensome process because the relationship is now one of teacher-student. There may be an imbalance in how information is shared and who benefits, which leads to the relationship becoming impersonal and education-oriented. It is no longer a friendship or place of escape or comfort.

The accounts of Pride (2020) and Belk (2020) are not universal, but they are very common and offer evidence that interracial friendships are vital to our public discourse on race and racism in that prejudices and biases can be conquered through our relationships (Killen et al., 2021). More specifically, it is the *quality* of those relationships that matters most. When there is relational substance to these interactions, they move beyond superficiality and become more personal, allowing the relationships to evolve from stranger to associate to acquaintance to *true* friendship. Communication scholars separate these relationships into two dominant categories: social relationships and personal relationships (VanLear et al., 2006). Social relationships are nonintimate, do not always meet our needs, and involve partners who are largely independent of each other. There is nothing or very little that binds them together, which is frequently evident in our relationships with coworkers, which occasionally meet our needs but lack the closeness and interdependence of personal relationships (VanLear et al., 2006). Personal relationships are the opposite because they meet many of our needs—emotional, relational, and instrumental—and are characterized by intimacy, closeness, and interdependence (VanLear et al., 2006). Examples of these relationships are best friends, family members, and romantic partners. Both voluntary and involuntary relationships can fall into either category, and for our purposes, we will focus on voluntary relationships. Friendships deserve attention because they require different kinds of commitment, dedication, and effort than familial (see chapter 3) and romantic relationships (see chapter 5). The focus is on voluntary relationships because partners are *choosing* to be connected to each other. In theory, they are willing to do the work to nurture and preserve that connection, but in practice that might be more difficult to do because of external stressors coming from family, other friends, or society.

Unfortunately, interracial relationships of all types are tainted by the residue of institutional and systemic racism. As such, this chapter will address the far-reaching effects of racism on our relationships and challenge us all to be reflective about our connections to others and how we have been socialized to perceive and interact with people from racial groups different from our own. The ultimate goal is to destigmatize interracial relationships and encourage us all to do our part in breaking the generational curse of racial segregation and racism. We live in a country that not only sanctioned and was founded upon slavery but also fully endorsed and legalized the separation of people groups according to their race after slavery was abolished in 1865. It would be foolish to believe or assume that racist ideologies died with the abolishment of slavery, particularly considering the racial unrest of the summer of 2020. Racism is thriving and wreaking havoc on race relations in society and in our personal and professional lives; therefore, it is our ethical and moral responsibility to collectively work to normalize interracial friendships and other interracial relationships. Toward that end, this chapter addresses Jim Crow laws and the sanctioning of racial segregation, the stigmatization of interracial relationships, the ineffectiveness of a colorblind ideology, the hard truths about and barriers to interracial friendship, and the optimal qualities of interracial friendships.

The necessary disruption in society also permeated some areas of communication scholarship, with some calling for social justice in our research because of the racial unrest witnessed in real time (Kurtz, 2021; Smith-Jones & Jones, 2022). Communication activism research (Frey et al., 2020) and critical communication pedagogy (Harris, 2017), for example, are research areas that became even more socially relevant. They challenged the discipline to be more race-centric (i.e., inclusive) and proactive in the fight against racism through theory and application to real-world contexts. This book is an excellent example of scholarship that was birthed in response to the 2020 racial unrest. It is in keeping with the author's long-standing history of doing interracial communication research and commitment to challenging scholars and members of society to explore how our interracial relationships are a vital part of the fight against systemic racism. The heart of the book is in keeping with Frey et al.'s (1996) social justice applied communication research (ACR) perspective by promoting "engagement with and advocacy for those in our society who are economically, socially, politically, and/or culturally underresourced" (p. 110) "based on a 'social justice sensibility'" that "(1) foregrounds ethical concerns, (2) commits to structural analyses of ethical problems, (3) adopts an activist orientation, and (4) seeks identification with others" (p. 111). Toward that end, this chapter pushes us to think critically about the unnecessary barriers that prevent interracial relationships from forming and how the field of interpersonal communication would greatly benefit from developing new and modifying existing theories designed to explain communication phenomena within this relational context. More importantly, the aim is to encourage scholars and society members to reconceptualize interracial friendships and recognize the tremendous potential therein to dismantle racism through interpersonal communication processes. This chapter proposes a six-stage friendship diversity inventory inspired by the limited amount of existent research on and emerging data on real-time experiences with interracial friendship. Since 2020, people are "reassessing many close interracial friendships" and, as Chingaipe (2020) notes, are "no longer interested in being friends with anyone who either refuses to engage with conversations around race or is dismissive of these experiences" (para. 22). Thus, this chapter and the book in its entirety are filling a long-standing void that must be filled.

THE STIGMATIZATION OF INTERRACIAL RELATIONSHIPS AND JIM CROW LAWS

Family networks are where we are socialized to interact with the world (see chapter 3), and through them we understand our different roles at home and in society as well as how we are to interact with each other. Familial norms are largely an extension of the societal norms that guide—or dictate—intergroup interactions. Data continue to show that interracial friendships remain less common than same-race or intraracial relationships (Plummer et al., 2016). People avoid intimate interracial relationships due to stereotypes (Wu, 2021), familial socialization (Orbe & Harris, 2022), mistrust (Chingaipe, 2020; Pride, 2020), and the normalization of same-race affiliations (Cox et al., 2016; Ramaih et al., 2015), among other reasons. People are either intentionally or unintentionally choosing to not have friends of a different race, suggesting that societal barriers such as residential segregation and school systems (Kim et al., 2015) and normalizing of same-race relationships (Al Ramiah et al., 2015) have collectively created a schism between racial groups that is somewhat impermeable. Why then are there not more interracial friendships? More importantly, why are people so afraid of what might come from them?

This pattern of interracial communication, or lack thereof, can be traced back to the Jim Crow laws beginning around 1865 that legally mandated physical boundaries between races (Little Fenimore, 2021). Jim Crow laws were designed to regulate "social, economic, and political relationships between whites and African-Americans," in an effort "principally to subordinate blacks as a group to whites and to enforce rules favored by dominant whites on non-conformists of both races" (Kousser, 2003, p. 479). (Slavery and Jim Crow laws are parts of our country's past, and we would be remiss if we did not acknowledge and address how these two travesties set the foundation for current race relations.)

Jim Crow laws were established in response to the Thirteenth Amendment, which abolished slavery in the United States. Prior to Jim Crow laws, local and state laws in the South adhered to informal rules or Black codes "as a legal way to put Black citizens into indentured servitude, to take voting rights away, to control where they lived and how they traveled and to seize children for labor purposes" (History.com, 2018). They were created by southern legislators committed to Black oppression. These legislators instituted Jim Crow laws (i.e., "separate but equal") that officially maintained and mandated the separation of Blacks and whites. This was done to preserve whites' "economically superior status" through practices such as requiring yearly labor contracts for Blacks, higher labor taxes for Blacks, and forced apprenticeships for Black minors (Robinson, 2017, p. 556). Although slavery no longer existed, there was an enslavement ideology (i.e., institutional racism) preserving the severest forms of racial disparities between Blacks and whites, not to mention the physical abuse, incarceration, discrimination, and prejudice to which Blacks were subjected in every aspect of their lives (Robinson, 2017). The Black codes effectively paved the way for Southern legislators to establish the Jim Crow laws, allowing them to use the judicial system to control interracial interactions and "protect" whites from Blacks and other racial/ethnic groups. These systems successfully preserved Blumenbach's racial hierarchy (see chapter 3) and created a society where comingling between whites and nonwhites was illegal and strongly discouraged. While consequences for violating these codes and laws varied in severity, the message was strong and clear that interracial relationships were unacceptable due to the alleged genetic superiority of whites, and hence the inferiority of Blacks (e.g., the one-drop rule). This also deemed all interracial interactions and relationships immoral, unnatural, and potentially illegal. Below are examples of Jim Crow laws from Alabama, Arizona, Florida, North Carolina, and South Carolina that literally and figuratively separated Blacks from whites in every way imaginable:

- Alabama: "The [railroad] conductor of each passenger train is authorized and required to assign each passenger to the car or the division of the car, when it is divided by a partition, designated for the race to which such passenger belongs."
- Alabama: "It shall be unlawful to conduct a restaurant or other place for the serving of food in the city, at which white and colored people are served in the same room, unless such white and colored persons are effectually separated by a solid partition extending from the floor upward to a distance of seven feet or higher, and unless a separate entrance from the street is provided for each compartment."
- Arizona: "The marriage of a person of Caucasian blood with a Negro, Mongolian, Malay, or Hindu shall be null and void" (antimiscegenation law).
- Florida: "The schools for white children and the schools for negro children shall be conducted separately."
- North Carolina: "Books shall not be interchangeable between the white and colored schools but shall continue to be used by the race first using them."
- South Carolina: "No persons, firms, or corporations, who or which furnish meals to passengers at station restaurants or station eating houses, in times limited by common carriers of said passengers, shall furnish said meals to white and colored passengers in the same room, or at the same table, or at the same counter." (Ferris State University, 2022).

These examples highlight how public spaces and private relationships were dictated by law and, after being outlawed, ultimately transformed into societal norms for interracial relationships. Though cross-race interactions are no longer illegal, these racist laws set the tone for societal expectations of how people from different races and ethnicities were expected to interact.

WHY A COLORBLIND MENTALITY DOES NOT WORK

Looking at the world through "rose-colored glasses" or a colorblind mentality has been one way many people have chosen to deal with racism. This kind of makes sense when a person has not lived a life of awareness when it comes to a racialized reality. They are "just a person," void of any cultural markers such as race, gender, ethnic, or sexuality and perceive others in the same way. Such a perspective is simultaneously idealistic and problematic (Wu et al., 2020). It is idealistic because it envisions a world in which socially constructed identities are benefits or meaningless rather than barriers. Our lives are believed to be experienced according to meritocracy; therefore, our positive and negative experiences are attributed to our effort. This is quite similar to a "bootstrap mentality." This way of thinking is very problematic because it rejects the reality of systemic oppression and its impact on everyone, including its beneficiaries. It ignores and negates the material experiences of BIPOC and other historically marginalized group members who are forced to view, experience, and navigate the world through two different lenses. This is what W. E. B. Dubois ([1903] 1965) referred to as double consciousness to explain how African Americans must simultaneously live in and understand the rules of white-dominant society and live life as a member of a microcultural group. The dual lenses inform each other and equip Blacks to live life as a Black person in a white world.

Bonilla-Silva (2006) argues that *colorblind racism* is a racial ideology that "justifies race-based social realties" (Zhang, 2021, p. 340). Through this process, people are taught that otherness is to be invisible (Wu et al., 2020). Colorblind ideology exists on an individual level (through our relationships) and through social structures and social institutions (Zhang, 2021). This way of thinking is an expression of white privilege that fails to acknowledge the racial background of others and leads to avoidance of race-based discussions (Durand & Tavaras, 2021). Colorblindness promotes the exact opposite of what many people believe it is, which is that ignoring racialized identities will make things better. Instead, it obfuscates interracial interactions by refusing to admit society is built on racial disparities that overprivilege whites and underprivilege BIPOC. Thus, such an ideology encourages one to believe "skin color does not play a role in interpersonal interactions and institutional policies/practices" (Neville et al., 2016, p. 5). This ultimately makes interracial interactions nearly impossible and disingenuous if they occur with a colorblind ideologist.

Chapter 4

RELATIONAL FISSURES AMID RACIAL UNREST

Yet another lesson that the 2020 racial unrest taught us was that we, as a country, are failing at interracial communication. It was evident from the many social media platforms flooded with op-eds, blogs, tweets, posts, and thirty-second videos of people expressing a range of emotions around police brutality, racial profiling, social justice, white privilege, racial unrest, and other related issues (Belk, 2020; Chingaipe, 2020; Pride, 2020). The looming issue of systemic oppression (i.e., racism) shifted from the political to the personal as people began to reassess their relationships and who they believed themselves and others to be. Their usually likable and lovable relations were no longer so, as the upholding of oppressive systems came to light. Conversations about racial injustices became a part of everyday conversations and revealed people's true character or a version of themselves that was troubling. Proverbial lines in the sand were drawn that forced people to determine which relationships to sever and which to save, the primary criterion being whether said partner was willing to fight racial injustices. Relational partners of all kinds ultimately found themselves at odds and questioning the feasibility and appropriateness of their connections to each other. It was only a matter of time before these oppositional and sometimes hostile attitudes trickled down from digital spaces into people's real-world relationships. Partners experienced intense levels of conflict threatening to terminate relationships or, at minimum, prompting long overdue frank conversations about racism. More importantly, the partner's willingness to stand up against social injustice became changed spoken and unspoken expectation of those in their networks for doing the same (Chingaipe, 2020).

No longer were people willing to silently stand by and allow heightened or egregious acts of racism to be condoned. Many took to social media to confront friends, acquaintances, and family members who resisted, hesitated, or remained silent about the fight for racial justice. The callout, per se, was a clarion call imploring everyone to do their part in addressing racism, both beneficiaries and victims of systemic oppression. Beneficiaries largely saw this as a personal attack and an accusation of being racist, which was not necessarily the case. Rather, they were being asked to acknowledge the hard truth that institutions throughout the United States had been and continued to be designed to maintain imbalances in societal power and access to opportunities primarily based on race. (This is also the case for sex, ethnicity, class, heteronormativity, and others forms of oppression.) Instead of placating ambivalence, there was an expectation that everyone take social responsibility for this serious issue. The act of calling out was not to engender guilt, but to encourage whites to prioritize social and racial consciousness to do the right thing in light of race-based social inequities. Doing so requires an acknowledgment not just of racism but also of the injustices it creates and its material effects on white and BIPOC alike. This means actively choosing to have uncomfortable and difficult conversations with people in one's interpersonal network because it is a safe space and a judgement-free zone (Ramasubramanian et al., 2017; see chapter 7).

Such conversations can and do happen, but for some people a lack of racial and ethnic diversity within their interpersonal network means they do not. These relationships have not been initiated or established because of societal or familial socialization against forming them and an expectation of homogeneity or connecting with people who are as similar as possible. A fear of differences (i.e., the other) driven by prejudice, racism, and implicit bias also prevents interracial friendships and other relationship types from developing. As such, a person may choose the familiar by insulating themselves with same-race friends under the assumption that there will be more commonalities with them than with their different-race friends. Such thinking is faulty because it is grounded in unhealthy attitudes and ideologies that sustain racial divisions plaguing society.

CONDUCTING A RELATIONAL INVENTORY

People have the freedom and right to form whatever relationships they want and need, and we each have discretion over who we allow into our lives; however, our relational choices ultimately reflect socialization processes. In the case of interracial relationships, separatist ideologies are covertly and overtly perpetuating oppression (i.e., racism) by discouraging relationships between whites and BIPOC by communicating messages that BIPOC are "less than" and "undesirable" or whites are "not to be trusted." Whether we consciously ascribe to this thinking or not, its existence is apparent in the lack of diversity within our interpersonal networks, showing us the far-reaching impact society has on our relational choices. We are encouraged to pursue same-race relationships, and the rationale for these choices will vary; however, one overarching pattern suggests that this desire to maintain racial segregation may be due to a fear of BIPOC and racial/ethnic difference by whites and a desire to protect oneself from the race-based power imbalance shaping lived experiences of BIPOC. In other words, whites have been socialized to view BIPOC as a physical and financial threat to their status as the majority group. As such, the desire to maintain literal and metaphorical social distance is heightened. Motivations for avoidance among BIPOC may be attributed to operating in a world where they have limited or no societal power and are subjected to bias, prejudice, and discrimination in interracial interactions with whites. Unfortunately, both scenarios heighten racial tensions and perpetuate the continued intergroup mistrust that continues to plague interracial relationships, professional and personal alike.

Jim Crow laws set the stage for what we are seeing now, which should be of no surprise, and if we are to reverse their profound impact on current race relations, we must be willing and committed to having difficult conversations with each other and being active participants in dismantling these systems. It is for this reason that a relational approach to disrupting these systems and ideologies must be taken. Doing so elucidates the interpersonal and communicative nature of systemic oppression, laying bare the fact that these ideologies were created through message exchanges by those in power. Naturally, contemporary iterations of those ideologies are also maintained through the interpersonal communication occurring among the powerful and their (sub)conscious focus on ways to preserve the racial hierarchy. Interracial communication is also how those interests are preserved, which warrants a shift in how we conceptualize diversity in every sense of the word. Thus, the first step in this tremendous yet achievable process is through a proposed multilayered relational inventory.

Understanding the Process

The first step toward normalizing interracial friendships and having healthy relationships with people from other races must be for every person to conduct a relational inventory. This means that we must *all* take a step back and assess how racially/ethnically diverse our friend groups are. Some may argue that doing so is making the personal political, but this is not the case at all. Instead, it is an opportunity to consider the extent to which we are socialized to manage, think about, and respond to racial differences. Our interpersonal networks are a direct reflection of this process and attest to the influence that society and, more importantly, our family and friends have on whom we choose to have a close connection with. For various reasons, we tend to surround ourselves with people who are very similar to us, one of those similarities being race. Similarities provide us with familiarity and common ground and potentially solidify the relationship. They also give partners a sense of comfort and assurance that they are connected to someone who is predictable and relatable. These relational qualities are perceived as being potentially lost in interracial friendships, which is not true. Racial differences and race-related experiences might not necessarily resonate with partners, but they can add nuances and qualities to the relationship that same-race relationships cannot. Rather than using a colorblind mind-set, partners have the opportunity to become racially sensitive and culturally competent in a trusting and caring space.

Unfortunately, the communication field has not prioritized research on interracial communication, let alone interracial friendships. There are a few scholars who have done research on intercultural communication and friendship, but limited attention has been given to race (Davis, 2018; Orbe & Harris, 2022); therefore, the relational inventory advanced here is informed by interracial and interpersonal communication research across the spectrum. Hopefully, it will inspire scholars to conduct the kind of research that has real-world application and relevance in ways that the field historically has not for BIPOC as well as white people. Communication scholars have the potential to revolutionize the field by redefining generalizability through exploring communication phenomena that include BIPOC experiences and realities too often ignored in our existing research. Additionally, *all* people should feel represented by the research, and the findings must be applied in ways that transform how we communicate across and through our racial differences.

There are five steps below that make up a relationship inventory. The primary goal of this process is to provide a template for diversifying interpersonal networks, specifically friendships, and challenging structural systems opposing the normalization of interracial friendships. Researchers benefit by adapting existing and developing new research programs that explore various aspects of interracial friendships unexamined in the field. Society members benefit by being self-reflective and proactive about changing how we should think about these relationships and the changes we can make on an individual and a societal level regarding interracial relationships. The five steps are (1) evaluate friendship racial/ethnic diversity, (2) assess interracial ideological indoctrination, (3) identify individual contributions to structural segregation, (4) commit to a relational approach to advancing racial justice efforts, and (5) identify essential qualities for interracial friendships. The five steps most likely would be achieved in chronological order.

Evaluate Friendship Racial/Ethnic Diversity

The first step in this inventory is to *evaluate the racial/ethnic diversity within one's interpersonal network*. The evaluation process sounds very simple but may prove a bit challenging. The simplicity lies in doing a survey of the number of close friends one has from an outgroup (i.e., different race), which might not take very long; however, the process becomes difficult when one begins to evaluate the degree of intimacy and connection of those relationships as compared to relationships one has with ingroup members. This was evidenced in the midst of the 2020 racial unrest. Social media platforms were inundated with public, heated arguments between family members and friends, or sometimes strangers, and ultimatums were issued, forcing people to choose a side in the fight against racial injustices against African

Americans, Asian Americans, and Latinx Americans. Being silent, privately offering support, and virtue signaling (i.e., a performative act of allyship) were all viewed as unacceptable because they were directly contributing to systemic oppression, whether intentional or not. Some were so outraged by what they believed was blatant opposition that the only recourse was to terminate those relationships informally. Unbeknownst to many, the racial unrest and reactions to it forced them to perform this very inventory. Realizing that the beliefs and values once shared between emotionally connected people were now diametrically opposed meant the relationship stood zero chance of surviving. This applied to both same-race and interracial relationships.

The racial unrest generated new relationship rules or at least revealed some that seemed to be lying dormant and needed to be articulated to remove doubt and confusion about what one expected in a friendship and from a friend. These rules go against the grain by chipping away at antiquated ideologies about interracial friendship, one of which is the "one friend rule" (Munn, 2018). The "one friend rule" is the practice of whites limiting their nonwhite friends to just one Black friend, as if having more violates an interpersonal or social norm of some sort. Adopting this approach to interpersonal connections communicates to others a perceived commitment to diversity. It also reveals biases and prejudices that spill over into other areas of life, such as service organizations and the workplace. The belief that racial groups should be separated, or at the very least have minimal contact, is very dangerous because it ensures that racial disparities will continue to exist in all areas of society, thereby perpetuating the imbalance in societal power.

In conducting a relationship inventory, a person should *divide their nonfamilial and nonromantic relationships into one of two categories: friendship or acquaintance.* A friendship is a voluntary, reciprocal, and egalitarian relationship where "both partners acknowledge the relationship and treat each other as equals" (Rubin & Bowker, 2018, p. 2). In contrast, an acquaintance is "a state of having at least some constituent knowledge of another person—their name, appearance, and so on" (Eckberg, 2013, p. 2). These two categories are critical because they force a person to be very honest with themselves about the kinds of connections they are making with others.

There is no expectation of there being more relationships in one category or other; rather, a tally provides a visual image of what a person believes constitutes closeness and relationships. This also sets the stage for a demographic assessment of those relationships, which entails subcategories of same-race and interracial relationships. The interracial subcategory could include multiple subcategories that identify the race of the friend and group those relationships together. For example, the racial pairings could be white/Black, white/Korean, or white/Dominican. Based on research, the total of same-race friendships most likely will be higher, and when compared to the interracial friendships, it may reveal a significant racial disparity or a preference for friends from a particular race or ethnicity (Davies et al., 2011; Diggs & Clark, 2002; Greenland et al., 2020). These observations should prompt one to consider the reasons behind these patterns, which may include asking questions about one's interpersonal network on the following topics: extent of its racial diversity, why the majority of friends are same-race, the biases or prejudices preventing interracial friendships from forming, why friends of color are more like acquaintances, familial and friend opinions about interracial friendship, extent of concerns about friend-perceptions of interracial friendship, differences in acceptability of friends from certain racial groups, quality of time spent with each other's friend groups and families and in each other's homes, and reasons for not diversifying one's friend group.

These questions are but a few of many one might ask while conducting a relationship inventory. Davies et al. (2011) identify six categories of cross-group friendship assessment, and they are (1) time and activities spent with outgroup friends, (2) self-disclosure to outgroup friends, (3) feelings of closeness to outgroup friend, (4) perceived inclusion of outgroup friend in one's sense of self, (5) number of outgroup friends, and (6) percentage of one's friendship circle who are outgroup members (p. 333). While there is overlap bewteen the question topics advanced in this book, all of these initial queries should give one pause while considering the influence of race on one's friendships. Assigning relationships thus to categories and subcategories quantifies one's interpersonal connections, making real the extent to which we do or do not choose to be racially inclusive when it comes to those closest to us. It also serves as a springboard for a path toward rethinking interracial relationships and being involved on an interpersonal level in addressing racism, *if* a person is willing to do so.

Having few or no interracial friendships is hurtful for whites and BIPOC because it reinscribes ideologies and behaviors that continue to fracture our society. It normalizes racial separation and sends a message that the other is not to be trusted solely based on the color of their skin. Whites and Blacks have historically had a troubling relationship, largely due to slavery and subsequent Jim Crow laws, and while neither no longer exists, each racial group continues to have stereotypes of the other that make interracial relationships nearly impossible (Leonard & Locke, 1993). Unfortunately, this prevents many from developing connections with people from a different race even though these can be and oftentimes are just as healthy, enriching, and gratifying as same-race friendships (Diggs & Clark, 2002). More importantly, people are robbing themselves of the wonderful opportunity to engage in perspective-taking on a more personal and intimate level and in a judgement-free space. The friends are bringing their respective racial identities and worldviews to the relationship, and because they inform their sense of self, it is inevitable that the knowledge and experiences gained from them will influence and emerge in the relationship. The relationship itself and each partner will definitely be impacted, as they will learn from each other about communicating across and through their differences, which will ultimately lead them to become more culturally competent and racially sensitive. Frequent and meaningful interactions engender open communication, trust, and honesty, among other relational qualities, because each partner is learning more about the other as people and products of systemic oppression.

BIPOC are more likely to have more interracial friendships than whites or majority group members because they are in the numerical minority and are operating in a world where whites have the most societal power (Davies et al., 2011; Du Bois, [1903] 1965) and more control over how the world functions. They are navigating two worlds at once and have double consciousness or an awareness of how both worlds operate (Du Bois, [1903] 1965). Most white people have not been socialized to view the world through a racial lens, which also means that they do not have the pressure or expectation to have relationships with people from other races. The age-old adage "birds of a feather flock together" captures this division (Al Ramiah et al., 2015; Policarpo, 2015) and speaks to the normalization of same-race friendships and the avoidance of interracial relationships. This interpersonal racial bias, whether intentional or not, becomes more apparent when a person literally calculates how many friends they really have who are from a different racial group. Taking an inventory will create an opportunity to reflect on how one has been socialized to establish interpersonal relationships and the degree to which interracial relationships possess the same relationship qualities as same-race relationships. In order to achieve any of these goals, we must first establish what is a friendship.

Qualities that typically define this type of relationship include, but are not limited to, being egalitarian, nonhierarchical, and reciprocal (Allan, 2003) as well as being personal or absent of "social roles or positions within the social structures," authentic, voluntary, and noninstrumental (Policarpo, 2015, p. 174). Friends provide each other with emotional and social support. Instrumental support (i.e., transportation, money) is something that is occasionally provided but is not a motivating factor. Collectively, these characteristics create expectations we have for our friends and friendships and impact our level of satisfaction. These expectations also carry an assumption that both partners will commit to the relationship, knowing that great effort is expected and required if the relationship is to work. The relationship qualities can make the relationship demanding and difficult to manage (Policarpo, 2015); however, the partners must both work to establish open lines of communication if they are to succeed.

Assess Interracial Ideological Indoctrination

After evaluating one's friendships, the second step is to *assess interracial ideological indoctrination*. It is during this stage in the inventory process that one turns attention to the sources of racial ideologies, which are institutions, people, and the media, who are the vessels through whom messages about race are communicated. The weightiness or level of importance given to the message is largely determined by the relationship the person has with the source and how credible that source is considered to be. Religions, political standpoints, education systems, and families, for example, are institutions that are oftentimes times directly tied to the attitudes, beliefs, and values we ultimately adopt as our own and use to guide us in life and in the decisions we make. Bandura's (1977) social learning theory tells us that we learn from the sources around us through observation and ultimately model those behaviors. This also applies to cognition or ways of thinking. We mirror those behaviors and attitudes and adopt them as our own until we have experiences that force us to understand *why* we do and believe certain things. This may include being exposed to different lifestyles, belief systems, and ideologies through interactions with other people, reading books, being exposed to other cultures, and having your own positionalities challenged. In the end, you have a better sense of what you believe and why.

Assessing interracial ideological indoctrination is a very specific phenomenon and requires one do a reality check on how one has been socialized by any or all of the aforementioned institutions when it comes to attitudes about race and racism. As a new concept, this assessment is being introduced to stress how important it is for people to recognize and be aware that they have certain attitudes and beliefs about race that shape their perceptions about outgroup members and how they should interact with them. These influences ultimately dictate whether or not relationships will be established and the level of intimacy they will have. The socializing agents use different approaches and mediums to indoctrinate people to think a certain way about different racial groups. Because family—however one may define that—is the first interpersonal network to which we are introduced and with whom we have strong emotional ties, we place great weight and value on what they teach us. In the case of a family with parents or adults at the helm, they have certain beliefs, values, and traditions they believe are important and verbally pass them down to their children. If they believe racial groups should remain segregated or that interracial relationships should be superficial and lack depth or intimacy, then that message might be overtly or covertly communicated to family members. A child might unknowingly conform to this way of thinking and consider it normal or typical until they encounter someone whose thinking is different or who challenges them about their beliefs. The same message might be communicated through film, schools, or the workplace, but much more subtly, and because they do not hold as much weight or influence as family and are less personal, their impact might occur through repeated exposure. Collectively, these sources dictate our thinking and expectations about interracial relationships and other matters related to race.

Much like the first stage, assessing interracial ideological indoctrination will prompt much self-reflection. Although attention is directed at sources outside the self, such as family members, friends, organizations, companies, and media, it still might be unsettling and uncomfortable to realize our own passive or active role in perpetuating racist ideologies. This apprehension is supported by research in which participants report hesitation in having intergroup contact or developing interracial friendships due to contact avoidance messages or apathy or lack of interest (i.e., modern racial prejudice) or the cultural capital of whiteness (Al Ramiah et al., 2015; Wu, 2021). Such behavior can be interpreted as equally troubling as active or overt espousal of racist, stereotypical, and prejudiced ideals since they fail to challenge these systems of oppression. This stage is very similar to how students enrolled in multiculturalism or interracial communication classes respond when they become more knowledgeable about and aware of racism (Harris & Abbott, 2011; see chapter 7). They experience a variety of emotions, thoughts, and feelings as they come to realize that the ideologies they have known all of their lives are inaccurate and faulty. Society members choosing this path and doing the relationship inventory will likely experience similar cognitive dissonance and an array of emotions.

Identify Individual Contributions to Structural Segregation

The third step is to *identify individual contributions to structural segregation*, which is potentially as daunting as stage two. It requires a person to make an inventory of the times when they directly or indirectly were racist, prejudiced, or discriminatory against someone of a different race. Much like stage one, stage three requires taking the time to identify moments either already known or yet to be discovered that may span one's entire lifetime. While this might take some time, it is important to reflect on these instances without parameters to encourage a wholistic approach to understanding the impact of racism on one's life and what role one has played in perpetuating it.

This stage was inspired by the Harris and Abbott's (2011) study on critical race theory in the interracial communication classroom. The study generated the Confronting Racial Microaggressions Model (CRaMM), which they contend is a critical tool for preparing students and society members to be global citizens engaging with an increasingly diverse world. The data in the study were student essays evaluating their own behavior in addressing an observed or experienced racial microaggression occurring outside of the classroom. This involved identifying an incident, describing it, reflecting on their response to it, and noting what, if anything, they might do differently if given the opportunity. The goal was to guide students through the process of recognizing racist and prejudiced behaviors and identifying "best practices" for confronting racism while also recognizing the relationship between course content (i.e., theory) and its application to real-world contexts. An analysis of the study reflection papers revealed a four-stage process they experienced in connection to the observed encounter: (1) identify the racial microaggression; (2) identify three cues that precede the process: (a) relational, (b) contextual, and (c) emotional; (3) process their reaction to racial microaggression; and (4) the outcome.

This multistage process is an excellent exercise for this stage because it provides the opportunity to determine where a person is on their journey toward being more racially sensitive and equips them to have (or maintain) healthy and productive interracial connections with friends. This can also be applied to romantic and work relationships. Although the data that created the CRaMM approach (Harris & Abbott, 2011) was related to pedagogy, it still has practical implications for other populations or communities—or individuals—genuinely concerned about racism and what they can do to combat it. Identifying past mistakes and successes will inspire people to remain in the fight and to seek opportunities to become a better ally or coconspirator against racism.

An individual- and institutional-level barrier that might emerge during this stage is *ethnic resegregation* occurring in public spaces (Fischer, 2008; Moody, 2011). Research has shown that teenagers and young adults, when they are in racially integrated or diverse spaces, typically seek same-race friendships despite opportunities to form relationships with people of other races. BIPOC people have higher friendship diversity than whites in general; however, those differences decrease when there is increased school diversity and increased opportunities for interracial interactions (Moody, 2011). In other words, the diversity needs to be more proactive and integrative rather than performative since many schools, companies, and organizations express a commitment to diversity, equity, and inclusion (DEI) but do little to embody the spirit of true inclusivity. As Rastogi and Juvonen (2019) note, long-lasting interracial friendships are possible when efforts are made early in life to immerse people in racially diverse environments where positive intergroup attitudes can occur (Killen et al., 2021).

Commit to a Relational Approach to Advancing Racial Justice Efforts

Step four speaks to the level of commitment a person has to *fighting racism and making more interracial connections and relationships.* Moving to this stage is critical because it marks a transition from cognitive change to behavioral change, both of which are equally important to the larger movement of dismantling racism. Committing to a movement is a very personal act, and because it is a promise of future behavior, it cannot be easily measured or reported on. Additionally, there is no research of note addressing this aspect of interracial communication, not to mention what it entails, how it is perceived by outgroup members, and how it leads to racial justice. There also is no qualitative or quantitative research on any combination of the terms *commitment, interracial communication,* and *racial justice* as interpersonal phenomena, demonstrating a crucial need for research in these areas within communication studies.

From a real-world perspective, a person can contribute to the racial justice movement through volunteerism, protests, and other forms of engagement to address racial inequities. They can also channel that interest into developing interracial relationships with like-minded people with whom they also have similarities and a connection. It is very important that, in this stage, a person avoids being performative, which requires that the relationship's origins are organic. The partner will be able to determine if a person's intentions are genuine, and if they are not, then the relationship will fail; therefore, the person needs to be aware of and willing to take the risks involved with committing to advancing racial justice and diversifying their interpersonal network. Similarly, communication scholars are in the unique position of conducting research that has the potential to transform the world and make contributions to racial justice.

Step four involves a person—either the one going through the process or a scholar—*having a "joyful commitment"* (Hartnett, 2010) *to racial justice and diversifying their interpersonal network*, which can come in various forms. Joyful commitment "asks us to work for social justice and for personal growth, to be both radical in our demands and gentle in our demeanor, both outraged by inequality and oppression and joyous in our commitments to end them" (Hartnett, 2010, p. 71). While "us" refers to communication scholars, it can also apply to real people in the real world. Real people can be catalysts for change, as evidenced by the historic worldwide response to police brutality in the United States in 2020. People took to the streets to express their outrage, and in doing so illustrated the power of protest, engagement, and relationship across differences to ignite change in society. Waymer (2021) addresses the importance of transformative scholarship by arguing that communication education scholars in particular should "engage in action research on diversity and other issues of societal import whereby we critically reflect and then seek transformative change via the simultaneous process of taking action and doing research" (p. 115). Thus, conducting research on experiences with this stage of the process can radically transform the field and empower people to be the change they want to be.

Identify Essential Qualities for Interracial Friendships

Step five is critical to the interpersonal component of this process. The process proposes that *a person have a clear understanding of what qualities are essential for an interracial friendship.* First, it is imperative to acknowledge that interracial friendships are very much like same-race friendships. The primary factor distinguishing them is that the partners' racial difference must be seen as shaping their identities as individuals and partners. Those differences might cause miscommunications between the partners, and instead of viewing these as barriers, partners should see them as learning opportunities. Partners will learn about the other and themselves as well as how to manage their relationship in light of the differences. The uniqueness they bring to the relationship will undoubtedly make for a fulfilling relationship.

Close relationships, such as friendships, are transactional due to processes such as self-disclosure, trust, and closeness (Davies & Aron, 2016). Davies et al. (2011) explain that research should explore feelings of closeness, willingness to self-disclose, and partner responses to efforts to facilitate closeness and the other's responses to and interpretations of them. These qualities are important for interracial relationships because, without them, partners might be unwilling to share themselves with others. Other qualities critical to interracial relationships are intimacy through self-disclosure and perceived responsiveness (Shelton et al., 2010), felt understanding (Chen & Graham, 2017; Reis & Shaver, 1988), validation, caring, and multicultural sensitivity (Hunter & Elian, 2000). In order to achieve these qualities, partners need to be aware that stereotypes (Leonard & Locke, 1993), mistrust (Munn, 2018), lack of relational commitment (Diggs & Clark, 2002), and intentionality (i.e., purposefully hurtful or harmful actions) versus emotionality (i.e., emotions elicited from offending behaviors) (Orbe & Harris, 2015) may be barriers to the friendship.

The five steps lay the groundwork for people to intentionally seek opportunities for interracial relationships. Hudson (2022) refers to this as "interpersonalizing" cultural difference, which is comprised of four central subprocesses necessary for developing and sustaining interracial friendships: "(1) cultivating trust and establishing a silent contract, (2) embracing similarity without forgetting difference, (3) exploring other cultures, and (4) bridging difference to connect" (p. 267). This means that such relationships can become normalized by partners becoming knowledgeable of the many benefits of and potential barriers to interracial friendships and nurturing their commitment to and passion for developing connections with people of other races. Doing so also requires remaining humble, being willing to learn, and having dedication to maintaining a healthy connection to outgroup members. This is not a guarantee of a perfect interracial friendship, but it does inspire someone to actively reflect on their interpersonal networks and what they can do to be more inclusive on an individual and societal level.

INTENTIONAL INTERRACIAL INTEGRATION STRATEGIES: THE CASE FOR INTERRACIAL FRIENDSHIP

In response to the racial unrest of 2020, there has been an influx of books, diversity workshops, lectures, master classes, and documentaries on the importance of racial diversity and interracial communication, and by extension interracial relationships. There is a thirst and desire for understanding across racial differences in an effort to engage in racial justice. Intentionality is critical to interracial friendships and requires *both* partners to be proactive in learning more about each other and racism (Shropshire, 2021). People are learning about the privileges and disadvantages of racism from both perspectives and have a nuanced understanding of systemic oppression that they otherwise would not have. All of this takes place in a safe space where trust and honesty have been established.

While intentionality on the individual level is essential to dismantling racism (see chapter 7), the same is true for organizations and institutions that are willing to get into "good trouble" by creating a more inclusive society. Placing members of different racial groups within close proximity to each other increases the likelihood of interracial interactions, which are imperative to dismantling racism (Gaither & Sommers, 2013; Kim et al., 2015; Shropshire, 2021). Organizations such as schools, churches, and businesses prioritizing racial diversity are creating physical spaces where people from different races/ethnicities have greater opportunities for interracial interactions and, more importantly, interracial relationships. When intentional integration is a priority, relationships are somewhat inevitable, along with "increased learning and satisfaction in college," "cognitive development," "growth in leadership skills and cultural awareness," "higher levels of civic interest," "civic engagement," "positive feelings towards other racial/ethnic group, prejudice reduction, and access to non-redundant information" (Kim et al., 2015, p. 59), and discrimination reduction (Greenland et al., 2020). Such structures also incentivize individuals to take an active role in addressing racial justice from a more informed and authentic perspective.

Chapter 5

Interracial Romantic Relationships and the Trickle-Down Theory

RACISM: THE FORCED MARRIAGE METAPHOR

The best metaphor to describe racism in the U.S. is that African Americans are like an abused partner in a forced marriage. The marriage was not entered into with joy and excitement (read slavery) as it typically should be. Instead, the bride is forced into a relationship with a partner who belittles her, believes she is less-than, and does everything in his power to torment her mentally and keep her under his subjection. He occasionally does something nice for her to appease her, but soon does something to undo that with various forms of abusive behavior, breeding even more distrust. Her children watch this and learn coping mechanisms to deal with the abuse. They vow to not repeat the cycle or fall victim to it, and sadly, the partner passes this behavior on from generation to generation. It becomes normalized.

Some "wives" reach their tolerance level and lash out. The expressions of frustration will vary in intensity, and there may come a point when she lashes out in violence because nothing else has worked to stop the abuse. She has gone to family, friends, agencies, and others to report the abuse, but everyone has turned a deaf ear and blind eye because they don't believe her, despite the glaring truth that lies before them. Others witness the abuse and become equally angry and frustrated. While some respond internally, others take on the pain of the other and join in the fight, however that may be. It is a never-ending cycle unless the family members of the abuser intervene and use their relationship or position in society to stop egregious behaviors that have become normalized within the family. While they didn't commit those abusive behaviors themselves, they are complicit because they stood by and did nothing.

The preceding metaphor was prompted by a request for help from a white female student who was recently in the author's multiculturalism and the media course in the spring of 2020. She was having difficulty explaining to her family the myriad emotions driving the protests of 2020 after the murder of George Floyd. Her family believed the protestors were looters, "antifa" (i.e., antifascists), antiracist allies, and "unnecessarily" angry Black people destroying their own neighborhoods and property. The metaphor captures the diabolical nature and historicity of racism and its irreparable effect on Blacks in the United States. It speaks to the boiling point that thousands—possibly millions—reached regarding police brutality against African Americans, who are often subjected to racial injustices while doing mundane things such as walking home, driving, or sleeping in their own homes, to name a few. Marriage was chosen because it speaks to the synergetic nature of race relations and the violence to which African Americans have been subjected (e.g., slavery, police brutality) for centuries at the hands of whites due to colonialism and their subsequent societal power. While marriage usually involves choice and is seen as a joyous union between two people, the imagery of a "forced marriage" conjures up the violent origins of Black-white race relations, which are not to be forgotten, and the residue of racism that continues to taint contemporary race relations. Such imagery is crucial if we are to fully uproot the racism entrenched in our nation's DNA and create a country where its racial hierarchy is obsolete. Envisioning a world where power imbalances do not exist might be idealistic, but it is imperative if social justice is to be realized. More importantly, we will finally realize the promise of the Pledge of Allegiance to provide "liberty and justice for all."

Since its writing, this metaphor has been shared more than 6,000 times on Facebook, suggesting that it resonates with people from a variety of backgrounds who are thirsting for healing, reconciliation, and understanding between racial groups. For the purposes of this chapter, the metaphor is a foundation for the argument that interracial romantic relationships are a window into the soul of the United States when it comes to race relations and interracial communication. People have a lot of opinions about and attitudes toward interracial romantic relationships (IRRs) even though they are very much like same-race romantic relationships. Partners are seeking a connection with someone who has similar values, beliefs, and interests, to whom they are attracted, and with whom they are choosing to build a life. For some, this becomes a problem when the person is of a different race or from a particular racial group. Antimiscegenation laws were another iteration of the Jim Crow laws, designed to legally separate racial groups, and in this case the motivation was to illegalize interracial relationships and interactions between whites and nonwhites for fear that white bloodlines were becoming impure by intermixing of the races. Thus, interracial marriages were criminalized and treated as if they were immoral, which was in striking contrast to same-race relationships. It was not until 1967 in *Loving v. Virginia* that the Supreme

Court overturned the first of several antimiscegenation laws in the country. Mildred (a Black woman) and Richard (a white man) Loving were legally married in Washington, DC, but lived in Virginia. In 1958, the state ruled they were violating its Racial Integrity Act of 1924, a law that criminalized marriages between whites and "colored" people, and ordered the Lovings to leave the state for one year. (Whites were defined as people having only Caucasian blood, the so called one-percent rule [Wolfe, 2021]). This movement was a part of eugenicist propaganda espoused by white supremacist Walter Plecker, who also served on the Virginia Bureau of Vital Statistics board (Yudell, 1971). The Lovings' appeal took them all the way to the Supreme Court, resulting in their conviction being overturned and antimiscegenation laws being ruled unconstitutional and in violation of the Fourteenth Amendment. This historic ruling resulted in an additional 16 other states overturning antimiscegenation laws; 26 other states had already done so (Oyez, n.d.).

Overturning antimiscegenation laws was a legal means for addressing inequities, but they did little to mitigate the racist ideologies driving institutions and systems that have become a cornerstone for nearly every aspect of public and private life. As noted in chapter 3, these belief systems were incredibly potent and successful in creating a racial divide between whites and BIPOC, while also preserving societal power for whites, who had secured it through colonialism (Orbe & Harris, 2015). These beliefs played a critical role in shaping societal attitudes about racial differences, with whites being situated as the most desirable, acceptable, and influential racial groups and all others being less so. This racial hierarchy is very evident when it comes to IRRs. Opinions about and attitudes toward IRRs offer insight into the broader issue of racial socialization and racist ideologies, as they are both responsible for how we choose to interact with and perceive each other as outgroup members. In other words, IRRs are a true gauge of race relations and how much progress or not we have made when it comes to the issue of race. People may disavow racist, prejudiced, and ethnocentric ideals on principle, but those very principles might be challenged or do not apply when it comes to IRRs. Whether in real or hypothetical situations requiring a decision about becoming romantically involved with an outgroup member, people's true feelings about race eventually emerge, calling into question their overall attitudes about diversity and race.

Data continue to show an upward trend in interracial romantic relationships and marriages. They also offer evidence that IRRs are placed under unnecessary and unwarranted scrutiny in ways that same-race relationships are not. As a result, partners are subjected to both internal (i.e., individual and partner) stressors and external stressors (e.g., disapproving family, friends, society) leading to relational instability or termination. These stressors are outside of typical relationship issues and cast a negative light on IRRs, framing them as unnatural and to be avoided at all costs. Race and ethnicity are closely tied to culture, which means that culture-based differences are likely to exist in IRRs; therefore, it is plausible these differences might be too significant for the partners to overcome or work through. If said differences are directly linked to negative racial perceptions, stereotypes, and biases of one partner's racial group, then it may be best to dissolve the relationship. After all, a relationship is supposed to be gratifying and affirming, and once it ceases being a safe and enjoyable space for either partner, then it is no longer fulfilling its purpose and should be terminated. Unfortunately, IRRs are not always given this opportunity due to the long-standing stigma associated with them, unfairly framing them as relationships that are to be avoided. Simply put, people are socialized to avoid, disapprove of, or terminate IRRs because of a person's race, all of which is done to maintain racial order. The racial order protects the interests and power of whites and forces less powerful people of color and whites who forfeit their cultural (i.e., racial) capital to remain powerless in both their public and private lives.

This chapter advances the argument that IRRs offer a unique window into the soul of a person or society regarding human diversity. The Trickle-Down Theory (TDT) is proposed in this chapter rather than earlier ones because of the history surrounding laws designed to criminalize interracial romantic relationships. Friendships and work relationships were strongly discouraged and regulated by Jim Crow laws, as discussed in chapters 4 and 7, but the greatest objectionable relationship was (and is) the IRR because it was seen as the greatest threat to the racial hierarchy; therefore, the best way to control them was through antimiscegenation laws. Under such laws, whites could remain the majority group, retaining their societal power. A loss of control due to interracial unions would radically shift the racial hierarchy and more evenly distribute power, resources, and opportunities across all racial groups. As antimiscegenation laws show, racist ideologies do not occur in a vacuum; rather, they are human constructs created to perpetuate a power imbalance in society that benefits the dominant group. These constructs ultimately infiltrate ingroup/outgroup perceptions and dictate how intergroup relationships should be managed and whether they should even exist.

TRICKLE-DOWN THEORY (TDT): RETHINKING AND NORMALIZING THE IRR

Trickle-Down Theory brings our attention to the fallacious thinking of a "pure" white race and its evolution over time from an overt to a covert oppressive racist ideology driving race relations. The purpose of TDT is to illustrate the interconnectedness between racist ideologies and IRRs, the general premise being that IRRs bring to the surface a person's and a society's true attitudes about race, serving as a barometer of sorts regarding the racial tensions of the country. This is of particular importance for people who see themselves as progressive or forward thinking. Sometimes it is not until people are faced with IRRs as a topic or real-life situation that their true feelings about race or specific racial groups emerge.

IRRs are intrinsically different from friendships and family relationships because they involve romance and sex and have relational expectations and norms imposed on them that are different from same-race romantic relationships. Although stigmatized as unnatural and unhealthy, IRRs provide partners with the intimacy or relational needs they are seeking in a romantic partner and are not innately dysfunctional (Orbe & Harris, 2022). It is not until others outside of the relationship interfere that IRRs become problematic and "abnormal." People as well as societies as a whole can state they are supportive or "tolerant" of diversity and inclusivity, suggesting to others they are progressive, but it is their disapproval of IRRs that tells the true story. Their expressed beliefs about IRRs offer a counternarrative to what is being communicated publicly, revealing a profound fissure in the public façade of a racially diverse and inclusive society. Toward that end, TDT challenges readers to think more critically about the far-reaching, microlevel impact society, family members, friends, and others have on how we think about IRRs.

Presumably, we like to think that our decisions to form relationships are made independently of others, but history has shown us that laws, lessons, and rules are handed down from generation to generation through governments and interpersonal networks that stigmatize cross-racial relationships. It is within this context that we have a better understanding of how every aspect of human life is controlled by oppressive ideologies designed to separate races by any means necessary. On a macrolevel, government and society have socialized citizens to perceive different racial groups as "the enemy," dictating how we should navigate the world and manage our relationships. This is all directly tied to race-based power. Racist ideologies are so powerful that they have trickled down to the microlevel, shaping how families, individuals, and others choose to establish or avoid outgroup relationships. Consequences for violating these laws and norms include legal sanctions (e.g., jail, lynching) and relational sanctions (e.g., disowning someone, alienation, isolation) that ultimately support the fact that racist ideologies from the macrolevel of society have infiltrated our microlevel spaces, namely, our personal relationships, which is a profound statement about our world and its racist leanings. It also offers evidence that a postracial society has always been a myth.

Being introspective about one's racial beliefs might be a difficult task for someone from a historically racially marginalized group or who believes themselves to be an ally or coconspirator supportive of human diversity.

Nevertheless, it is necessary that we work collectively to dismantle systems of oppression. This can (somewhat) easily and effectively be done by examining how we respond to IRRs as a topic of discussion or a possible relational option for ourselves or others. Whether real or imaginary, the scenario forces people to confront their own racial biases and prejudices. Granted, they probably have an idea that IRRs exist, but when placed in such a situation, latent beliefs will either intentionally or unintentionally surface. The opinions people hold about IRRs speak not only to their morals and values but also to the stranglehold that racist ideologies have on our society.

Racism and Eugenics

Contemporary iterations of these ideological frameworks are grounded in a belief in a racial hierarchy that is not to be disturbed, leading to disapproval of IRRs and anything disrupting the status quo. To be fair, there are some people who frown on such unions because of the criticism, prejudice, and discrimination to which relational partners of different races will or may be subjected. They see themselves as operating from a place of care, love, and protection. Nevertheless, their disapproval ultimately contributes to further stigmatizing IRRs, reiterating the erroneous narrative that IRRs are a threat to the racial hierarchy and are dysfunctional, less satisfying than, and more sexual than same-race romantic relationships.

Racism and eugenics are but two forms oppressive ideologies that historically and contemporarily continue to infiltrate race relations. Eugenics was a scientific movement created to "improve human heredity by the social control of human breeding, based on the assumption that differences in human intelligence, character and temperament are largely due to differences in heredity" (Leonard, 2005). In other words, a society with a eugenic agenda is committed to breeding "the best," which was widely believed to be people of European descent. This is also referred to as selective breeding, a movement that has had a far-reaching effect on the world since the late 1800s by way of leaders and intellectuals committed to advancing "eugenic beliefs and policies based on common racist and xenophobic attitudes" that still exist in the United States and beyond (National Human Genome Research Institute [NHGRI], 2022). Governments and societies espousing eugenics in theory and practice include but are not limited to Germany, the United States, Great Britain, Italy, Mexico, and Canada. Its pervasiveness is largely due to the "statisticians, economists, anthropologists, sociologists, social reformers, geneticists, public health officials and members of the general public [who] supported eugenics through a variety of academic and popular literature" (NHGRI, 2022). Communities that have been directly affected by this often deadly way of thinking are people of color (i.e., nonwhites), people with disabilities, LGBTQ+ individuals, and others deemed less than. Into and throughout the 20th century, the U.S. victims and targets of eugenics have been Latinxs, Native Americans, African Americans, poor whites, and people with disabilities (NHGRI, 2022). The most notorious proponent of eugenics was Adolf Hitler, who saw "racial hygiene" as the answer to society's problems and used sterilization and genocide to carry out this deadly agenda against Jews, the mentally ill, the racially inferior, the poor, and homosexuals. They were all believed to be a danger to the national community and a financial burden to society (Gopalakrishnan, 2022).

Of note is South Africa's seeming rejection of eugenics and adoption instead of ethnic nationalism through the ruling National Party, whose argument was that racial apartheid as a formalized system of racial separation was "good for all ethnic groups, white as well as black" (Klausen, n.d., para. 7). During this era, the state used legislative policies to criminalize interracial sex and racially categorize all South Africans through measures reminiscent of eugenic thought. The Population Registration Act No. 30 of 1950 is responsible for establishing three main racial groups—Whites, Natives (Blacks), Indians, and Coloured people (people of mixed race)—"for political, social and economic purposes" (South African History Online, n.d., para. 2). Such strategies "were updated versions of the kinds of discourse and policies promoted in the name of eugenics" (Klausen, n.d., para. 7). At the time, white supremacy in the form of a racial hierarchy had already been naturalized, which meant that eugenics "was never of primary importance to the production or maintenance of a racial state" (Klausen, n.d., para. 6). Thus, white supremacy was manifested through racial apartheid and embraced by white South Africans, who saw poor whites as "the enemy within" and were set on combating two racial threats: "'swamping' by the black majority, and the proliferation of 'unfit' whites" (Klausen, 2014, para. 3). The fear of the Black peril was that the majority Black population would have all of power; hence the need for a racial hierarchy and a system of subjugation directly benefiting powerful whites.

The Rationale for TDT

Eugenics and racism are discussed together because they are intimately interconnected, reflecting what some might call the extremes or degrees of racist ideologies governing human relations for centuries. While some might denounce the current existence of either, racist ideologies continue to shape societal perceptions of and attitudes toward IRRs, sometimes with deadly consequences. TDT stresses the fact that these ways of thinking are passed down from generation to generation and become either external or internal stressors on interracial partners, ultimately preventing otherwise healthy, normal, and necessary human connections from occurring. External stressors, such as family, friends, and society members, exert pressure and stress onto partners and the relationship with the goal of ending the relationship (Orbe & Harris, 2022). Internal stressors occur when one or both relational partners allow external stressors and normal relational pressures to cause difficulties for themselves, their partner, both partners, or the relationship itself. Taken together, external and internal stressors manifest on the microlevel through interpersonal relationships, originate on the macrolevel via racist ideologies, and are created by institutions in order to maintain racial power imbalances.

Figure 5.1 contains a visual illustration of TDT. The faucet with falling droplets of water represents the systemic nature of racist ideologies that are present in society and exist within institutions such as political systems, families, organizations, government policies, schools, and religions. Those institutions then propagate negative attitudes, beliefs, and values through people, who in turn become external stressors for people in IRRs. While the messages communicated can be positive, particular attention must be given to the negative ones since racist ideologies designed to suppress and oppress people of color find their way into our most intimate relationships, which is disturbing. These messages create external and internal stressors that ultimately impact the partners and the relationship. Granted, some partners and relationships can withstand these stressors. Yet these same pressures obstruct and destroy many relationships that might actually be good for the partners. As such, we must turn a critical eye to external and internal stressors if we are to understand the far-reaching impact racism has on our personal relationships and our decisions to avoid them, judge them, withhold support, or punish people when they make the decision to be romantically involved with a person of a different race.

The first and second tiers of the figure are the external and internal stressors, respectively. The external stressors exist on the societal level and can work either in concert with or independent of internal stressors. External stressors are created by systems and attempt to dictate beliefs about, attitudes toward, and behaviors associated with IRRs. They function to stigmatize these relationships and maintain norms and expectations about how people from different racial groups should interact with each other, the end goal being to discourage the initiation, maintenance, and preservation of these intimate connections. Internal stressors exist on the interpersonal level within the IRR itself and are introduced into the relationship by one or both partners. Both stressor types have the potential to temporarily strain the partner(s) and relationship, and if not properly addressed, then they can lead to relationship dissatisfaction and dissolution. External and internal stressors can feed off each other or exist independently and be experienced to varying degrees by interracial partners, or not at all. The very fact that they exist tells us that

Figure 5.1. Trickle-Down Theory of Interracial Romantic Relationships

racist ideologies are much more powerful and entrenched in our collective psyche than we realize or care to admit.

The bottom tier is the IRR and is one of several primary targets of racist ideologies. In order to reach the relational partners, these oppressive belief systems first go through society (e.g., mass media, organizations, religion, politics) to create the dominant narrative about race relations and IRRs to which people are expected to ascribe. From there, those ideologies are reified within interpersonal networks, making the messages more believable and seemingly legitimate despite being grounded in prejudiced, biased, and white supremacist thinking. Family members and friends are trusted and assumed to have our best interests at heart; therefore, when they express concern about or disapproval of an IRR, it may give us pause, causing us to reconsider or reject the idea of romantic involvement with an outgroup member. They also sometimes have the power to issue sanctions to achieve that same goal, such as disowning, cutting off communication, removing them from a will, or refusing financial support. The partners respond by either complying with or rejecting the multilayered influences on what should be a personal choice. In either case, it is in this relational context that we can see the pervasiveness of racist ideologies and their active role in making the political personal.

TENETS OF TDT

To date, the subfield of interpersonal communication research has given limited attention to interracial romantic relationships (Brummett, 2017; Brummett & Afifi, 2019; Castle Bell, 2019; Foeman & Nance, 2002; Harris & Kalbfleisch, 2000). Failure to include racially, ethnically, and culturally diverse couples in our research calls into question the assumption of social science research that study findings with a large sample size are generalizable. (For the purposes of this chapter, we are focusing on heterosexual relationships.) They are not applicable to all relationships because those differences assuredly influence how the partners communicate; hence the need for more inclusivity and representation. Also, exploring how partners in IRRs communicate and deal with relational issues can dispel myths that they are dysfunctional, unhealthy, and violent relationships when compared to same-race or white-only romantic relationships.

The Trickle-Down Theory is being proposed as a new theoretical framework designed to illustrate the pervasive nature of racist ideologies. More specifically, the argument is that people's attitudes toward and beliefs about IRRs are the direct result of societal and institutional beliefs about racial differences and racial hierarchy. While people are very unlikely to admit espousal of taboo ways of thinking, their covert and sometimes overt opinions about IRRs reveal socialized ways of thinking about different racial groups and racial pairings. TDT is an important theory because it illuminates the long-term and unfortunate success governments and social institutions have had in perpetuating a racial divide between the powerful and the powerless based solely on skin color. To that end, the three tenets below speak to the profound impact of governmental/societal systems on personal relationships.

Tenet #1: IRRs Are a Barometer of Societal Attitudes toward Race and Racial Difference

The first tenet lays the foundation for the others and is very clear in the supposition being advanced. While it may appear to be common sense, the tenet draws attention to the fact that our individual attitudes toward race and racial differences ultimately reflect the attitudes of society at large. As previously discussed, antimiscegenation laws were established to maintain the "purity" of the white race (Orbe & Harris, 2022), and while they have been overturned, there is ideological residue impacting contemporary perceptions of IRRs both by society and by the partners within those relationships. As such, the attitudes partners and society members hold about IRRs tell us a great deal about institutional-level ideologies about race. The abolishment of these incredibly invasive laws did not, however, obliterate arcane ways of thinking, as evidenced by the fact that many still believe IRRs are unnatural, dysfunctional, unhealthy, or a product of low self-esteem (Orbe & Harris, 2022). These assessments remain a barrier to IRRs.

We are socialized to have certain perceptions of IRRs, and people become aware of this socialization process in different ways and at different times in their lives. The lessons learned might be overt, covert, or a mixture of the two and become evident, for example, when a person becomes involved in an IRR (Lemay & Teneva, 2020). Interracial partners often have distinct biases in their racial metaperceptions, which are *assumed reciprocity*, *projection*, and *confirmation bias*. Racial metaperceptions are the perceptions a person has of their partner's attitude toward their racial group. Although this occurs within the relationship and between the partners, it is a product of their racial socialization and how they believe racial differences are managed in their interactions with outgroup members. Assumed reciprocity is the partner's assumption that their "attitudes toward their partners' racial group are reciprocated by their partners" (Lemay & Teneva, 2020, p. 1380). The assumption is that the partners will have the same attitude about each other's racial groups, which means that if one person has a negative attitude about their partner's racial group, then they assume the partner will hold the same for their racial group. Projection is the partner's assumption that the two have the same attitudes toward that person's racial group. There is a belief in an assumed similarity in that, for example, the partner has positive associations between "private collective self-esteem (i.e., personal evaluations of one's racial group) and public collective self-esteem (i.e., beliefs regarding other people's evaluations of one's racial group)" (Lemay & Teneva, 2020, p. 1382). Confirmation bias occurs when a partner perceives the other's racial attitudes as "consistent with their chronic expectations about being the target of prejudice" (p. 1382). The partner expects others to have racial biases against them because of their racial group membership and processes information from that perspective. The biases suggest that partners engage in their relationships and with their partners in ways that reflect how they have been consciously and subconsciously socialized to think and believe about their own and others' racial group membership.

Partners' racial metaperceptions have a direct impact on the quality of the relationship. Specifically, partners' "relationship satisfaction, perceived regard, relationship commitment, and prosocial behavior" can be influenced by the partners' attitudes toward race (Lemay & Teneva, 2020, p. 1380). The attitudes are the direct result of their racial socialization by family and society. Those beliefs trickle down into their relationship and ultimately impact their partner and the unit. Lemay and Teneva (2020) found partners who felt dissatisfied with and devalued in the relationship attributed it to their partner's negative attitude toward their racial group. This also held true for those partners who misperceived their partner's attitude. Across all situations, partners are consciously or subconsciously internalizing societal beliefs about racial groups and IRRs that manifest in their relationships, causing stress for them and their partner. Lemay and Teneva (2020) also explain that, based on their findings, lower relationship quality for an IRR is not necessarily due to inherent racial differences but internalization of negative societal attitudes toward racial groups and IRRs. Thus, if one or both partners allow biases, discrimination, and stereotypes (i.e., racial metaperceptions) to enter their thought process (regardless of the source), then there will surely be an adverse effect on the relationship itself. The researchers also support previous findings that a positive racial regard for self extends to the ingroup and contributes to better IRRs (Frey & Tropp, 2006; Tropp, 2007). When that regard is negative, it feeds into insecurities about their partner's regard and care, which become heightened when racial identity is deemed salient in how others view and treat the partner (Lemay & Teneva, 2020). This is particularly true for Blacks, who typically tend to have stronger racial identities in comparison to whites, leading to a hyperawareness of race within interracial interactions (Crocker et al., 1994; Lemay & Teneva, 2020; Wong & Cho, 2005).

Tenet #2: IRRs Are a Catalyst for Racial Identity Development Processes That Do Not Occur in Same-Race Relationships

The second tenet draws our attention to how an IRR is a catalyst for partners' racial identity development process, which is less likely to occur in a same-race romantic relationship. It is different from tenet #1 in that there is an emphasis on the IRR being a catalyst for racial identity development (Hill & Thomas, 2000; Roy et al., 2020). In terms of race, the macroculture is the numerical majority of a population, and in the United States that is whites. Macrocultures have a majority group status that remains largely unnamed and uninvestigated (Orbe & Harris, 2022). Members rarely, if ever, reflect on their raced, gendered, feminine/masculine, or able-bodied identities in comparison to microcultures who are forced to do so. The racial microculture is the numerical minority comprised of African Americans, Asian American and Pacific Islanders, Indigenous Americans, and Latinx Americans. Because they live life from the margins, they are subject to systemic oppression and must manage both their public and private lives from the perceptive of their marginalized status. Microcultural group members are attuned to the impact their race and that of others has on their lived experiences. They must also engage the world through what Du Bois ([1903] 1965) termed "double consciousness," which is "a sense 'of always looking at one's self through the eyes of others'" as a Black person (Meer, 2019, p. 54).

When macrocultural and microcultural group members choose to enter an intimate relationship, they not only violate societal norms but become vulnerable to the relationship being a catalyst for their racial identity development process. Partners of color have likely been on this journey for a much longer time; therefore, it is very likely the white partner's racial identity development that is being explored for the first time (Roy et al., 2020). This self-discovery increases awareness of their and their partner's racial identities because of discrimination, privilege and oppression, role expectations tied to culture, and lack of familial support of the relationship, for example (Orbe & Harris, 2022). For white partners, they are becoming more knowledgeable about what their whiteness means in society and, more importantly, in relation to their partner. Their whiteness may elicit white guilt, denial of race, a heightened sensitivity to race, or a journey toward self-discovery and antiracism. Whatever path they choose, it is fair to assume that, were it not for the relationship, the partner would not be compelled to explore their racial identity. Either partner can respond by "restoring constraining narratives of racial identity" that transform them into empowering identities through "three types of strategies: blocking strategies, transforming strategies, and generating strategies" (Hill & Thomas, 2000, p. 193). Blocking strategies involve deflecting oppressive or inconsistent narratives of self-definition; transforming strategies involve a defensive posture and forming empowering identities; and generating strategies are formed independently and also lead to empowering identities.

While the white partner is likely experiencing this for the first time, the partner of color is either having their identity affirmed or questioned, forcing reconceptualization of their racial identity. Their compounded experiences with racial discrimination, stereotyping, and prejudice as both an individual *and* a partner in an IRR are redefining for them what it means to be a member of their racial group. The partner of color is forced to identify or create new coping strategies beyond normal relationship obstacles as well as redefine their sense of self because of the external pressures placed on them, their partner, and the relationship. These are adaptations that would be absent from a same-race relationship. This means IRR partners face problems and issues directly associated with race that they do not have to deal with if they share their partner's racial identity (Holoien et al., 2015; Orbe & Harris, 2022). They are also engaging in identity negotiation and management because of their relationship, which very likely would not happen in a same-race relationship. Their racial differences are problematized and treated as insurmountable barriers to relationship satisfaction. This journey of self-discovery is foisted upon the partners, and for the partner of color, this is somewhat familiar terrain given they have lived life as a racially marginalized person. This is new for the white partner, who has likely lived a raceless life in which their racial identity has not been examined. While the white partner can choose whether or not to embark on this journey, ignoring or remaining ignorant of how whiteness and otherness are fundamental to the couple creates a considerable barrier to the relationship.

Tenet #3: External Factors (i.e., Family, Friends, Society) and the Racial Hierarchy Exert Undue Pressure and Stress on Partners in IRRs, Forcing the Development of Coping Strategies for Relationship Turbulence

The third tenet addresses the undue pressure that external factors (i.e., family, friends, and society) and the value-laden racial hierarchy exert on interracial partners, forcing them to create coping strategies to deal with relationship turbulence. Unlike same-race couples, interracial couples are at risk of having their relationship judged and disrupted due to others "internalizing racial homogeneity or a homogamy perspective" (Brooks et al., 2018, p. 2685) and expecting them to do the same. The partners direct their attention to those factors, which ultimately impacts their relationship (Roy et al., 2020). Specifically, "interracial couples become more aware of their surroundings and more conscientious about who they surround themselves with, likely because of the historical social opposition to such relationships" (p. 46). These factors are influential because they are important to one or both partners; their opinions are valued and carry considerable weight. The opposition is driven by a racial hierarchy in which whites are considered superior to all other racial groups (Ranzini & Rosenbaum, 2020), followed by Asians, Latinxs, and Blacks in descending order. People's sensibilities are disrupted when the hierarchy is challenged, thereby feeding into antimiscegenation beliefs. Beliefs against IRRs include preoccupation with "impure races," preserving culture (i.e., traditions, values), protection from discrimination, inevitable relationship dissolution, unnatural unions, and decreased personal value. Opposition from external others is often driven by love and a desire to protect loved ones from a racially intolerant society; however, many other sources of opposition are racist, racially prejudiced, or driven by negative feelings and attitudes regarding race. Regardless of the motivation, opposition to IRRs is born out of a shared ideology: race matters when it comes to love.

Family and friends interrupt the relationship because they are important to the partner; in turn, the partner is a child, sibling, or friend who cares about their opinions. Thus, their racist ideologies directly insert themselves into the marriage and force the partners to work toward "understanding the dynamics of their relationships" (Roy et al., 2020, p. 43). Whether it is as a partner or a unit, the couple is subjected to racial discrimination, prejudice, or stereotyping that forces them to realize the gravity of the historical opposition to IRRs, especially between Blacks and whites. Ideally, the couple blocks out those factors and determines how to respond to this ill-treatment; however, that is not always the case. They must contend with loved ones, employers, and strangers attempting to determine the worth of their relationship.

Dyadic coping in IRRs results from external factors projecting stigma onto the relationship, causing depressive symptoms and the development of new coping strategies (Rosenthal et al., 2019). Dyadic coping becomes an effective buffer against family and society members causing relational stress and was confirmed through in-depth interviews with Black-white couples about their communication (Foeman & Nance, 1999, 2002). Foeman and Nance discovered four *stages of relationship development* that typify how interracial couples deal with these external factors: (1) racial awareness, (2) coping, (3) identity emergence, and (4) maintenance. In the first stage, racial awareness, partners become aware of their attraction and the possibility they may become intimately involved. They are sensitive to each other's racial status and to having their backgrounds and attitudes challenged. This stage involves the couple "work[ing] through their interpersonal attraction," addressing the "social frames for their attraction," and deciding how they are going to "come out of the closet" to external others (Foeman & Nance, 2002, p. 239). Moving forward requires the partners to have frank discussions about their different worldviews, cultures, and relationship goals.

Coping, stage 2, involves weaving together their very different realities "into one fabric" (Foeman & Nance, 2002, p. 243). The couple prioritizes their coupledom and pulls away from others while learning how to integrate their lives. This occurs either by choice or force from others and involves the development of reactive and proactive strategies insulating the couple from people and situations potentially causing them harm (Foeman & Nance, 2002). The partners also turn to each other for greater understanding of perspectives to help with the coping process. The third stage, identity emergence, is where the couple activates strategies allowing them to be self-sustaining and facilitating a healthy life together. Instead of focusing on their differences and the barriers erected to dissolve their relationship, "interracial couples view the unique racial configuration of their families as a positive source of strength: 'Being biracial is a gift,' or 'We are the inevitable family of a truly multicultural society'" (Foeman & Nance, 2002, p. 246). Maintenance is stage four, in which the couple views their relationship as a lifetime commitment that they must work toward, which is essential. Open communication becomes a natural part of who they are and is evident to others and how they communicate with them. Throughout this process, the couple reframes how they and society think about IRRs by challenging racist ideologies on a very intimate level.

DISCUSSION

IRRs are very intimate and bring together two people from different races, cultures, and worldviews who simply want to be in a healthy loving relationship. Unlike same-race relationships, partners in IRRs are subjected to barriers grounded in racist ideologies that are inserted into and foisted on the relationship by external factors and potentially have the power to dissolve the relationship. Antimiscegenation laws were overturned in 1967 with the *Loving v. Virginia* Supreme Court case, which paved the way for people from all races to legally marry just like same-race couples. Despite this monumental moment in U.S. history, the legalization of interracial marriages did not erase the vestiges of racism that continue to define race relations in every aspect of public and private life for so many people whether they realize it or not. Racism is systemic, and though it will be difficult (some say impossible) to completely extract it from society, it is critical that we all pause and identify the ways we are individually and collectively contributing to systemic racism and the racist ideologies preserving it. This is very evident when it comes to IRRs.

IRRs are on the rise, which suggests that societal attitudes toward them are changing; however, the summer of 2020 tells us racial tensions in all other areas of society are at an all-time high. Thus, it is reasonable to assume that current approval rates of IRRs are at a standstill or on a slow decline. The racial unrest when George Floyd was murdered had nothing to do with IRRs and everything to do with racial justice and, by default, interracial communication and how Blacks and whites and other racial groups view and experience the world from very different vantage points. While Blacks, BIPOC, and allied whites were very aware of the racial disparities and race-centric violence overtaking the country, many remained in denial of the gravity of racial tensions impacting every relationship. Racism is not a phenomenon affecting only people of color; it is impacting us all in very fundamental and distressful ways.

The United States remains a country in cultural crisis when it comes to the issue of race, and it is imperative that every citizen give careful thought to what their role is in dismantling systemic racism. One way is it so think critically about our attitudes toward IRRs and actively work toward removing the stigma from what should be a healthy relationship. To hit home the severity of the situation, this chapter focused on IRRs to demonstrate how the ways we engage and communicate with each other are the direct result of racist frameworks sanctioned for decades in public and private spaces. IRRs are of focus because they are the one intimate relationship the U.S. government outlawed for fear of disrupting the racial hierarchy and redistributing societal power to create a more equitable and just society. Overturning antimiscegenation laws was certainly a step in the direction, but more must be done. It is incumbent on everyone to do their part in overturning racist ideologies that have governed our society and the world for far too long. We must look deep within our souls to determine how we can be part of the solution and not the problem of systemic racism.

The TDT was developed as a means for making the abstract concept of systemic racism concrete and accessible by focusing on interpersonal relationships as the greatest purveyors of racist ideologies. Racist ideologies are part of a tragically flawed, complex value system whose sole purpose is to perpetuate systemic oppression according to long-held racial hierarchies that intentionally disenfranchise the powerless on institutional and individual levels. These ideologies primarily exist in our communication, which on its most basic level involves the exchange of implicit or explicit messages through relationships, groups, organizations, cultures, and mass media. The messages themselves convey negative attitudes (i.e., prejudice, biases, xenophobia) that ultimately translate into discrimination and limit or prohibit access to opportunities or resources that should be provided to all in a true democracy. The communication involves relaying messages that pointedly privilege whites over other groups. The racial hierarchy was propagated during the era of Manifest Destiny, disseminating a global message of the racial superiority of white Christians (Orbe & Harris, 2022). Driven by racist ideologies, these messages have had an enduring effect on how racial groups interact with and perceive each other. In this chapter, this was evidenced within IRRs, where the partners are subjected to pressure from external factors to conform to societal norms of racial segregation. The three tenets underscore the degree to which this way of thinking is entrenched in our society and makes interracial communication more complex than necessary.

Tenet #1 states that "IRRs are a barometer of societal attitudes toward race and racial difference." IRRs elicit certain attitudes in people that otherwise may not surface. Racial socialization processes are revealed through the attitudes people express to loved ones and even strangers intermixing with different racial groups. In other words, we learn how people's families, society, and the media have taught them to adopt certain ways of thinking about romantic relationships that cross racial lines. This is subsequently indicative of their attitudes about interracial interactions in general. According to tenet #2, "IRRs are a catalyst for racial identity development processes that do not occur in same-race relationships." External factors are aware of the impact their negative views will have on partners in an IRR; however, they may be unaware that the opposition can trigger a path of self-discovery regarding the racial identity for one or both partners. This racial development process might have the opposite effect desired by drawing the partners closer as they make a concerted effort to better understand themselves and each other as racial beings. The process can eventually result in a stronger relationship, improved communication, increased empathy, and greater commitment for the partners now that they are more knowledgeable about themselves and each other and about how race has impacted their realities as individuals and as a couple. Lastly, tenet #3 states that "External factors (i.e., family, friends, society) and the racial hierarchy exert undue pressure and stress on partners in IRRs, forcing the development of coping strategies for relationship turbulence." The couple responds to pressure from external factors by developing coping strategies that insulate them from the discrimination, prejudice, and stereotypes to which they are subjected. The external factors are responsible for this stress, but because of their commitment to each other, the partners can again focus on each other and aim to protect the relationship while learning to cope with life in a racially intolerant world.

While these tenets might not relate to all IRRs, they apply to many and help us to understand how racist ideologies permeate society in ways that are undeniable. IRRs are allegedly the result of individual choices and the desire for love, connection, and belonging; however, racial ideologies and systemic racism are so ingrained in the fabric of society that interracial relationships remain taboo. The only way to extract this toxic and potentially deadly way of thinking is to communicate. *Communicate, communicate, communicate.* We must all be willing not only to cross the proverbial aisle and engage in true dialogue with racially different others but also to have difficult conversations with our same-race family members, friends, neighbors, and colleagues. Those relationships have contributed to our opinions about IRRs and other race-related issues; therefore, that is where the most difficult conversations must take place. In order to do that, we must treat racism like a cancer. When doctors discover cancer in a patient, they use radiation or perform surgery to excise the cancerous tissues and hope that the patient will live a cancer-free life. They take these measures to prevent the potentially deadly disease from spreading. Fear that the cancer will return is always there, but hope has been provided through the valiant effort expended to provide the patient with a healthy, fulfilling life. Much like a cancer patient (this is not to minimize this horrific health crisis), a post-op process ensues that involves chemotherapy and other medical care to ensure a successful operation. The patient will be on a long road to recovery, and it is made easier with the help of loved ones committed to being there. The same is true for those choosing to join the fight against racism. Recovering racists and antiracists must commit to a lifetime of unlearning and learning that keeps them and others engaged in breaking the cycle of systemic oppression by any means necessary.

Chapter 6

Making Interracial Communication Possible in the Workplace

Just like family and friend relationships incurred significant change and in some cases were dissolved because of the 2020 racial unrest, workplace relationships also experienced change in response to the murders of Ahmad Aubrey, Broanna Taylor, and George Floyd, among others. Employees, consumers, healthcare practitioners, and concerned citizens expressed disquiet about what companies, universities, and other institutions were not doing in response to the rampant racial and social injustices in the United States (Battaglio, 2020; Bongiovanni, 2020). The primary institution involved in this ongoing social issue is police departments, which were heavily criticized for what many believed was the sanctioning of police brutality against Black and Brown communities. Sadly, this is a crisis that has been plaguing society for decades. In 2020, movements such as the Black Lives Matter movement demanded the government defund the police. This specific demand for racial justice was initiated to address the structural—both material and ideological—systems reinscribing racist ideologies and resulting in the abuse, incarceration, and deaths of people of color at markedly higher rates than whites (Clement & Meyer, 2020). While some supported such drastic measures, others criticized them for being another form of prejudice and created the Blue Lives Matter countermovement, falsely equating racial and professional identities when they are not the same thing.

Racial identities are born into, whereas professional identities are chosen (Orbe & Harris, 2022). In other words, a person's race is assigned to them at birth; it is a human quality that cannot be altered. Because society is driven by a racial hierarchy, a person's quality of life will be significantly influenced by their racial identity, through no fault of their own (Morrison, 2010). Conversely, being a police officer or member of any other profession is a chosen identity. A person has the freedom to choose their profession, which means they also have a choice in whether that profession becomes an integral part of who they are. A racial identity is assigned at birth, and a professional identity can be disavowed or ascribed to at will. Given these drastic differences, the public discourse around Black Lives Matter and Blue Lives Matter illuminated for many the disconnect between racial groups and widened the ideological gap regarding what constitutes racism and its impact on certain groups. At the end of the day, the cry for racial justice rang louder (Clement & Meyer, 2020; Loller & Crary, 2021; Weaver & Walsh, 2021), as did the rejection of any such claims of systemic oppression. Police departments, the government, citizens, companies, and religious organizations (e.g., the Southern Baptist Convention) were all called on to either take accountability for or reject all accusations of racism whether directly or indirectly tied to the murders (Loller & Crary, 2021). This groundswell of racial unrest was a testament to the longstanding history of racism in the United States, which was no longer to be tolerated.

Another resounding message of racial conflict reverberating throughout these public discourses was that organizations, companies, and universities needed to up their game, so to speak, regarding diversity, equity, and inclusion (DEI) and belonging. Twitter, Ben and Jerry's, NASCAR, Disney, Apple, BabyNames.com, and Nike are a few of the companies that released strong statements on social media or their website supporting BLM and demanding racial equity (Ben & Jerry's, n.d.; D'Souza, 2020; Hessekiel, 2020; Marcin, 2020; Wade, 2020; Yep, 2020). Twitter and Square made June 19 (i.e., Juneteenth) a company holiday in celebration of the end of slavery (Rodriguez, 2020), and the producer of the television show *Law & Order: SVU* released a statement promising that a future episode would show "'how justice should be handled'—even if that isn't always the reality" because of his frustration with shows that "glorify cops who don't follow the law" (Trepany, 2020, paras. 7 and 6). The Black Lives Matter movement even brought understanding for some whites and Blacks who held opposing views on the issue of race. The USA Today Network's diversity committee responded by immediately mandating capitalizing "B when describing Black culture, ethnicity and communities of people" (McCarter, 2020, para. 4). Prior to and during the protests, universities and the U.S. Navy responded to calls for racial equity by removing the names of racists from buildings (Brooks, 2020; Nicholson 2020). While these may seem like significant victories, they are "the lowest of the low-hanging fruit" (Nicholson, 2020), further demonstrating the potentially performative nature of racial justice.

During the protests, some whites became less pro-white and Blacks became less pro-Black, achieving what Sawyer and Gampa (2018) call an egalitarian "no preference" position. Their findings demonstrate the possibility of change and the tremendous value of social protests. For organizations, there were varying degrees of expressed or implied commitments to DEI. There was also an expectation that more needs to be done. Lip service was no longer sufficient. Companies were expected not only to publicly express racial solidarity with communities of color but also to expend the financial and personnel resources necessary for establishing an ethic of inclusivity (Clement & Meyer, 2020; Loller & Crary, 2021; Patel, 2020). Moreover, there was an expectation that a position of solidarity and support of racial justice beyond a public statement would lead the country on a path toward racial reconciliation (Ben & Jerry's, n.d.). Informal observations of digital media, news broadcasts, blogs, vlogs, and other public platforms offered further proof of the depth of the seas of discontent regarding racial inequality. People from all races, cultures, ethnicities, political orientations, and faiths throughout the world reached their limits with legislators, police, and the criminal justice system and expressed their outrage over the racist inhumanity being broadcast for the world to see (Carman, 2020). There were also people from across the proverbial aisle who vehemently disagreed with this interpretation of the events unfolding before our eyes. They felt the police were being wrongly accused of racial discrimination and brutality and that the issue took place on an individual level rather than being systemic. There was an assumption that individual citizens were choosing to engage in seemingly criminal or actual criminal behavior and were reaping and suffering the consequences of their actions.

From this unrest arose an even greater moral issue surrounding humanity and the ethical treatment of people from historically marginalized groups in the workplace. Our attention was specifically directed to African Americans and Asian American Pacific Islanders (AAPI), the latter of whom became the target of hate crimes at a horrifying rate after former President Trump deliberately called the coronavirus "the Wuhan virus." Unsurprisingly, his racist and xenophobic moniker for this deadly disease coincided with an astounding increase in hate crimes against AAPI people (Orbe & Harris, 2022). To date, there is no data to definitively link Trump's and his supporters' racist behaviors to these hate crimes; however, it has been made abundantly clear that hate, racism, and xenophobia are intricately woven into the DNA of U.S. culture. To alter this genetic roadmap, as a society, we must force ourselves to confront the truth about the pervasiveness of racism and, more importantly, the ways institutions become warehouses for racist ideologies.

At the nexus of the pandemic and 2020 protests was a harsh reminder that racism is a cancer that has been plaguing the United States and the world for centuries, and now it was time for citizens, businesses, employers, politicians, activists, educators, and policymakers—everyone—to take a bold stand against racial justice. This meant moving beyond performative allyship

(Carson, 2020). Such was the case with former University of Iowa football coach Kirk Ferentz, who publicly called for more interracial dialogue about race yet was heavily scrutinized because of the hostile environment he created for his Black athletes by his racist comments and demeaning coaching style (Emmert, 2020). Instead, there was an expectation that everyone would do the morally and socially conscionable thing by educating themselves about racism through reading credible sources, having difficult conversations with family and friends about racism, and committing to unwavering advocacy for racial justice.

These expectations become a bit complicated when we consider the workplace and other professional contexts. Institutions like these often provide a service or product that does not reflect cultural sensitivity or racial inclusivity, which means racial equity and racial justice will not be a priority there. Resistance may be grounded in racist positionalities or fear of being perceived as "too woke" (i.e., too socially conscious) (Sonnemaker, 2020), ultimately translating to losses of revenue, loyal customer base, or relationships with organizational members and business partners. Three specific types of threat that are instrumental in helping explain advantaged groups' opposition to DEI policies are "(1) resource threat, or concern about losing access to outcomes and opportunities; (2) symbolic threat, or concern about the introduction of new values, culture, and expectations; and (3) ingroup morality threat, or concern about their group's role in perpetuating inequality" (Iyer, 2022, p. 1). In short, the risks that come from actively seeking inclusivity might be seen as far outweighing the rewards (Plaut et al., 2018), leading some institutions to explicitly distance themselves from or assume a neutral stance on racial justice issues. Either response is troubling because it positions institutions and people "on the wrong side of history" and exacerbates the many racial disparities and inequities ingrained in our national DNA. Thus, it is essential that institutions, individuals, and groups commit to becoming educated on racism and how to eradicate it and apply that knowledge to their relationships, societal norms, policies, and practices (Darling-Hammond et al., 2020). Efforts on such a global level can only increase the likelihood that progress will be made in achieving social justice on behalf of groups subjected to systemic racism and others treated unjustly because of their marginalized status.

WHY INSTITUTIONS SHOULD CARE ABOUT SYSTEMIC OPPRESSION

Businesses and universities are two kinds of institutions that have attempted to address racial inequities by advancing the issue of diversity. While the concept suggests an appreciation of identities from diverse racial, ethnic, and cultural backgrounds, there is minimal recognition that diversity can "impact potentially harmful or beneficial employment outcomes such as job opportunities, treatment in the workplace, and promotion prospects" (Mor Barak, 2005, p. 132). One solution among many to resolve this is diversity training. It has been touted as an answer to the problem of racism in the workplace; however, the limited research available says otherwise. According to Wiggins-Romesburg and Githens (2018), diversity training is guilty of focusing too much "on the legal and financial consequences of discrimination," thereby limiting opportunities for greater "creativity, learning, and innovation that may result from establishing more equitable norms" (p. 181). The research on diversity training programs has found that many have been designed to "manage diversity" and have either no effect or a negative effect on race relations within organizations (Dobbin & Kalev, 2018; Rynes & Rosen, 1995). The characteristics typically associated with such ineffective training include "lack of attention to (a) skill building and transfer, (b) visible leadership and financial support, (c) front-end needs assessment, and (d) long-term evaluation" (Wiggins-Romesburg & Githens, 2018, p. 181). The primary issues are the intensity and duration of diversity training, which suggests that such training is more effective and impactful if it is ongoing and uses an intensive curriculum (Dobbin & Kalev, 2018).

Rather than perceiving diversity training and other interventions as impediments to organizational culture, institutions and their members must recognize them as imperative to their survival and success in an increasingly diverse world (Patrick & Kumar, 2012). This requires an admission that racism is inherently systemic and perpetuated by structures (Kornbluh et al., 2021; Sisco, 2020), including the organization using the training. To that end, there is an element of complicity for institutions because the structures in question are maintained by past and present organizational members, and the organizational culture has very likely normalized and encouraged workplace segregation. This is also due in part to the failure of the organization to prioritize belonging, particularly for members from historically marginalized groups (Kornbluh et al., 2021; Wiggins- Romesburg & Githens, 2018). In theory, members most likely want to feel connected to the organization and each other, and for BIPOC, that need is exacerbated since they often are the only minority and/or are treated like outsiders (Morrison, 2010). This isolation or minimal engagement (which is not their fault) creates feelings of detachment and limits access to opportunities for professional growth and networking (Brown & Grothaus, 2019). It also risks perpetuating hypervisibility or tokenizing, for example, Black women, especially when they have excelled in the workplace (Brown & Grothaus, 2019; Dickens et al., 2019). Whenever opportunities for advancement have been limited due to systemic oppression, the fallout or shards from the glass ceiling worsen organizational experiences for BIPOC (Kornbluh et al., 2021). Neglecting belonging and an acknowledgment of inherent racism ultimately function to preserve power imbalances and socialize Black employees and other BIPOC to be high-achieving (i.e., resilient) in order to reach similar or the same level of success as their white counterparts (Kornbluh et al., 2021; Plaut et al., 2018; Sisco, 2020). Recognizing these inadequacies is a form of reflexivity or critical consciousness that will work in an organization's favor, allowing it to operate from a place of honesty and be better positioned to identify its strengths and weaknesses in its culture and how to actively pursue and create inclusivity. Additionally, all organizational members must have a working understanding that racist ideologies impact all organizations, how they function, and how members interact and communicate with one another (Milner et al., 2020). Otherwise, any efforts toward inclusivity will fail.

Understanding the interconnectedness of racism and institutions begins with an awareness of the fact that institutions are both physical and ideological structures with specific functions and goals. They are physical spaces that allow institutional members and consumers to come together in a mutually beneficial relationship to produce and use products or services, such as education, employment, clothing, books, food, or social networking, provided to a target population. Institutions' ideological structures are both abstract and material in the way they manifest in the culture. Organizational culture is created through communication among the leadership and members. Because of the nature of their positions, leaders have unearned and earned powers that allow them to determine, maintain, and preserve the organization's beliefs, values, and traditions (Davis, 2018). This is fundamentally dependent on organizational members executing and espousing these ideologies and ensuring they are adhered to as expected. Despite the leaders having most, if not all, of the power and control, members have a modicum of power that can be used to influence change if the leaders see its direct benefit for them. The power imbalance becomes clear when decisions about racial diversity and systemic oppression are made. As organizations work toward racial diversity, racial equity and racial justice will undoubtedly and necessarily emerge as compounding issues to be addressed in order to ensure true inclusivity and representation.

Beyond having employees, students, and customers from racially diverse backgrounds, institutions also need to address deeper issues that come along with diversifying an organization that consciously or unconsciously perpetuates systemic oppression. Most leaders would deny such allegations or assumptions, as admitting so would make them culpable. For those leaders who do take ownership of these failings, they must also be ready to move the organization forward by developing a strategic plan that actively addresses racial equity and racial justice (Plaut et al., 2018). Racial equity is "a process of eliminating racial disparities and improving outcomes for everyone" (Race Forward, n.d., para. 3). The efforts involved in achieving racial equity involve the "continual practice of changing policies, practices, systems, and structures by prioritizing measurable change in the lives of people of color." Making things fair for all people eventually (and hopefully) results in a fight for racial justice, which means a society committed to eliminating racial hierarchies and advancing collective liberation for the direct benefit of "Black, Indigenous, Latinx, Asian Americans, Native Hawaiians, and Pacific Islanders, in particular, [to] have the dignity, resources, power, and self-determination to fully thrive" (Race Forward, n.d., para. 2). Taken together, these three different phenomena underscore the degree of change that will and must come because organizations are making the right choice to be more inclusive. An organization taking on the challenge and responsibility of evolving into a racially inclusive institution will inevitably change in some very fundamental ways (Carter, 2020). Not only will traditions, policies, and other practices change, but so will workplace communication. Organizational members must now consider that their racial identities are playing a more prominent role in the workplace, school, or volunteer program than has been recognized in the past. To be clear, members should not be expected to serve as racial spokespersons or representatives of their respective racial groups. Rather, the organization should be so welcoming and inviting that all voices will be heard and members will feel generally comfortable enough to share ideas and thoughts about the organization, their responsibilities, and other issues related to the organization, allowing them to share racialized views and experiences as warranted (Darling-Hammond et al., 2020).

Being able to manage change in the power dynamics of a socially conscious institution is a delicate dance because it forces leaders to either make existing organizational structures more stringent, maintain the existing organizational structures as they are, or create changes within the organizational culture in response to concerns about racial equity (Fitzhugh et al., 2020). Unfortunately, not all institutions are able or willing to invest the financial resources, personnel, and time required to redefine themselves to reflect their social consciousness. Regardless of the reason, organizations resisting change will be seen as racist and supportive of racist ideologies that harm historically oppressed racial groups, thereby upholding racist systems (Patrick & Kumar, 2012; Plaut et al., 2018). Hopefully, the organizations that do mobilize are doing so out of a genuine concern for the many inequities impacting communities, such as in education, healthcare, and employment, and are committing to doing their part to make opportunities more equitable and accessible (Patrick & Kumar, 2012). These efforts can only be successful if organizational leaders and members are willing to work together to become the inclusive community they aspire to be.

Chapter 6

THE INEVITABILITY OF INTERRACIAL COMMUNICATION IN THE WORKPLACE

Workplace relationships and interactions are vastly different from those occurring in other less formal contexts. The relationships formed in the workplace are typically involuntary and require organization members to work together as a team to achieve micro- and macrolevel goals (Brown & Grothaus, 2019). Voluntary relationships do exist and possess a high level of trust between relational partners. They choose to be connected to each other for various reasons, most of which are not tied to their respective roles in the workplace. Microlevel goals are specific to each member's role or position in the organization and the tasks they are expected to fulfill. Those goals also include the ones a member sets as a person with an identity that exists apart from the organization. Professional identity is an important part of who workers are and likely impacts their commitment to the organization and the way they perform as a member. Macrolevel goals are fueled by and dependent on the microlevel goals achieved by the members. The two entities work together as a system, an ecosystem dependent on each other to survive. While the macrolevel goals are determined by the higher-ups, they are also influenced by the microlevel goals of the members and the teams that emerge among them.

According to Lu et al. (2020), the most powerful people in the United States are responsible for "pass[ing] our laws, run[ning] Hollywood's studios and head[ing] the most prestigious universities" and "they own pro sports teams and determine who goes to jail and who goes to war" (paras. 1 and 2). A closer look at institutions across the country reveals an unsurprising pattern whereby most powerful positions are held by whites. Institutions where this is true include but are not limited to the Supreme Court, Fortune 500 companies, universities, government agencies, military ranks, major news organizations, book publishing companies, most-read magazines, major recording labels, and TV networks and Hollywood studios (Lu et al., 2020). A vast majority of the positions at the top of these organizations are occupied by white men who "enjoy the benefits of enhanced mobility chances (the glass escalator)" (Maume, 1999, p. 500). And while these people have probably earned their position, they are direct beneficiaries of a system designed with them in mind, one that creates a "white man's vision of Utopia" (Epstein, 2020). Thus, it stands to reason that much is at stake in changing the status quo. The powerful very likely will be resistant to racial equity efforts because their share of societal power will be disrupted if power is redistributed and the playing field leveled. Most of these ideologies reflect white dominant culture, which is the most powerful group in society and has historically controlled and occupied the spaces significantly shaping organizational culture. Race and gender privilege are threatened by changes in the status quo, and because they are tightly interwoven, they create a dilemma for BIPOC navigating these institutions and spaces (Calvente et al., 2020; Gordils et al., 2021; Ouali & Jefferys, 2015).

The year 2020 was a catalyst for a social movement recentering racial justice in all public spheres in the United States, especially in the workplace. Since then, attention has galvanized around white citizens engaging in racial violence—verbal and physical—against BIPOC doing everyday activities in public spaces (e.g., neighborhoods, grocery stores), often resulting in physical harm, physical threat, and in extreme cases death. These perpetrators are people with jobs living in communities and patronizing businesses that very likely cater to BIPOC, and it is unsettling, at the very least, to learn that such behaviors are tolerated and sometimes encouraged by employers through silence and inaction. Some may argue that an employee's behavior outside of work has nothing to do with their job or the company, but many others would beg to differ. These behaviors are egregious and demonstrate how systemic racism and other forms of oppression are preserved. The racial indoctrination received throughout one's life does not disappear in the workplace (Davis, 2018). This is especially true if an organization does not have a system in place clearly denouncing racist ideologies and outlining consequences for them. Instead, the organizational culture becomes malleable to them and either intentionally or unintentionally creates an intolerable work environment at best or a hostile one at worst.

These structures house the people who embrace racist ideologies. What has also been revealed is that "everyday" people are a fundamental part of the everyday racism that people of color are experiencing on a regular basis. Racism cannot exist without people espousing these ideologies, indoctrinating others to believe the same, and engaging in racially discriminatory practices that preserve the very institutions perpetuating these inequities. This was encapsulated in the hashtag #LivingWhileBlack, created by writer Black Aziz in 2018 (Thompson, 2018), which continues to gain traction as Black Americans provide digital evidence of the unfathomable, enumerable forms of racial microaggressions they experience while engaging in normal activities such as birdwatching, walking in their neighborhoods, shopping, playing golf, or attending a wine tasting tour. Other racial/ethnic and cultural groups also experience egregious racial microaggressions and injustices; however, the emphasis here is on race relations between African Americans and white Americans, given America's history of slavery and systemic oppression in the public space, education, healthcare, the workplace, and more. These injustices continue to impact the contemporary realities and experiences of African Americans in every aspect of life, including the mundane. Institutional reform and policy change are but two avenues for addressing racial equity (Enos et al., 2019; Fitzhugh et al., 2020), and coupled with education, engagement, and allyship, these allow organizations and governments attainable solutions for inclusive workplace environments where diversity is affirmed, valued, and nurtured.

STRUCTURAL BARRIERS TO INTERRACIAL COMMUNICATION IN THE WORKPLACE

For authentic and productive interracial communication to occur in the workplace, leaders and members must acknowledge that everyday racism, sexism, and other systems of oppression are real (Bourabain, 2021; Cletus et al., 2018; Cornileus, 2013; Milner et al., 2020; Plaut et al., 2018) and develop a plan for redressing them within the organization (Loller & Crary, 2021). There must also be an acknowledgment that the organization is knowingly or unknowingly maintaining inequality regimes (Acker, 2009), which are "loosely interrelated practices, processes, actions, and meanings that result in and maintain class, gender, and racial inequalities within particular organizations" (p. 201). Measures to remedy inequities within these organizational structures and their environments are resisted by many because of the perceived threat to the status quo (Gordils et al., 2021; Ouali & Jefferys, 2015). Dominant cultural narratives indifferent toward or positioned against diversity are driving these attitudes and have a profound impact on the "relational dynamics of oppression in the workplace" (Hasford, 2016, p. 158). In other words, how members from different races communicate with each other and with those of varying degrees of power may be significantly hampered (Sondel et al., 2019). These narratives will also affect identity performance and how members manage those identities in the workplace (Hasford, 2016; Morrison, 2010; Vallejo, 2015). Unsurprisingly, racial and ethnic differences in white spaces create a heightened sensitivity to one's difference and concern with being watched (Calvente et al., 2020), which Hasford (2016) (citing Foucault) refers to as panopticism or "the internalized gaze" (p. 169). Hasford explains that "social institutions regulate human behavior through subtle mechanisms, such as instilling people with a sense of being under surveillance or under threat of punishment, and that the internalization of the gaze of the Other functions to control subordinate peoples" (p. 169). The ways most organizations are structured make interracial communication nearly impossible due to a lack of trust from BIPOC in both people and a system that does not have their best interests at heart and seems to actively work to further oppress them (Brown & Grothaus, 2019). This is not universally true for all organizations; however, it illustrates how obstacles must be removed if interracial communication is to occur (Milner et al., 2019).

To that end, it is imperative that institutions choosing to change and be more diverse implement diversity initiatives that aggressively address four specific barriers that impede progress. While there are surely many other barriers, these are highlighted because they are specific to higher education and can apply to other organizational contexts. Bourabain's (2021) research focused on racism and sexism in academia among ethnic majority and ethnic minority women, and while the barriers discussed reflect women's experiences with sexism, they are also applicable to racism experiences. Barrier one is the "smokescreen of equality" and refers to a "paradoxical climate in which substantial attention is paid to the construction of an inclusive academia, but does not do so effectively" (p. 255). Research has shown that, while reporting offices for sexual assault have been installed, they are largely ineffective because they have "remained within the boundaries prescribed by and maintained the status quo" (p. 256). The actions of the organization are deemed performative and lead to no true change. A second barrier, "everyday cloning," is defined as explicit measures taken to exclude women "from academic tasks and opportunities that increase the chance of an academic career" (Bourabain, 2021, p. 257). The practice of cultural cloning involves supervisors seeking someone who looks like them and whom they can groom for professional success. The assumption is that they have similar characteristics, attitudes, and abilities, which makes it "easier" for the more senior person to predict their abilities and career success. In this study, women reported pressure to publish like their male colleagues (focused on number of publications, top journals, etc.), with significantly less "access to other academic opportunities such as teaching, going on a research stay, or conferences" (Bourabain, 2021, p. 258). Additionally, informal and formal exclusionary practices allow the cloning of white males to continue while also limiting the success of females and punishing them for personal decisions deemed disruptive of academic plans (e.g., motherhood). Barrier three is patronizing mechanisms and refers to "the undervaluation of women's presence and work by key constituents in a variety of ways" (p. 258). Patronization is communicated through a role, and the individual and is sometimes ambiguous. An example is when a female professor expressed frustration with male colleagues addressing each other by their honorific (i.e., professor, doctor) but referring to her as "Miss." The final barrier, paternalism disguised, differs from patronization and relates to actual superiors (i.e., supervisors) and those who believe they are superior and "act as a dominant authority figure with the intent to control the subordinates in an oppressive and repressive way" (Bourabain, 2021, p. 261). Male employees are treated better than and differently from female employees. An example is women being monitored by male superiors and colleagues, while men are given much more freedom to determine their work conditions and are unaccountable to supervisors.

These barriers, among others, are evidence organizations are structured to directly benefit the powerful, who are often white men. The organizations prevent all members from having equal access to opportunities for success and growth (Cletus et al., 2018; Kornbluh et al., 2021), which directly contributes to a hostile work environment where communication across differences is impossible. By extension, the goal development process for such organizations will trivialize or be dismissive of members' racial/ethnic identities and their influence on their culture, identity, and brand. Just as professional and gender identities shape the culture, so do race and ethnicity, as they are tied to lived experiences, traditions, beliefs, and values of all members, whether they realize it or not (Kornbluh et al., 2021). Society has made it impossible to escape the material consequences of racism and racial hierarchies that place greater value on whites and racial groups in close proximity to whiteness. These racist ideologies are also present in the workplace, not surprisingly. They produced racial and ethnic disparities that remain inextricably linked to the concept of race, which is a human construct that infiltrated humanity and established the status quo. Those disparities extend to the workplace because most businesses and institutions in the United States were directly designed to benefit the most powerful people, who in this case are whites. Hundreds of years ago, power was established and usurped worldwide by British colonialists through formal systems of oppression (e.g., slavery), and while the most extreme forms are largely nonexistent, evidence remains that white people as the majority group continue to hold power and influence in every sphere of society, especially in the workplace.

ORGANIZATIONAL RESPONSES TO SOCIAL AND RACIAL INJUSTICE

One overarching expectation born from the 2020 protests was that organizations and institutions abandon performative responses to racial injustices and implement true change for racial inclusivity and equity (D'Souza, 2020; ESPN Internet Ventures, 2020; Ben & Jerry's, n.d.). There was also an expectation and hope that opponents of racial justice would realize racism is systemic and perpetuated in every aspect of human life (Cornileus, 2013). More importantly, there was an even higher expectation that institution-level awareness—along with individual-level awareness—would finally translate into material changes in organizational environments and cultures, ultimately reflecting the ideals of DEI and belonging in organizations with a history of maintaining the status quo (D'Souza, 2020). Businesses, universities, and other organizations historically have played critical roles in establishing and maintaining institutional and systemic racism (Orbe & Harris, 2022) where the primary beneficiaries are white, heterosexual, Christian, cisgender males. This is evidenced, for example, by the fact that the United States has its origins in colonization and the practice of Manifest Destiny, under which white settlers believed they were divinely ordered by God to expand into "uncivilized" lands occupied by Indigenous people (Orbe & Harris, 2022). This pattern of expansion laid the foundation for what is contemporarily understood as institutional racism or structural racism. It established the template for white supremacy and the general idea of a racial hierarchy, ranking the value of people groups according to skin color, with white being most valued and all other nonwhite groups being less valued in varying degrees (Ouali & Jefferys, 2015). This value system has become normalized and continues to influence how interracial interactions and relationships can be managed.

The urgency in disrupting the status quo regarding racial justice was also fueled by the 2020 election of Joe Biden to the U.S. presidency, which preceded the racial unrest after George Floyd's murder. This victory "spurred action for achieving greater equity in government programs and identifying biases, discrimination, and other drivers of inequity in government practices" (de Souza Briggs & McGahey, 2022, para. 9). Upon taking office, President Biden took decisive action by issuing Executive Order 13985, the first-ever executive order designed to advance racial equity and offer support to historically underserved communities "through policies and practices used across the executive branch." There were already advocates and local governments working on initiatives designed to "promote racial equity assessment and generate new government practices and approaches to decisionmaking" (para. 9). Policy changes and plans include Democrats' introduction of the bills S. 2723 and H.R. 5018 in the Senate and House, respectively. The Biden-Harris administration has demonstrated its commitment to equity for historically oppressed groups, such as communities of color, tribal communities, rural communities, LGBTQI+ communities, people with disabilities, women, and girls, through equity action plans for federal agencies (White House, 2022). The White House Office of Management and Budget introduced multiple methods for assessing equity "(with respect to race, ethnicity, religion, income, geography, gender identity, sexual orientation, and disability) in federal agency 'policies and actions' and, crucially, for building the requisite data and capacity to effectively use the best methods to change outcomes" (de Souza Briggs & McGahey, 2022, para. 12).

Normalizing racial equity through policy is certainly necessary if institutional and structural racism are to be abolished (Fitzhugh et al., 2020); however, implementation of such changes will fail if we do not address communication across and between races (Milner et al., 2019). As de Souza

Briggs and McGahey (2022) note, operationalizing equity is "a dynamic field of knowledge and practice" (para. 18), and a critical component to its manifestation is communication. Everyone needs to have the appropriate knowledge about racial equity and communication skills necessary for being culturally competent (Milner et al., 2019; Orbe & Harris, 2022). Increased diversity in the workplace, for example, and equity initiatives will undoubtedly face resistance and interracial conflict (Epstein, 2020; Ouali & Jefferys, 2015), which means policymakers, organizational leaders, and organizational members must work together to ensure conditions are optimal for the pending changes.

The last few years have shown us that policy changes and institutional reform are obsolete if people are not appropriately educated about racism and its long-term effects on all sectors of society (Enos et al., 2019). In their research brief on racial equity through the Brookings Institution, de Souza Briggs and McGahey (2022) explain that

> community advocates and pathbreaking governments have gone from conceptual framework to concrete and innovative practice in just a few years and in a remarkable range of ways. But for the work to become broadly transformative and supported, governing for equity—and, specifically, embedding equity impact analyses—now needs more public sector capacity, more allies, and more generative projects that show the idea in action and deliver visible, valued results in communities. (para. 8)

The potential for this work to transform society also requires critical engagement by organizational members and leaders and society members across all racial, ethnic, and cultural backgrounds. Not only must we all be educated on the numerous equity issues plaguing society, but we must also be knowledgeable about racism, its consequences, and how best to implement solutions leading to long-term change. This process requires centering communication, taking individual and institutional responsibility for our roles in combatting racism, and normalizing racial equity in the workplace and beyond (Milner et al., 2019).

Making Sense of Five Forms of Racism

Regardless of whether organizations have implicitly or explicitly conformed to racist ideologies, they have all been complicit in perpetuating systems that maintain inequities based on very superficial human qualities, the result being a profound impact on how people experience life due to racism. In the wake of the 2020 racial unrest, there was an expectation that all institutions be held accountable for their role in either maintaining or challenging these oppressive systems. What emerged from the public discourse around this long-standing issue was the need for a fundamental understanding of several concepts illuminating power imbalances in society and how they are maintained. This shared knowledge sets the groundwork for effective interracial communication (Milner et al., 2019). Similar to the concepts discussed in chapter 2, there are five types of racism that contribute to the racial divisions and contention that exist today. They are discussed in this chapter because they underscore how vital it is for organizations to acknowledge their contributions to this long-standing social issue and identify ways to be actively involved in dismantling racism. The five types of racism pertinent to interracial communication in the workplace are (1) individual racism, (2) interpersonal racism, (3) systemic racism, (4) institutional racism, and (5) structural racism (Abraham, 2021; National Museum of African American History and Culture [NMAAHC], n.d.; University of Southern California [USC], 2021). Although these forms of oppression are interrelated, it is imperative that we take a multipronged approach to eradicate racism on the micro- and macro-level. More specifically, having knowledge about the origins, characteristics, and impacts of racism on BIPOC and whites will allow leaders and members to understand that racism predates contemporary society. Organizations must be able to promote knowledge via education and experience as a vital precursor to all structural and ideological changes leading to racial equity. Otherwise, future efforts toward DEI and belonging will only be met with resistance and opposition.

Individual racism and *interpersonal racism* occur on the microlevel and are the most common ideologies espoused by the public. *Individual racism* is defined as "beliefs, attitudes, and actions of individuals that support or perpetuate racism in conscious and unconscious ways" (NMAAHC, n.d., para. 3). This definition of racism, if it is the only type recognized, fails to account for systemic racism. *Interpersonal racism* involves "public expressions of racism, often involving slurs, biases, or hateful words or actions" (para. 4), arising from an individual's personal racism. Reducing racism to micro- or individual-level oppression is calamitous because it minimizes the macro-level forms of oppression at the root of racism or racial prejudice and societal power (Orbe & Harris, 2022). *Systemic racism* refers to the discrimination that occurs in a system grounded in racist principles or practices, an example being a department lacking diversity in its faculty, staff, and students "despite training them to service communities of color" (USC, 2021). This is not to be confused with other types of racism, as it would trivialize the depth and breadth of racist systems. The complexities of this concept were evidenced by a March 2021 national debate in the United Kingdom that ensued after an independent report from the Commission on Race and Ethnic Disparities concluded institutional racism does not exist, which warranted further discussion of how this term is defined and how it relates to structural racism. *Institutional racism* is far-reaching and involves "discriminatory treatments, unfair policies, or biased practices based on race that result in inequitable outcomes for whites over people of color and extend considerably beyond prejudice" (NMAAHC, n.d., para. 5). Kehinde Andrews, professor of Black studies at Birmingham City University in the UK, explained that institutional racism is *how* racism is practiced in and through "institutions such as schools, universities, workplaces in ways that maintain structural racism" (Abraham, 2021, para. 11). Relatedly, *structural racism* is "the systematic oppression of ethnic minorities that leads the disparities that we see in terms of income, employment, health etc." (para. 7). Thus, *structural racism* can be viewed as an umbrella term encompassing all other forms of racism.

As these terms demonstrate, understanding and ultimately dismantling the various forms of racism is complex and intense and will require *everyone* to do their part. Organizations must be part of this process. The end goal is not only to achieve true DEI and belonging in every facet of society but also to ensure that schools, businesses, and other institutions completely abandon racist ideologies and systems designed to perpetuate racial inequities and disparities. Organizations as institutions and the individuals who make them up are perfectly situated to change the racial ideologies driving our current conceptions of humanity. Most organizations do not blatantly state one racial group or gender is better than another; those messages are more subtle yet evidenced in the extent to which organizations commit to raising their level of consciousness about racial justice and engaging in efforts toward that end. This also means organizations must move beyond performativity to create measurable, observable social reform that, at the very least, chips away at racism and alters the ideological landscape guiding these institutions.

DISCUSSION

Although organizational responses to the 2020 racial unrest varied, the truth about the reality of structural racism through police brutality against Black people was undeniable and laid bare for all to see. Dealing with race in the workplace is necessary for the reasons expressed in this chapter and many more; however, the primary reason is that racial diversity in United States and the world is an inevitability. By extension, interracial communication is going to happen, and people need to be properly equipped to understanding the nuances of these complex relationships. People often treat interracial interactions as if they should be avoided at all costs or will inevitably lead to interpersonal conflict. Both approaches and expectations are unfortunate because they set the stage for heightened racial tensions and reinforce the false assumption that racial groups are incapable of interacting with each other. One or both parties has been socialized to distrust the other, possibly due to misconceptions, lack of interracial contact, or social conformity. These reasons are not surprising given that we live in a country and world consumed by race, impacting how every facet of life is navigated and managed. While this might be more obvious for people of color who are keenly attuned to their oppression, white people are in the precarious position of rarely, if ever, having to worry about their race and how it is impacting the perceptions others have of them or how they are going to be treated. This does not mean that all whites are oblivious to their whiteness and its inherent privileges. Rather, their racial identities are rarely a part of their identity socialization, which would entail an acknowledgment of structural racism and its impact on all racial groups and its critical role in normalizing racial hierarchies. Conversely, BIPOC typically learn about race at a very young age. Parents, extended family members, and communities take an active role in educating their children about their racial identities, racism, prejudice, and discrimination so that they will be equipped to deal with a world that is not always kind to them. Given the disparate experiences with and realities of race, it stands to reason that interactions between racially different people will potentially lead to misunderstandings, discomfort, and miscommunication. Thus, being culturally competent and knowledgeable about race and all that it entails are skills everyone should be seeking, especially in the workplace.

Positive, effective interracial communication in all spaces is only possible if everyone is willing to do their part. There must be a commitment to working through differences, an appreciation of those differences, and an acceptance that we are better together than we are apart. This is just as important in the workplace. Racial/ethnic diversity has the potential to enhance the organization's performance "by broadening the group's perspectives" (Patrick & Kumar, 2012, p. 1) and bringing together members from diverse backgrounds (Williams, 2020). Ideally, all voices will be given the opportunity to be heard in a welcoming and comfortable environment. Toward that end, organizations striving for true diversity must be dedicated to valuing difference, which means abandoning all colorblind and color- and gender-neutral approaches born of discrimination prevention and fairness paradigms that end up actively "suppress[ing] individual ideas, values, or perspectives" from diverse organization members (Wiggins-Romesburg & Githens, 2011, p. 185). This requires leaders to simultaneously "encourage positive focus on disadvantaged groups" and "emphasize positive aspects of advantaged group identity" (Iyer, 2022, p. 9). This will, in turn, reduce ingroup morality threat objections to DEI efforts and changes being made by the leadership that may be perceived as a threat to majority group members. Similarly, this will reduce the need for Black (and other BIPOC) members to explore self-preservation and coping strategies employed to help them overcome the many institutional barriers embedded within these institutions (Sisco, 2020).

Collectively, organizational leaders and members must focus on the benefits of racial, ethnic, and cultural diversity, which include but are not limited to enriched worldviews, experiential diversity, and ideological diversity (Cletus et al., 2018). Such efforts require an investment in diversity initiatives that work and that translate into successful retention of members of color (Iyer, 2022). On an interpersonal level, all members and leaders benefit from these interactions, which can lead to reduced prejudices and biases, cohesion among members, cultural competence, and meaningful engagement (Iyer, 2022). Regardless of position in the organization, everyone is a stakeholder and should be willing to do their part to create a race-conscious workplace (Sisco, 2020). Leaders have the power and resources required to implement change, but it is all for naught if they fail to work collaboratively with members to offer solutions that eliminate workplace incivility and hostility toward racial minorities. Thus, effective interracial communication and a willingness to work through differences and redress institutional barriers can lead to institutions that epitomize workplace diversity.

Chapter 7

Intentionality and the Fight against Racism

In order to fight racism, we must be intentional and put forth the time, energy, effort, and other resources necessary to change our relationships and the societal structures on which racial hierarchies and ideologies are based (Coleman, 2020). Being intentional means moving forward with a purpose and with a specific goal in mind. In this case, we are addressing how a person or institution can lead or join the fight against racism in practical and effective ways, ultimately leading to long-term, sustainable change (Erskine & Bilimoria, 2019). Intentionality requires a lifelong commitment from everyone since it has taken centuries for systems of oppression to be erected and maintained as they have been. In other words, change cannot happen overnight. It will take time, dedication, and commitment if true change is going take place. Uprooting racism will require a lot from *everyone*. Racism is embedded in nearly every aspect of life; therefore, the efforts must be far-reaching in order to have the desired impact. This process, though challenging, will require canvassing the ideological landscape to determine how best to transform people's thinking and behaviors such that respect for human diversity in all its forms is normalized.

Intentionality is at the core of dismantling racism. Before becoming involved in this process, a person must first recognize that there is a problem. They must go beyond the surface level, recognizing that BIPOC have vastly different experiences than white people (see McIntosh, 1998). Black people have learned to live simultaneously in a Black and a white world, which Du Bois ([1903] 1965) refers to as double consciousness. Other people of color experience this as well. They are not a part of the majority group, and their marginalized status is determined by their placement in the racial hierarchy; they, too, must learn to navigate the world from two worldviews. Although the origins of their oppression may be different (e.g., slavery, internment camps), the outcome is the same: BIPOC have intimate knowledge and experiences with race and racism that can only be understood from a standpoint of oppression. Their experiences with oppression are ongoing, manifested in the constant barrage of racial micro- and macroaggressions they face doing everyday things, including going to work. In contrast, white people rarely must be cognizant of their racial identity. They have access to opportunities and resources because of their racial privilege (McIntosh, 1998), and while obstacles are experienced, they are attributed to other issues such as classism, sexism, or sexual orientation. Thus, their race normally works to their benefit rather than their detriment (Horowitz et al., 2019). BIPOC and whites live markedly different lives, and when it comes to not only communicating about race but also joining the fight against racism *together* (Scaramuzzo et al., 2021), barriers may emerge that prevent both from occurring; therefore, it is imperative that everyone be in a continual state of reflexivity as they embark on this difficult yet essential, rewarding journey.

The previous chapters challenged us to confront all that we know about race, racism, and race relations—the good, the bad, and the ugly. The questions and information posed were designed to facilitate better understanding of a historically taboo topic and encourage a healthy curiosity about and commitment to establishing interracial connections in authentic and necessary ways (Ilchi & Frank, 2021). For this final chapter, the Racial Intentionality Roadmap (RaIR) (see figure 7.1) is introduced to help everyone do their part to eradicate racism. The three stages on the road to dismantling racism are progressive and can be adopted by individuals, communities, and organizations: (1) Racial Past, (2) Racial Present, and (3) Racial Future. Intentionality is the foundation of RaIR and must be present to begin the journey. Intentionality means a person(s) is deliberate or purposeful in their efforts to fight racism; their actions and ways of thinking move beyond performativity.

As will be explained throughout this chapter, different steps within the stages are key to the cognitive and behavioral changes society desperately needs. While structural transformations such as changes in administrative procedures, chain of command, redistribution of departmental responsibilities, reorganization of the management hierarchy, or job structures are a step in the right direction (Erskine & Bilimoria, 2019), particular attention must be given to the stakeholders—citizens and organization members—and how they adapt to said changes. They need to be 100 percent on board if these changes have any hope of happening. Moreover, individuals need to be willing to take a lifelong journey toward *racial enlightenment*, which will be of direct benefit to themselves as well as to the communities and organizations to which they belong. Racial enlightenment, for our purposes, is defined as an awareness and acknowledgment of racism as an oppressive force negatively impacting people of color while benefiting whites that evolves into a process of unlearning racist and oppressive ideologies. People who choose

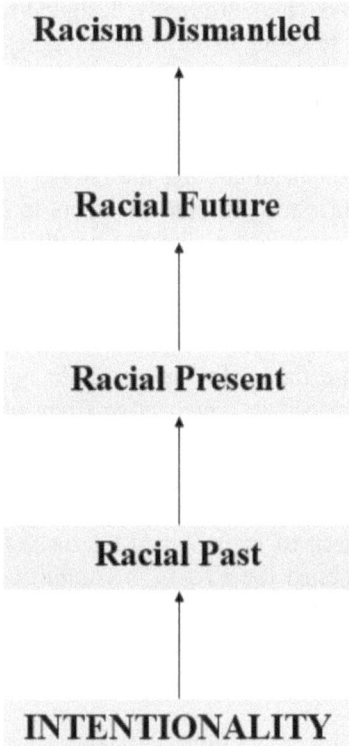

Figure 7.1. Racial Intentionality Roadmap (RaIR)

the path of racial enlightenment are motivated by their belief that everyone is responsible for doing their part in reducing racial inequities wherever they exist. Similarly, they commit to the lifelong journey of unlearning oppressive ideologies from the vantage point of the overbenefited (i.e., powerful) and the underbenefited (i.e., powerless, victim), regardless of their own positionality (Horowitz et al., 2019).

INTENTIONALITY AND POSITIONALITY

Before endeavoring on this journey toward self-awareness and activism, it is imperative to recognize our positionalities and their influence on how we engage with the world and the beautiful people within it. This requires us to be deliberately attuned to the aspects of our identities (i.e., race, gender, gender, sexuality) that define who we are and subsequently influence how others choose to perceive us. Relatedly, this must be done with the broader understanding that our identities as social constructions are inarguably grounded in power and racial hierarchies originally designed to assess the perceived value of people groups, resulting in harmful ideologies that continue to shape every aspect of human life. While some navigate the world and public spaces unaware of these racial inequities, others do so with a heightened wakefulness, but not of their own doing. Famed Black intellectual W. E. B. Du Bois ([1903] 1965) was prescient in coining the phrase *double consciousness* to capture what is oftentimes too difficult for others to comprehend. The term refers to the undeniable reality of simultaneously living in a Black and a white world. It has since been applied to other BIPOC and members of other similarly oppressed groups that do not fit into the dominant culture.

To be clear, double consciousness is not something that is to be debated, as that would invalidate the reality of systemic oppression. Rather, it is another important and necessary perspective from which to understand the world and all its flaws. Moreover, awareness of this universally understood reality should prompt reflexivity, particularly for those whose realities in relation to racism are born from unearned privileges they are oftentimes afforded through no merit of their own (McIntosh, 1998). From there, the person should be positioned for a *racial-consciousness wakening*—void of guilt and shame—where there is a genuine desire to become more knowledgeable about race and everything therein that evolves into a long-standing commitment to dismantling racism and establishing spaces and systems of racial equity.

Regardless of who joins in the fight, *everyone* must accept the reality that BIPOC have and continue to reap the incredibly negative consequences of systemic oppression that has been normalized and rarely challenged. To that end, there must be a strong command of the essential vocabulary discussed in chapter 2, with very careful attention given to the definition of racism and its direct connection to societal power, and a sure recognition that to ignore, deny, or minimize that connection is not only dangerous but also potentially lethal. This has been evidenced by the country's long history with lynchings and its contemporary iterations in the form of police brutality. Subtler forms of racism are evidenced by the lack of racial, ethnic, and cultural diversity in many organizations and institutions that either remain oblivious to or are hesitant to disturb the status quo for whatever reason. They also manifest in our interpersonal actions in the form of intentional and unintentional racial micro- and macroaggressions in grocery stores, places of worship, classrooms, and the workplace, among many other locations. Taken together, these data points offer various forms of evidence that dismantling racism is a gargantuan but necessary mission that must be undertaken by everyone, not just BIPOC. Thus, we must take baby steps before we can walk and then run, which requires that we commit to taking micro- and macrolevel approaches to addressing the wrongs in society and making them right as best we can. Not only does this mean acknowledging and accepting that systems were created primarily to benefit one group over others (Horowitz et al., 2019), but we must also undo the wrongs of the past to create a right and just present and future where everyone is *truly* equal. Accordingly, as individuals, communities, and industries, we must commit ourselves to a cause that is bigger than ourselves. Our collective responsibility will get us closer to breaking the cycle of systemic oppression (Scaramuzzo et al., 2021) and manifesting ways to actively promote and establish equity and equality for a better society where everyone is valued for who they are as complex, multidimensional beings.

RACIAL INTENTIONALITY ROADMAP (RaIR)

As a whole, this book aims to challenge everyone to make a long-term commitment to disavowing false and flawed information about race and becoming thoroughly educated about racism, its origins, and its long-term effect on society. Achieving these goals requires reading a considerable amount of information (i.e., facts and data) from credible sources as well as intentionally exposing yourself to the race-related experiences of people from groups different from your own. Additionally, BIPOC and whites need to engage in perspective-taking to see things from the vantage point of the other. Neither will be able to fully know what it is like to be a different race, and that must remain at the forefront of everyone's minds throughout this journey. Furthermore, one must be conscience of one's own racial identity and its influence on engagement with this process in order to be a productive contributor to dismantling racism. Although racial socialization happens differently for whites and BIPOC, this roadmap can be used by anyone and everyone.

In addition to being intentional, one must have an internal dialogue about the impetus for long-term involvement in fighting for racial justice. The questions to be asked are different for whites and BIPOC but equally important. They heighten sensitivity to the realness of what they are about to embark on and force them to be truthful with themselves about why they are choosing the road less traveled. Questions will be asked of BIPOC and whites that acknowledge their divergent lived experiences and subsequent worldviews. Additionally, the questions speak to how both groups are oriented differently to the realities of race, but with an understanding that they mutually inform each other and provide a broader picture of how systemic racism functions. The questions are not exhaustive, but they are a jump start for the journey to dismantling racism.

Questions to Ponder for BIPOC

Because of their racial identities, BIPOC are coming to this process with a history of racial experiences and will need to ask themselves questions that probe how those past experiences help or hinder their engagement with the process. They are probably experiencing varying degrees of racial trauma or racial fatigue after years, possibly decades, of racism and are trying to figure out how to be or remain engaged in the fight against racism.

Questions 1 and 2 ask the broader question of whether they should remain in the fight and if they are doing so in isolation. They may or may not have actual control of the impact those experiences have on them, but BIPOC do have power over their responses to them. Questions 3 and 4 address the impact of cumulative racism (see chapter 2) on one's mind, body, and spirit over time and how to prevent it in the future. Continuing to engage in racial justice but on a greater scale can take a toll on a person, which is why it is necessary to assess strategies for remaining committed to the cause. Question 5 forces BIPOC to be introspective about how they can or are recovering from past racist transgressions, which will be helpful as they cope with the ones that are bound to come. Questions 6, 7, and 8 direct our attention to whites and other people proclaiming to be allies and supporters of BIPOC in the fight for social justice. These are valid questions because BIPOC need to know if whites and others can be trusted and are authentic in their claim to help dismantle racism.

Questions to Ponder for BIPOC
1. Why must I continue to fight?
2. Am I in this alone?
3. How can I avoid battle fatigue?
4. How do I handle racial fatigue and racial trauma?
5. How can I heal from past racial infractions in order to be whole?
6. Whom can I trust?
7. How do I know allies are authentic?
8. How can I know for sure someone is not being performative?
9. What racial biases am I aware of within the BIPOC community?

Questions to Ponder for Whites

Unlike BIPOC, whites must make other considerations before they become involved in fighting institutionalized racism since they do not usually have to think about race in the same way, if at all. Dismantling racism means not only getting rid of the racial hierarchy but also losing the white privilege that comes with that, which some people might be unwilling to do (Hernández, 2020). Choosing to divest in a system that directly benefits you to the detriment of others is more common than we think when we consider the disparities and inequities in society today (Horowitz et al., 2019; Paleologos, 2021). While the following questions are related to race, they can also apply to class, gender, and sexual orientation, for example.

Question 1 prompts a person to be honest with themselves and explain why race should be important to them. This may encourage them to think more realistically about the reality of racism for BIPOC and their role and that of other whites in perpetuating racism, whether intentional or not. Questions 2 and 3 take that thinking a step further and essentially ask what is in it for them. Their motives should be pure and empathic, and the answers will reveal the level of altruism guiding their intentions in investing the time, energy, and effort into unlearning toxic ideologies that perpetuate systemic oppression. Questions 4 and 5 take that thinking further and address the risks and gains the person should anticipate by choosing to disrupt the status quo. For example, they may lose relationships or access to resources and opportunities, but if they are concerned with doing what is right and just, they will commit to the cause. Questions 6 and 7 deal with fear, which can be paralyzing if they are afraid to put themselves out there and of being perceived as a racist. By choosing to be vocal and active in the fight, others may believe they are acting out of guilt because of their whiteness. They must be willing to put aside such hinderances and focus on doing what they believe is right and seek justice with an altruistic heart. Question 8 challenges one to think about the potential of their actions being perceived as performative. They should take confidence in knowing they have good intentions that are not the norm, thus causing people to question them. Avoid taking a defense posture, as that will fuel the fire. Instead, take it as an opportunity to self-reflect and engage in corrective behavior if warranted. Question 9 reinforces the importance of being a part of the fight without choosing to speak on behalf of BIPOC. Doing so will muffle the voices that need to be amplified. Otherwise, their involvement will be in vain because they will be centering whiteness, thereby preserving systematic racism.

Questions to Ponder for Whites
1. Why should race matter to me?
2. Why am I invested?
3. What is in it for me?
4. What are the risks? Am I willing to take them?
5. What are the gains? Are they worth the risks?

6. How do I overcome my fear of getting involved?

7. How can I overcome my fear of being perceived as a racist?

8. How can I avoid people thinking my actions are performative?

9. How can I amplify voices without centering whiteness or myself?

THE STAGES OF RaIR

As previously noted, there are three stages of RaIR, and they are progressive in that they occur in chronological order. Each is a mental exercise in intrapsychic dialogue one must have for a lifetime to be serious about joining the fight against racism. A person can revisit stages, or recycle through them, should a situation arise that prompts them to do so. RaIR can be used by a person or a group of people (i.e., organizational leaders), and as will be demonstrated, dismantling racism must be done on the individual and institutional level between members. Racism is systemic and requires that *everyone* be involved in eradicating it. Individuals are a part of the system, and if they can change as people (Erskine & Bilimoria, 2019), then the system itself will change for the greater good.

Racial Past

Stage one of RaIR is Racial Past and involves a reflexive critical thinking exercise that gets a person to think about how they have been socialized to perceive and understand their racial identity and that of others. Racial socialization is the "transmission from adults to children of information regarding race and ethnicity" (Hughes et al., 2006, p. 748). This will take some effort because a person will have to think hard about their childhood or other times in the past in order to understand their racial socialization process. In other words, they will be reflecting on how their parents, other people, and society have shaped or influenced how their racial identity has evolved. It is assumed that everyone has had at least one defining moment in their lives when they became aware of their race. Maybe your parents had either no or very surface-level conversations about your race or you actually had The Talk when you were in elementary school. These conversations, or lack thereof, impact your level of connection to you racial/ethnic identity and how much you identify with it (Ade-Serrano & Nkansa-Dwamena, 2016; Galán et al., 2021).

Race and racial/ethnic identity conversations occur earlier in life for BIPOC than they do for whites (Ade-Serrano & Nkansa-Dwamena, 2016; Ayón, 2016; Minniear & Soliz, 2019). Black and Latino young adults recall receiving racial socialization messages from parents, extended family members, and community members who were instrumental in helping them understand the meaning of race. Minniear and Soliz (2019) conducted focus groups with young Black adults about the importance of these race messages and found three areas central to racial socialization: "(a) the content of familial messages regarding race, identity, and prejudice, (b) critical incidents that shaped individuals' understandings of Black racial identity, and (c) familial sources" (p. 329). The authors highlight how these findings are particularly important given today's social climate. Minniear and Soliz (2019) further stress how family communication is a major part of understanding one's racial identity. According to Ayón (2016), racial socialization for families of color also involves conversations affirming those identities through cultural retention and pride, "the value of empathy and diversity, ensuring safety through comfort, modeling advocacy, as well as fostering resiliency" (Padron Eberline & Shue, 2022, p. 175).

White families do have conversations about race and identity, but the dominant messages are about "egalitarianism and silence," which put greater emphasis on "hard work, virtue, and universal equality over the recognition of ethnic-racial divisions" (Eberline & Shue, 2022, p. 175; see also Hughes et al., 2006). Eberline and Shue (2022) found that white young adults and their parents are not communicating about white privilege and rarely, if ever, discuss their cultural heritage or ethnicity. Their findings support other research stating that failing to engage in these race conversations and explicitly discuss white privilege perpetuates a colorblind ideology, ignoring how racial socialization fits into the large picture of racism (Ayón, 2016; Eberline & Shue, 2022; Hughes et al., 2006).

The aforementioned communication inequities underscore the value of RaIR by demonstrating how racial socialization directly influences how prepared a person is to be culturally competent or engage in conversations about race. If individuals have no understanding of how these identities function and their impact on worldviews, then they will be equally uninformed about the realities of race and racism, thus serving as a barrier to social justice. The intentional person, the one who is actively trying to fight racism, must begin their journey by acknowledging how they have been socialized to understand their racial identity and its placement on the racial hierarchy. To be clear, the goal is not to elicit guilt or anger but to promote awareness and compassion as conduits for racial justice in a society consumed with race. This stage of RaIR involves reflexivity and requires a person respond to the following prompts with multiple examples, articulating specific messages they have received about their own racial socialization process:

- The moment and event that triggered awareness of your racial identity

- Lessons taught about the importance of being a member of your racial group
- Lessons taught about what it means to be a member of other racial groups
- Messages received from *society* about your racial group membership
- Messages received from *family* about your racial group membership
- Specific behaviors or decisions that are directly shaped by your racial socialization
- Specific messages family and society have communicated to you about how to interact with other racial group members

These prompts are critical to self-discovery as a person begins the journey toward fighting racism. If every person committed themselves to racial justice, then the systemic nature of racial oppression will surely erode. It is then that people will be able to comprehend the material implications of race and racism on everyone's life and how they can be part of the solution in advancing racial justice.

Racial Present

Stage two of RaIR is Racial Present and involves being cognizant and critical of how the activities you engage in and behaviors you enact are either advancing or impeding your contributions to the fight against racism. This ongoing process is an opportunity to conduct an inventory that determines exactly *what* you are doing that is assisting you in addressing racism on the micro- and macrolevels. During this stage, you are actively making the choice to assess the extent of your progress in fulfilling your commitment to the racial justice cause. In other words, you are "putting your money where your mouth is." Your intention to have a long-term commitment to the cause does not need to be announced, as that will appear disingenuous to others and minimize the importance of everyone doing their part. Instead, the ideological and behavioral changes you experience, along with increased self-awareness, should organically emerge and attest to who you are and who you are becoming. Your being selfless and centering others will allow people to see your authenticity, particularly in the case of majority-group members (Heinze, 2008; Ilchi & Frank, 2021).

Racial Present is different from Racial Past because you have, to some degree, moved beyond your racial socialization. You spent time understanding how your racial identity was formed, and now you are using that knowledge to inform your plans to be perpetually involved in the fight against racism. This can include but is not limited to immersing yourself in racism literature by BIPOC, addressing racial incidents in the moment, initiating conversations about race despite the discomfort, confronting others about their racist behaviors, and actively listening to victims' accounts of racism (Ade-Serrano & Nkansa-Dwamena, 2016; Harries, 2014). Each of these activities involves a person translating their intentionality into an observable act or behavior that produces somewhat measurable results.

Navigating this stage requires the use of Harris and Abbott's (2011) Confronting Racial Microaggressions (CRaM) model. The model was originally used as assignment guidelines for an interracial communication course in which students were required to reflect on an interracial encounter they either personally experienced or witnessed. This involved them describing the encounter, how they handled it, and what they would do differently if it happened again. The four steps are (1) identify the microaggression, (2) identify three cues, (3) react to the racial microaggression, and (4) assess the outcome. The model is an excellent exercise in behavioral evaluation in that you are reflecting on a recent encounter and determining if you did enough to confront racism in real time. The exercise forces self-evaluation, which should lead to the identification of effective communication strategies that can be used in future interactions. More importantly, you are assessing your decision-making and other related behaviors to determine how you can be the best coconspirator (Carson, 2020) while boldly confronting racism. This also includes using these encounters as teachable moments for other involved parties to pause and reflect on their own ideologies and roles in perpetuating racism in that situation and beyond. Ultimately, you are building an arsenal of weapons to be used in future interactions where race becomes a negative issue.

Step 1, identifying the microaggression, is fairly simple and requires that the person contextualize the encounter and be clear that the encounter was, in fact, race-centered. To illustrate the model, a student observation from the original study will be used in every stage (Harris & Abbott, 2011). A white female student shared a recent racist encounter with her grandparents who used the racial epithet "n-word toes" to reference Spanish nuts. She was stunned because she had never heard them use it and was appalled that they did it so comfortably and casually. She was easily able to identify the racial microaggression because it was overt and shocking, and although no BIPOC person was present, she felt compelled and empowered to confront the behavior due in large part to the knowledge about racism she was gaining through the course and the egregious nature of their behavior.

After identifying the racial encounter, a person moves on to step 2, which is to identify three cues. It is during this stage that a person determines what information to use in responding to the racial encounter or if they should respond at all (Harris & Abbott, 2011). *Relational cues* characterize the relationship the person has with the other people directly involved in the encounter. *Contextual cues* involve the physical environment (e.g., store, home, classroom) within which the racial encounter has taken place. *Emotional cues* are the emotional responses (e.g., anger, fear, frustration) that emerge as a direct result of the racial encounter.

For the female student, a relational cue was the fact that her grandparents were the perpetrators of the racist behavior, and despite this close relationship, she was willing to ignore this cue and directly confront them on their racism. The contextual cue was the grandparents' home; they were having lunch after some gardening. Similarly, she was not concerned that the encounter occurred in their home. Although she did not mention this, it is possible the student would have confronted them regardless of where the incident took place. It was the emotional cue that overrode the others and influenced her eventual response in the form of anger, which was accompanied by disappointment that her grandparents felt comfortable using racist language and doing so in front of her, as if she approved. The student responded to the situation because of the weight she placed on her emotional reaction to the racial microaggression. She wrote that she told her grandparents using the slur was racist and highly inappropriate and would have been even more so if used in the presence of a Black person. They responded that they did not know the slur was offensive and had been using it for as long as they could recall. She then had a long conversation with them about the history of the n-word and used information learned from the class to teach them about how troubling, offensive, and inappropriate their language is. After determining which cue weighed more in this scenario, the student then moved to step 3.

Step 3 is the reaction to the racial microaggression (RM) and involves the person replaying the interaction and reflecting on different aspects of how they handled it to determine their level of satisfaction with the chosen strategy (Harris & Abbott, 2011). This is done soon after the interaction so that the recency will allow for an accurate assessment. If that is not possible for whatever reason, then they should prioritize this step so that they can hone their interracial communication skills. Reflecting on the interaction will allow them to assess their comfort level with difficult race-related conversations (Ade-Serrano & Nkansa-Dwamena, 2016) and determine if they have truly been intentional in confronting racism. Collectively, these efforts will also give the person the opportunity to assess their commitment and dedication to fighting for racial justice and recalibrate if necessary.

The following prompts require that the person be very honest with themselves, which means being vulnerable. They may experience myriad emotions and thoughts as they critique, and that is totally fine. The most important thing is that they are open to the process and will use this as an opportunity to be a better communicator and ultimately co-conspirator in the fight against racism (Carson, 2020; Norander & Galanes, 2014). The prompts are as follows:

- How did I react?
- How comfortable am I with my response?
- How did they respond?
- How did I feel in that moment?
- What influenced my decision to respond in that way?
- What about the other person influenced how I chose to respond?

Step 4, the final stage, is assessing the outcome. In this step the person assesses whether the strategy used was successful in helping them reach their goal of confronting racism in a constructive and helpful way (Harris & Abbott, 2011). During this part of the model, the reaction or response of the other person involved can also be used to determine the effectiveness of the approach taken, but this should be done carefully, as the confrontation can easily be seen as an affront or attack. The other person might be closed off to being confronted about their behavior and learning about racism and the possible role they have had in perpetuating it. To be clear, the person going through CRaMM must be committed to following their moral compass, which means there are risks of being rejected. There must be an acknowledgment that the recipient of this message may not be in a space to receive the reality check, but the person must take comfort in knowing they are being true to who they are becoming. A seed has been planted that will hopefully blossom into a life-altering teachable moment.

These prompts are designed to help you post-hoc with evaluating the outcome of confronting or avoiding a race-related incident (Harris & Abbott, 2011). Although the outcome is out of your control, you should still be prepared to fulfill the vow you made to join the fight against racism. Evaluating the situation is a learning opportunity and will help you determine what you can or should do in the future should similar situations arise. Racial incidents are likely to happen, which means you need to regularly do this exercise. Answering the provided prompts and creating new ones can only improve your race-related communication skills, which will make you more adept at managing those difficult yet necessary conversations.

- How effective was your reaction?
- What emotions did you experience during and after the situation?
- How did the incident affect your relationship with that person?
- How might this interaction impact your future interactions with this person?
- What would you do differently if you have the chance?

- What lesson(s) did you learn from this interaction that has prepared you for how to best deal with future confrontations involving racism?
- What lesson(s) do you wish you had known before the confrontation that you think would have helped you better handle the situation?
- What are some of the risks you took in confronting the person?
- What are some of the consequences if you chose not to address the person or the situation?

CRaMM Strategies

Harris and Abbott (2011) identified nine reactions to racial microaggressions apropos for addressing contemporary manifestations of racism in what is considered a hostile sociopolitical climate. These reactions set the groundwork for what can potentially be a depository of responses for others to use in present and future interactions. They fall into three dominant categories: active strategies, protective strategies, and passive strategies. It may seem that the passive category is to be avoided; however, these responses are as important as active and protective strategies because they reveal communication barriers in need of correction in order to further empower the public and communication scholars to remain unwavering in the fight against racism.

Active Strategies

The four active strategies are the direct result of students thinking critically about their education on interracial communication and personal experiences addressing racial microaggressions. Despite this structured space for being reflective, this exercise provides compelling evidence of the power of communication in dismantling racism. It also demonstrates that being knowledgeable and informed about systemic oppression can be done both formally and informally. While others might not have been fortunate enough to be formally educated on racism, they have their own arsenal of experiences and self-education that can serve the same purpose. It also requires that credible information about race, racism, systemic racism, implicit bias, and discrimination be accessed through such places as online master classes, social media apps, or self-created curricula designed to educate and empower a person to become well versed on this complex issue (Clark, 2019).

Ideally, when using any of these strategies, a person will correct offensive behaviors fueled by racist ideologies by applying their knowledge to these interactions. In doing so, there is also the potential to inspire the offending party to become more educated themselves and less dedicated to their racism or racial prejudices. The four active strategies are as follows: (1) *casual consciousness*, (2) *aggressive confrontation*, (3) *active confrontation*, and

(4) *mediation*. Casual consciousness is a "pointed effort to apply classroom knowledge and *informally* educate others about race without invoking guilt, shame, or blame" (Harris & Abbott, 2011, p. 295). Similarly, aggressive confrontation involves a "deliberate effort to address the racist behavior of an offender regardless of the consequences" (p. 295). The third strategy, active confrontation, is also deliberate but involves the person addressing the offender's racist behavior with careful caution. Mediation, the fourth strategy, refers to when a person takes on "an assumed role as a mediator (between the offender and offended party) in an effort to resolve racial tensions while recognizing the offensive nature of the racial microaggression" (p. 296).

Protective Strategies

The two protective strategies in CRaMM are self-preservation and concerted self-reflection (Harris & Abbott, 2011) and speak to a person's acknowledgment of the difficulties with and consequences for confronting racism. At first glance, self-preservation might appear self-serving; however, a closer look suggests it is a way to protect one's mental or emotional well-being, akin to handling racial battle fatigue (RBF) (Smith, 2004). RBF addresses the constant exposure to stress a BIPOC experiences due to everyday racism (Chancellor, 2019). Smith et al. (2006) define RBF as "the stress associated with racial microaggressions [that] causes African Americans to experience various forms of mental, emotional, and physical strain" (p. 300). Self-preservation is "the decision to not engage in confrontational behaviors that risk one's face (e.g., avoiding embarrassment)" (Harris & Abbott, 2011, p. 296). Concerted self-reflection is a psychological strategy involving "a purposeful engagement in self-reflection on the topic of race and how to best understand its significance in real world contexts after being an outsider to or observer of a race-centered experience that warrants no direct response" (p. 296). This strategy may be necessary when you are a "helpless bystander," which is when there is "an inability to significantly impact the racist and inappropriate behaviors of others" (p. 296). When used by a BIPOC, these strategies are a necessary response to RBF, and for white people, while stress might not reach as high, it can still exist due to the risks associated with such confrontations.

Passive Strategies

Passive strategies are barriers to dismantling racism because a person is choosing to take the path of least resistant and act as if the racial microaggression did not occur or was insignificant. By employing a passive strategy, a person is absolving themselves of any responsibility and possibly becoming an impediment to dismantling racism. According to Abbott and Harris (2011), avoidance involves "purposeful (active) efforts to avoid confronting behavior which may include future interactions with the offender or perceived opportunities for confrontation" (p. 295). The person is essentially choosing to remove themselves from potentially confrontational situations. Self-censure is similar yet places greater emphasis on attempting to understand what is happening. While inaction is the response, the person chooses "to self-monitor for fear of being offensive" (Harris & Abbott, 2011, p. 295). In other words, the person is engaging in intrapsychic communication in order to cognitively process the event and to avoid being misperceived or saying the wrong thing and subsequently worsening the situation.

Racial Future

Stage 3 of RaIR is Racial Future and refers to the actions a person plans to engage in during future interactions with others to maintain their commitment to the fight against racism. Racial Future is like a game plan for what a person intends to do now that they have some experience and knowledge under their belt. Experiences have taught them what is effective and ineffective in addressing racism in a variety of circumstances and with an array of people. They may have learned that direct communication, indirect communication, or avoidance are the most common approaches used across different relationship types, such as family, friends, colleagues, and associates. Factors that might influence strategy choice are the three cues (i.e., emotional, relational, and contextual) identified in CRaMM (Harris & Abbott, 2011), personality, length of relationship, relational power, and immediate and long-term risks.

As previously noted, Harris and Abbott (2011) report nine identifiable reactions a person might have in response to a racial microaggression. These responses evolved from a class assignment but have practical implications for contemporary race communication and interracial communication. Race communication refers to intraracial (i.e., same-race) race-centered dialogue, whereas interracial communication occurs between two racially different people where race becomes a salient issue (Orbe & Harris, 2022). Race is the focal point of both forms of communication, and how the topic is managed very likely will be influenced by the racial composition of the interactants. BIPOC communicating among fellow BIPOC might be more comfortable because of shared racialized experiences, making such discussions somewhat easier to manage. These conversations may provide mutual support, understanding, and affirmation facilitated by shared negative (i.e., racial fatigue, distrust, racism) and positive (i.e., racial pride, self-respect) racial experiences. Conversely, whites might not have conversations with other whites or BIPOC due to their lack of awareness of or interest in race issues due to their own racial socialization (Harries, 2014; Heinze, 2008; Hernández, 2020). From their vantage point, their realities are less obviously shaped by race because of their privilege and placement in the racial hierarchy (Ade-Serrano & Nkansa-Dwamena, 2016; McIntosh, 1998); thus, it is reasonable to assume that they are not as incentivized to have these conversations as are BIPOC. For those who are enlightened, they can move beyond their feelings of ineptness or discomfort because they genuinely what to understand the systems that have created disparate racial realities for whites and BIPOC (Hernández, 2020; Paleologos, 2021). Nevertheless, they are open to the possibilities that may come from having these conversations despite how uncomfortable they might be (Harries, 2014). They also are unafraid of being perceived as racist and are emboldened to have these conversations with full knowledge of their racial privilege (McIntosh, 1998), how pivotal they are to the fight against racism, and their awareness of the consequences that come with going against the grain.

The Racial Future is a lifelong journey one embarks on after committing to active engagement in the fight against racism and refers to an appraisal of the future self. In short, the person has chosen to become involved in social activism related to racial injustice, and unlike the previous stages, Racial Future is more nuanced because the person now has data in the form of critical moments or events that can be used to determine their success in achieving their personal activism goals. The person has had the opportunity to apply what they have learned about confronting racism. Now they are engaging in a more intense form of reflexivity by evaluating their current racial ideologies and corresponding actions and the specific things they have done to become a sincere and committed advocate. It is during this stage that the person also receives or solicits feedback from orientational others (e.g., family, friends) and generalized others (e.g., associates, colleagues, strangers) (Orbe & Harris, 2022) about their progress on this journey. This may sound self-serving, but it is not, or at least it should not be. Rather, the person is using their critical moments as information to safeguard against them being a hindrance, distraction, or barrier in achieving short- and long-term goals for dismantling racism in their interpersonal networks.

Reflexivity in this stage is necessary even though it is potentially hurtful, as the person is learning truths about who they are and who they believe themselves to be. This part of the process involves having very challenging intrapersonal and interpersonal communication that might be uncomfortable; however, both are vital to growth and the ability to make substantive and long-lasting contributions to the fight against racism. In truth, this as an opportunity to continue the evolutionary process of being a global citizen. Time has lapsed between stages 2 and 3, and the person has likely moved from the theoretical to the practical. They have developed a plan to be more proactive in the fight in ways that are most comfortable and effective for them while also facilitating societal change. It is important to note that the person has very likely recommitted themselves to being a better person who uses their privilege(s) to better the lives of others or their own oppression-related experiences as a foundation upon which to continue building their activism (Bernstein, 2011).

While Racial Future is the last stage of RaIR, a person's racial justice journey does not end there. Instead, they will likely revisit stage 2 to replay past and prepare for future interactions where a confrontation is warranted. This also means that the person will continue to learn about who they are and whether they are achieving personal goals set for achieving racial justice. They will prioritize the relevancy and necessity of RaIR due to the pervasiveness of racism as a kind of highly coveted form of societal power. When considered along with the many others who have committed themselves to fighting racism, a person committed to RaIR will always be learning, reflecting, and devising new ways to do their part in this lifelong process.

NINE RULES FOR RaIR

There are nine rules an adherent of RaIR is strongly encouraged to prioritize. Each articulates the necessity of focusing on the fundamental reasons a person has chosen to get in the trenches and fight systemic oppression. Regularly revisiting these rules should not only serve as a reminder of one's commitment to the cause but also generate new strategies for maintaining dedication to a necessary and worthy social cause. They are as follows, in no particular order:

1. Remain intentional in your efforts to challenge racism despite the difficulties to come.
2. Maintain perspective-taking as you forge relationships with ingroup and outgroup members.
3. Pursue formal and independent continuing education opportunities to become well informed about racism and systemic oppression.
4. Own your activism; do not allow others or the process to become intimidating or overwhelming.
5. Engage on constant reflexivity; always be willing to assess where you are in your journey and determine what you can do to be a better antiracist
6. Hold yourself and others accountable in order to confront racial microaggressions in real time.

7. Practice perpetual empathy toward others; sensitivity is necessary for understanding to occur.
8. Be unwavering in your commitment to combating racism.
9. Identify ways to engage in community activism to dismantle racism on the local level.

WHAT NOW? ENACTING RaIR IN THE FIGHT FOR RACIAL JUSTICE

Dismantling racism is a tremendous task to undertake, and for any progress to be made, *everyone* must be involved in the effort to remove the long-standing barriers and the racial and ethnic disparities plaguing every aspect of human life. Indeed, BIPOC are more adversely impacted by racism than whites (Orbe & Harris, 2022; Scaramuzzo et al., 2021) due to the systemic nature of racial oppression. Most people are not actively or overtly expressing racist ideologies undergirding these inequities, as these disconcerting ways of thinking and acting have become normalized and are often difficult to identify and subsequently eradicate. Achieving change means disrupting the status quo, and many people are unwilling to do that because of the societal privileges that will be lost in the process. An important piece of the puzzle many people are missing or are choosing to ignore is the fact that racism has had a far-reaching effect on us all, whether we want to admit it or not, and has created inequities that are adversely impacting the quality of life for BIPOC. Frankly, racism is a blatant example of the lack of respect for humanity that has run rampant in the United States and across the world for far too long. Thus, it is hoped that this book will inspire many to do the necessary work of dismantling racism.

Hopefully, this final chapter has catapulted you into a journey of restoring humanity in the spaces and places you occupy that mislabel these efforts as being a part of "woke" culture. At its most basic level, woke needs to be operationalized and understood as an awareness of and attention to the respect and value that must be afforded *all* people. That is the impetus for RaIR and the end goal of this book: to take us to a place of respect, appreciation, and admiration of people groups so that we live in peace and authenticity. While this is idyllic, it can only manifest through our individual and collective work and commitment to promoting parity in all areas of life. The only way we can get there is through intentionality; we must each be intentional in our commitment to facilitating racial justice in every aspect of life. Intentionality means we are in this for the long haul and are taking a step in the right direction (Erskine & Bilimoria, 2019). Racial enlightenment is a lifelong journey we must all be willing to take.

An overarching theme of interracial communication in general and for the purpose of dismantling racism is to be consistently mindful of our own positionalities as well as those of others. This means that we must be willing to answer and reflect on the "Questions to Ponder" posed earlier in this chapter. Regardless of and because of our racial identities, we must be willing to be reflective and engage in intrapersonal communication as we consider how to have healthy intraracial and interracial interactions that lead to mutual understanding and societal change. Such an approach will ultimately render racial hierarchies moot and encourage a divestment from systems of oppression (Ayón, 2016; Eberline & Shue, 2022; Hughes et al., 2006). This can be achieved by adopting RaIR as well as intentionality, dedication, and vulnerability while trying to understand how to use our various relationships to address this larger societal issue. Ultimately, these will translate into an urgency for all to include helpful CRaM strategies (Harris & Abbott, 2011) in their communication tool kit.

The summer of 2020 taught the world a plethora of lessons regarding racial equity. Sadly, these are not new, as civil rights activists, citizens, and allies have been active in resisting disparities for decades. Rather than be complacent and accept the status quo, it is a matter of life and death—literally and figuratively—that we all join forces to do the right thing when it comes to the issues of race and racism. This cannot be done by one person, one racial group, or one organization. It will take *all* of our individual and collective efforts to level the proverbial playing field and address racial microaggressions along with other barriers that preserve antiquated and troubling ideologies that hurt us all. Thus, we must normalize strategies of resistance, such as RaIR and CRaMM, that boldly address imbalances in societal power and encourage healthy conversations about racism within our intraracial and interracial interactions and relationships. The Talk that occurs within our BIPOC communities should become a natural part of white communities as well if we are to see true change in how we perceive and engage with people who are racially different from us. Instead of stigmatizing and avoiding these conversations and interactions, we must be bold enough to be a part of the societal change we wish to see in this increasingly diverse world. We must actively engage with each other with pure intentions and a commitment to dismantling racism, one relationship at a time.

References

Abraham, E. (2021, April 1). What is the difference between institutional and structural racism? *Independent*. https://www.independent.co.uk/life-style/institutional-racism-structural-racism-report-b1825596.html
Acker, J. (2009). From glass ceiling to in equality regimes. *Sociologie du Travail, 51*(2), 199–217.
Ade-Serrano, Y., & Nkansa-Dwamena, O. (2016). Guest editorial—Voicing the uncomfortable: How can we talk about race? *Counselling Psychology Review, 31*(2), 5–9. https://doi.org/10.53841/bpscpr.2016.31.2.5
Agyeman, J., & Erickson, J. S. (2012). Culture, recognition, and the negotiation of difference: Some thoughts on cultural competency in planning education. *Journal of Planning Education and Research, 32*(3), 358–66. https://doi.org/10.1177/0739456X12441213
Ahmed, R., & Bates, B. R. (2017). Patients' fear of physicians and perceptions of physicians' cultural competence in healthcare. *Journal of Communication in Healthcare, 10*(1), 55–60. https://doi.org/10.1080/17538068.2017.1287389
Allan, G. (2003). Friendship. In K. Christensen & D. Levinson (Eds.), *Encyclopedia of community: From the village to the virtual world*. Sage.
Al Ramiah, A., Schmid, K., Hewstone, M., & Floe, C. (2015). Why are all the white (Asian) kids sitting together in the cafeteria? Resegregation and the role of intergroup attributions and norms. *British Journal of Social Psychology, 54*(1), 100–124. https://doi.org/10.1111/bjso.12064
American Medical Association. (n.d.). *Covid-19 health equity initiatives across the United States*. https://www.ama-assn.org/delivering-care/health-equity/covid-19-health-equity-initiatives-across-united-states
Asare, J. G. (2021, April 22). How the adultification bias contributes to black trauma. *Forbes*. https://www.forbes.com/sites/janicegassam/2021/04/22/how-the-adultification-bias-contributes-to-black-trauma/?sh=53c4fd062b08
Ayón, C. (2016). Talking to Latino children about race, inequality, and discrimination: Raising families in an anti-immigrant political environment. *Journal of the Society for Social Work and Research, 7*(3), 449–77. https://doi.org/10.1086/686929

Bahk, C. M., & Jandt, F. E. (2008). Explicit and implicit perceptions of non-whiteness and interracial interaction reluctance in the United States. *Human Communication, 11*(3), 319–39.

Bandura, A. (1977). Self-efficacy: Toward a unifying theory of behavioral change. *Psychological Review, 84*(2), 191–215. https://doi.org/10.1037/0033-295X.84.2.191

Bartoli, E., Michael, A., Bentley-Edwards, K. L., Stevenson, H. C., Shor, R. E., & McClain, S. E. (2016). Training for colour-blindness: white racial socialisation. *Whiteness and Education, 1*(2), 125–36.

Battaglio, S. (2020, June 11). Tucker Carlson's Black Lives Matter remarks alienate Fox News advertisers. *Los Angeles Times.* https://www.latimes.com/entertainment-arts/business/story/2020-06-11/tucker-carlson-black-lives-matter-remarks-alienate-fox-news-advertisers

Bauder, D. (2020, July 20). AP says it will capitalize Black but not white. *Associated Press.* https://apnews.com/article/entertainment-cultures-race-and-ethnicity-us-news-ap-top-news-7e36c00c5af0436abc09e051261fff1f

Beck, K. (2018, July 21). City rallies behind 13-year-old entrepreneur after a racist moron calls the cops. *Mashable.* https://mashable.com/article/minneapolis-13-hot-dog-stand

Belk, J. (2020, June 27). Op-ed: Interracial friendships can be gratifying, but they're also complicated. *Los Angeles Times.* https://www.latimes.com/opinion/story/2020-06-27/interracial-friendships-black-white

Ben & Jerry's. (n.d.). *Silence is not an option.* https://www.benjerry.com/about-us/media-center/dismantle-white-supremacy

Bernstein, S. (2011). Interracial activism in the Los Angeles Community Service Organization: Linking the World War II and civil rights eras. *Pacific Historical Review, 80*(2), 231–67. https://doi.org/10.1525/phr.2011.80.2.231

Black, L. L., & Stone, D. (2005). Expanding the definition of privilege: The concept of social privilege. *Journal of Multicultural Counseling and Development, 33*(4), 243–55. https://doi.org/10.1002/j.2161-1912.2005.tb00020.x

Blumenbach, J. F. (1865). *The anthropological treatises of Johann Friedrich Blumenbach.* (T. Bendyshe, Trans.). Longman, Green, Longman, Roberts, and Green. https://doi.org/10.1037/13883-000

Bongiovanni, D. (2020, June 3). Doctors join the protests in support of Black lives, calling racism a health crisis. *Indianapolis Star.* https://www.indystar.com/story/news/local/indianapolis/2020/06/03/indianapolis-protests-doctors-demonstrate-call-racism-health-crisis/3140936001

Bonilla-Silva, E. (2006). *Racism without racists: Color-blind racism and the persistence of racial inequality in the United States.* Rowman & Littlefield.

Bourabain, D. (2021). Everyday sexism and racism in the ivory tower: The experiences of early career researchers on the intersection of gender and ethnicity in the academic workplace. *Gender, Work & Organization, 28*(1), 248–67. https://doi.org/10.1111/gwao.12549

Brooks, J. E., Ogolsky, B. G., & Monk, J. K. (2018). Commitment in interracial relationships: Dyadic and longitudinal tests of the investment model. *Journal of Family Issues, 39*(9), 2685–2708. https://doi-org.libezp.lib.lsu.edu/10.1177/0192513X18758343

Brooks, K. (2020, June 10). Middleton Library to be renamed, pending approval, LSU announces with Black student leaders. *Advocate.* https://www.theadvocate.com/baton_rouge/news/education/middleton-library-to-be-renamed-pending-approval-lsu-announces-with-black-student-leaders/article_a51f8b56-ab80-11ea-8940-43c9ae158546.html#:~:text=LSU%20announced%20with%20black%20student,his%20name%20in%20the%20building.

Brown, E., & Grothaus, T. (2019). Experiences of cross-racial trust in mentoring relationships between Black doctoral counseling students and white counselor educators and supervisors. *Professional Counselor, 9*(3), 211–25. https://psycnet.apa.org/doi/10.15241/emb.9.3.211

Brummett, E. A. (2017). "Race doesn't matter": A dialogic analysis of interracial romantic partners' stories about racial differences. *Journal of Social and Personal Relationships, 34*, 771–89. https://doi.org/10.1177/0265407516658790

Brummett, E. A., & Afifi, T. D. (2019). A grounded theory of interracial romantic partners' expectations for support and strain with family members. *Journal of Family Communication, 19*(3), 191–212. https://doi.org/10.1080/15267431.2019.1623220

Burch, A. D. S. (2018, October 26). How "gardening while Black" almost landed this Detroit man in jail. *New York Times.* https://www.nytimes.com/2018/10/26/us/white-women-calling-police-black-men.html

Calvente, L. B., Calafell, B. M., & Chávez, K. R. (2020). Here is something you can't understand: The suffocating whiteness of communication studies. *Communication and Critical/Cultural Studies, 17(*2), 202–9. https://doi.org/10.1080/14791420.2020.1770823

Campisi, J., Smith, E., Levenson, E., & Hutcherson, K. (2018, June 26). *After internet mockery, "permit Patty" resigns as CEO of cannabis-products company.* CNN. https://www.cnn.com/2018/06/25/us/permit-patty-san-francisco-trnd/index.html#:~:text=After%20internet%20mockery%2C%20'Permit%20Patty'%20resigns%20as,CEO%20of%20cannabis%2Dproducts%20company&text=The%20woman%20who%20threatened%20to,as%20CEO%20of%20TreatWell%20Health

Cargile, A. C., & Kahn, A. S. (2021) System justification in communication: A study of imagined dialogue receptivity. *Communication Research Reports, 38*(2), 103–11. https://doi.org/10.1080/08824096.2021.1891039

Carman, A. (2020, June 5). *Facebook groups are falling apart over Black Lives Matter posts.* Verge. https://www.theverge.com/2020/6/5/21279319/facebook-group-moderation-black-lives-matter-movement

Carson, E. (2020, June 14). *How to be an ally in the fight for racial justice: Here's what white allyship actually looks like.* CNET. https://www.cnet.com/culture/in-the-fight-for-racial-justice-heres-what-white-allyship-looks-like/

Carter, E. R. (2020, October 12). Restructure your organization to actually advance racial justice. *Harvard Business Review.* https://hbr.org/2020/06/restructure-your-organization-to-actually-advance-racial-justice

Castle Bell, G. (2019). "There's a difference between Black people and n*gg*rs": A cultural contracts exploration of interracial communication barriers. *Communication Quarterly, 67*(3), 243–70. https://doi.org/10.1080/01463373.2019.1573744

Cava, M. D. (2020, June 8). Jesse Jackson says white Americans are finally "awakening" to the nation's racial crisis. *USA Today.* https://www.usatoday.com/story/news/nation/2020/06/08/white-americans-finally-confronting-racism-jesse-jackson-says/5322012002/

Centers for Disease Control. (2021, April 19). *Health equity considerations and racial and ethnic minority groups.* https://stacks.cdc.gov/view/cdc/108144

Chancellor, R. L. (2019). Racial battle fatigue: The unspoken burden of Black women faculty in LIS. *Journal of Education for Library and Information Science, 60*(3), 182–89. https://doi.org/10.3138/jelis.2019-0007

Chen, X., & Graham, S. (2017). Same-ethnic, interethnic, and interracial friendships among Asian early adolescents. *Journal of Research on Adolescence, 27*(3), 705–13. https://doi.org/10.1111/jora.12309

Chingaipe, S. (2020, August 30). *Why I still struggle to talk about race with my non-Black friends.* ABC Everyday. https://www.abc.net.au/everyday/why-i-still-struggle-to-talk-about-race-with-non-black-friends/12593792

Christian, M., Seamster, L., & Ray, V. (2021) Critical race theory and empirical sociology. *American Behavioral Scientist, 65*(8), 1019–26. https://doi.org/10.1177/0002764219859646

City University of New York. (2021, July 14). *"The Racial Contract" by Professor Charles Mills retains its influence after more than two decades.* CUNY Graduate Center. https://www.gc.cuny.edu/news/racial-contract-professor-charles-mills-retains-its-influence-after-more-two-decades

Clark, M. D. (2019). White folks' work: Digital allyship praxis in the #BlackLivesMatter movement. *Social Movement Studies, 18*(5), 519–34. https://doi.org/10.1080/14742837.2019.1603104

Clement, O., & Meyer, D. (2020, June 5). How have off-Broadway theatre companies responded to black lives matter? *Playbill.* https://playbill.com/article/how-have-off-broadway-theatre-companies-responded-to-black-lives-matter

Cletus, H. E., Mahood, N. A., Umar, A., & Ibrahim, A. D. (2018). Prospects and challenges of workplace diversity in modern day organizations: A critical review. *Journal of Business and Public Administration, 9*(2), 35–52. https://doi.org/10.2478/hjbpa-2018-0011

Cohen, L. (2021, May 28). Teen who recorded George Floyd's death speaks out: "It made me realize how dangerous it is to be Black in America." CBS News. https://www.cbsnews.com/news/darnella-frazier-george-floyd-black-america/

Cohn, N., & Quealy, K. (2020, June 10). How public opinion has moved on Black Lives Matter. *Salt Lake Tribune.* https://www.sltrib.com/news/nation-world/2020/06/11/how-public-opinion-has/

Coleman, J. (2020, June 7). *Black Lives Matter co-founder says defunding the police means invest in the resources our communities need.* Hill. https://thehill.com/homenews/sunday-talk-shows/501541-black-lives-matter-co-founder-says-defunding-the-police-means

Compton-Lilly, C. (2020). Microaggressions and macroaggressions across time: The longitudinal construction of inequality in schools. *Urban Education, 55*(8–9) 1315–49. https://doi.org/10.1177/0042085919893751

Cornileus, T. H. (2013). "I'm a Black man and I'm doing this job very well": How African American professional men negotiate the impact of racism on their career development. *Journal of African American Studies, 17*(4), 444–60. https://doi.org/10.1007/s12111-012-9225-2

Cox, D., Novarro-Rivera, J., & Jones, R. P. (2016). *Race, religion, and political affiliation of American's core social networks*. PPRI. https://www.prri.org/research/poll-race-religion-politics-americans-social-networks/

Crocker, J., Luhtanen, R., Blaine, B., & Broadnax, S. (1994). Collective self-esteem and psychological well-being among white, Black, and Asian college students. *Personality and Social Psychology Bulletin, 20*(5), 503–13. https://doi.org/10.1177/0146167294205007

Crowley, C. (2020, June 3). *Fast-food companies still don't care*. Grub Street. https://www.grubstreet.com/2020/06/fast-food-companies-blm-statements.html

Daniels, N. (2021, February 18). What students are saying about race and racism in America. *New York Times*. https://www.nytimes.com/2021/02/18/learning/what-students-are-saying-about-race-and-racism-in-america.html

Darling-Hammond, S., Lee, R. T., & Mendoza-Denton, R. (2020). Interracial contact at work: Does workplace diversity reduce bias? *Group Processes & Intergroup Relations, 24*(7), 1114–31. https://doi.org/10.1177/1368430220932636

Dastagir, A. E. (2020, June 4). George Floyd, Lea Michele and the problem with performative outrage. *USA Today*. https://www.usatoday.com/story/news/nation/2020/06/04/george-floyd-lea-michele-and-problem-performative-outrage/3137994001/

Davies, K., & Aron, A. (2016). Friendship development and intergroup attitudes: The role of interpersonal and intergroup friendship processes. *Journal of Social Issues, 72*(3), 489–510. https://doi.org/10.1111/josi.12178

Davies, K., Tropp, L. R., Aron, A., Pettigrew, T. F., & Wright, S. C. (2011). Cross-group friendships and intergroup attitudes: A meta-analytic review. *Personality and Social Psychology Review, 15*(4), 332–51. https://doi.org/10.1177/1088868311411103

Davis, J. F. (2018). Selling whiteness? A critical review of the literature on marketing and racism. *Journal of Marketing Management, 34*(1–2), 134–77. https://doi.org/10.1080/0267257X.2017.1395902

Davis, S. M. (2019). When sistahs support sistahs: A process of supportive communication about racial microaggressions among Black women. *Communication Monographs, 86*(2), 133–57. https://doi.org/10.1080/03637751.2018.1548769

Delgado, R., & Stefancic, J. (2001). *Critical race theory: An introduction*. New York University Press.

Desormes, I., & Miller, C. (2020, November 9). *Seeing race through another's eyes: Two SLPs do the work*. ASHAWire. https://leader.pubs.asha.org/do/10.1044/leader.OTP.25112020.44/full/

de Souza Briggs, X., & McGahey, R. M. (2022, October 11). *Keeping promises while keeping score: Gauging the impacts of policy proposals on racial equity*.

Brookings Institute. https://www.brookings.edu/research/keeping-score-measuring-the-impacts-of-policy-proposals-on-racial-equity/

Dickens, D. A., Womack, G. Y., & Dimes, T. (2019). Managing hypervisibility: An exploration of theory and research on identity shifting strategies in the workplace among Black women. *Journal of Vocational Behavior, 113*, 153–63. https://doi.org/10.1016/j.jvb.2018.10.008

Diggs, R. C., & Clark, K. D. (2002). It's a struggle but worth it: Identifying and managing identities in an interracial friendship. *Communication Quarterly, 50*(3–4), 368–90. https://doi.org/10.1080/01463370209385673.

Dobbin, F., & Kalev, A. (2018). Why doesn't diversity training work? The challenge for industry and academia. *Anthropology Now, 10*(2), 48–55. https://doi.org/10.1080/19428200.2018.1493182

Docan-Morgan, S. (2011). "They don't know what it's like to be in my shoes": Topic avoidance about race in transracially adoptive families. *Journal of Social and Personal Relationships, 28*(3), 336–55. https://doi.org/10.1177/0265407510382177

D'Silva, M. U. (2021). Colorblind ideology and othering in our time: A mindfulness pathway. *Intercultural Communications Studies, 30*(1), 15–19. https://www.kent.edu/stark/ics-2021-vol-30-no-1-dsilva

D'Souza, D. (2020, June 1). *How corporate America is reacting to the protests.* Investopedia. https://www.investopedia.com/how-corporate-america-is-reacting-to-the-protests-4846547

Du Bois, W. E. B. ([1903] 1965). *The souls of Black folk.* Longmans, Green and Co.

Durand, T. M., & Tavaras, C. L. (2021). Countering complacency with radical reflection: Supporting white teachers in the enactment of critical multicultural praxis. *Education and Urban Society, 53*(2), 146–62. https://doi.org/10.1177/0013124520927680

Edwards, F., Lee, H., & Esposito, M. (2019). Risk of being killed by police use of force in the United States by age, race-ethnicity, and sex. *Proceedings of the National Academy of Sciences of the United States of America, 116*(34), 16793–98. https://doi.org/10.1073/pnas.1821204116

Ekberg, S. (2013). Maintaining shared knowledge of acquaintance: Methods people use to establish who knows whom. *British Journal of Social Psychology, 53*(4). https://www.researchgate.net/publication/257750496_Maintaining_shared_knowledge_of_acquaintance_Methods_people_use_to_establish_who_knows_whom

Ellis, B. R., & Branch-Ellis, N. (2020). Living in an age of colorblind racism and police impunity: An analysis of some high-profile police killings. *Phylon, 57*(2), 105–25. https://www.jstor.org/stable/26990925

Emmert, M. (2020, June 12). Iowa Hawkeyes football coach Kirk Ferentz: "We must be more inclusive and more aware." *USA Today.* https://www.usatoday.com/story/sports/ncaaf/bigten/2020/06/12/kirk-ferentz-iowa-program-culture-chris-doyle/3179731001/

Enos, R., Kaufman, A., & Sands, M. (2019). Can violent protest change local policy support? Evidence from the aftermath of the 1992 Los Angeles riot.

American Political Science Review, 113(4), 1012–28. https://doi.org/10.1017/S0003055419000340

Epstein, G. (2020, June 13). *So you want to talk about race in tech with Ijeoma Oluo.* TechCrunch. https://techcrunch.com/2020/06/13/so-you-want-to-talk-about-race-in-tech-with-ijeoma-oluo/

Erskine, S. E., & Bilimoria, D. (2019). White allyship of Afro-diasporic women in the workplace: A transformative strategy for organizational change. *Journal of Leadership & Organizational Studies, 26*(3), 319–38. https://doi.org/10.1177/1548051819848993

Espinoza, A. R. (2021, June 15). *False claims of critical race theory in Virginia schools spark resistance.* VPM. https://vpm.org/news/articles/22982/false-claims-of-critical-race-theory-in-virginia-schools-spark-resistance

ESPN Internet Ventures. (2020, June 10). *NASCAR bans Confederate flags from all racetracks.* ESPN. https://www.espn.com/racing/nascar/story/_/id/29293767/nascar-bans-confederate-flags-racetracks

Ferris State University. (2022). *Examples of Jim Crow Laws—Oct. 1960—Civil Rights.* https://www.ferris.edu/HTMLS/news/jimcrow/links/misclink/examples.htm

Fischer, M. J. (2008). Does campus diversity promote friendship diversity? A look at interracial friendships in college. *Social Science Quarterly, 89*(3), 631–55. https://doi.org/10.1111/j.1540-6237.2008.00552.x

Fitzhugh, E., Julien, J. P., Noel, N., & Stewart, S. (2020, December 2). *It's time for a new approach to racial equity.* McKinsey Institute for Black Economic Mobility. https://www.mckinsey.com/bem/our-insights/its-time-for-a-new-approach-to-racial-equity

Foeman, A. K., & Nance, T. (1999). From miscegenation to multiculturalism: Perceptions and stages of interracial relationship development. *Journal of Black Studies, 29*(4), 540–57. http://www.jstor.org/stable/2645869

Foeman, A., & Nance, T. (2002). Building new cultures, reframing old images: Success strategies of interracial couples. *Howard Journal of Communications, 13*(3), 237–49. https://doi.org/10.1080/10646170290109716

Follman, M. (2021). How Trump unleashed a domestic terrorism movement—and what experts say must be done to defeat it. *Mother Jones.* https://www.motherjones.com/politics/2021/02/trump-stochastic-terrorism-us-capitol-mob-incitement/

Ford, K. A. (2012). Shifting white ideological scripts: The educational benefits of inter- and intraracial curricular dialogues on the experiences of white college students. *Journal of Diversity in Higher Education, 5*(3), 138–58. https://doi.org/10.1037/a0028917

Fox, G. (2020, March 1). *"Pull yourself up by your bootstraps": An American mythology.* Leading Women of Tomorrow. https://www.leadingwomenoftomorrow.com/blogposts/2020/3/1/pull-yourself-up-by-your-bootstraps-an-american-mythology

Franco, M., Katz, R., Pickens, J., & Brunsma, D. L. (2020). From my own flesh and blood: An exploratory examination of discrimination from family for Black/white multiracial people. *Qualitative Social Work, 19*(2), 246–66. https://doi.org/10.1177/1473325018815734

Frey, F. E., & Tropp, L. R. (2006). Being seen as individuals versus as group members: Extending research on metaperception to intergroup contexts. *Personality and Social Psychology Review, 10*(3), 265–80. https://doi.org/10.1207/s15327957pspr1003_5

Frey, L. R., German, J., & Russel, V. (2020). Communication activism for social justice research. In H. D. O'Hair & M. J. O'Hair (Eds.), *The Handbook of Applied Communication Research* (pp. 731–46). John Wiley & Sons. https://doi.org/10.1002/9781119399926.ch40

Frey, L. R., Pearce, W. B., Pollock, M. A., & Artz, L. (1996). Looking for justice in all the wrong places: On a communication approach to social justice. *Communication Studies, 47*(1–2), 110–27. https://doi.org/10.1080/10510979609368467

Gadson, C. A., & Lewis, J. A. (2021). Devalued, overdisciplined, and stereotyped: An exploration of gendered racial microaggressions among Black adolescent girls. *Journal of Counseling Psychology, 69*(1), 14–26. https://doi.org/10.1037/cou0000571

Gai, F. (2014). The application of autonomous learning to fostering cross-cultural communication competence. *Theory and Practice in Language Studies, 4*(6), 1291–95. http://dx.doi.org/10.4304/tpls.4.6.1291-1295

Gaither, S. E., & Sommers, S. R. (2013). Living with an other-race roommate shapes whites' behavior in subsequent diverse settings. *Journal of Experimental Social Psychology, 49*(2), 272–76. https://doi.org/10.1016/j.jesp.2012.10.020

Galán, C. A., Yu, A. C., O'Connor, J. P., Akinbola, D. T., & Anderson, R. E. (2021). Having the talk when our little ones just learned to walk: Racial socialization with young children in contemporary times. *Infant and Child Development, 31*(1), e2276. https://doi.org/10.1002/icd.2276

Gallagher, C. A. (2003). Miscounting race: Explaining whites' misperceptions of racial group size. *Sociological Perspectives, 46*(3), 381–96. https://doi.org/10.1525/sop.2003.46.3.381

George, J. (2021, May 26). *Critical race theory isn't a curriculum. It's a practice*. Education Week. https://www.edweek.org/leadership/opinion-critical-race-theory-isnt-a-curriculum-its-a-practice/2021/05

Gopalakrishnan, M. (2022, July 3). Why language needs to be decolonized. *Deutsche Welle*. https://www.dw.com/en/why-language-needs-to-be-decolonized/a-62286311

Gordils, J., Elliot, A. J., & Jamieson, J. P. (2021). The effect of perceived interracial competition on psychological outcomes. *PLOS One, 16*(1), e0245671. https://doi.org/10.1371/journal.pone.0245671

Greenland, K., Augoustinos, M., Andreouli, E., & Taulke-Johnson, R. (2020). Cross-group friendships, the irony of harmony, and the social construction of "discrimination." *Ethnic and Racial Studies, 43*(7), 1169–88. https://doi.org/10.1080/01419870.2019.1648845

Griggs, B. (2018, May 12). *A Black Yale graduate student took a nap in her dorm's common room. So a white student called police*. CNN. https://www.cnn.com/2018/05/09/us/yale-student-napping-black-trnd/index.html

Guardian. (2017, January 27). Woman at center of Emmett Till case tells author she fabricated testimony. https://www.theguardian.com/us-news/2017/jan/27/emmett-till-book-carolyn-bryant-confession

Gudykunst, W. B. (1995). Anxiety/uncertainty management (AUM) theory. In R. L. Wiseman (Ed.), *Intercultural communication theory* (pp. 8–58). Sage.

Guerrero, L., & Afifi, W. A. (1995a). Some things are better left unsaid: Topic avoidance in family relationships. *Communication Quarterly, 43*(3), 276–96. https://doi.org/10.1080/01463379509369977

Guerrero, L. K., & Afifi, W. A. (1995b). What parents don't know: Topic avoidance in parent–child relationships. In T. J. Socha & G. H. Stamp (Eds.), *Parents, children, and communication: Frontiers of theory and research* (pp. 219–45). Lawrence Erlbaum.

Harries, B. (2014). We need to talk about race. *Sociology, 48*(6), 1107–22. https://doi.org/10.1177/0038038514521714

Harris, T. M. (2017). Performing otherness as an instructor in an interracial communication classroom: An autoethnographic approach. In A. Atay and S. T. Toyosaki (Eds.), *Critical intercultural communication pedagogy* (pp. 131–52). Routledge.

Harris, T. M. (2021a). Being our sister's keeper: Rethinking allyship amid multiple pandemics. Special issue, *Women's Studies in Communication, 44*(2), 146–50. https://doi.org/10.1080/07491409.2021.1923332

Harris, T. M. (2021b). Performative activism: Inauthentic allyship in the midst of a racial pandemic. In J. Bauer & S. Blithe (Eds.), *Badass feminist politics: Exploring radical edges of feminist theory, communication, and activism* (pp. 97–102). Rutgers University Press.

Harris, T. M., & Abbott, B. (2011). Reframing the rhetorics of race through classroom discourse. In Deborah Brunson, Linda Lampl, and Felicia Jordan (Eds.), *Interracial communication: Contexts, communities, and choices* (pp. 286–306). Kendall Hunt.

Harris, T. M., Harris, R., & Stanley, K. (forthcoming). Surthrival skills: Surviving and thriving in academic white spaces. In M. Y. Byrd & C. Scott (Eds.), *Handbook of antiracism research, theory, and practice in human resource development.* Palgrave Macmillan.

Harris, T. M., Janovec, A., Murray, S., Gubbala, S., & Robinson, A. (2018). Communicating racism: A study of racial microaggressions in a southern university and the local community. *Southern Communication Journal, 84*(2), 72–84. https://doi.org/10.1080/1041794X.2018.1492008

Harris, T. M., & Kalbfleisch, P. J. (2000). Interracial dating: The implications of race for initiating a romantic relationship. *Howard Journal of Communication, 11,* 49–64. https://doi.org/10.1080/106461700246715

Harris, T. M., & Lee, C. N. (2019) Advocate-mentoring: A communicative response to diversity in higher education. *Communication Education, 68*(1), 103–13. https://doi.org/10.1080/03634523.2018.1536272

Harris, T. M., & Moffitt, K. (2019). Centering communication in our understanding of microaggressions, race, and otherness in academe and beyond. *Southern Communication Journal, 84*(2), 67–71. DOI: 10.1080/1041794X.2018.1515978

Harris, T. M., & Weber, K. (2010). Reversal of privilege: Deconstructing privilege and power in the film *White Man's Burden*. *Communication Law Review, 10*, 54–74.

Hartnett, S. (2010). Communication, social justice, and joyful commitment. *Western Journal of Communication, 74*(1), 68–93. https://doi.org/10.1080/10570310903463778

Hasford, J. (2016). Dominant cultural narratives, racism, and resistance in the workplace: A study of the experiences of young Black Canadians. *American Journal of Community Psychology, 57*(1–2), 158–70. https://doi.org/10.1002/ajcp.12024

Heinze, P. (2008). Let's talk about race, baby. *Multicultural Education, 15*(1), 2–11.

Herda, D. (2017, September 25). "To hell with them all!": Perceived discrimination, interracial contact, and racial attitudes. *Sociological Focus, 51*(2), 111–29. https://doi.org/10.1080/00380237.2017.1370939

Hernández, L. H. (2020). Silence, (in)action, and the downfalls of white allyship. *Women & Language, 43*(1), 147–52.

Hessekiel, D. (2020, June 4). Companies taking a public stand in the wake of George Floyd's death. *Forbes*. https://www.forbes.com/sites/davidhessekiel/2020/06/04/companies-taking-a-public-stand-in-the-wake-of-george-floyds-death/?sh=665b13ea7214

Hill, M. R., & Thomas, V. (2000). Strategies for racial identity development: Narratives of Black and white women in interracial partner relationships. *Family Relations: An Interdisciplinary Journal of Applied Family Studies, 49*(2), 193–200. https://doi.org/10.1111/j.1741-3729.2000.00193.x

History.com. (2018, April 28). *Jim Crow laws*. https://www.history.com/topics/early-20th-century-us/jim-crow-laws

Holoien, D. S., Bergsieker, H. B., Shelton, J. N., & Alegre, J. M. (2015). Do you really understand? Achieving accuracy in interracial relationships. *Journal of Personality and Social Psychology, 108*(1), 76–92. https://doi.org/10.1037/pspi0000003

Hooghe, M., & Dassonneville, L. R. (2018, July). Explaining the Trump vote: The effect of racist resentment and anti-immigrant sentiments. *American Political Science Association, 51*(3), 528–34. https://doi.org/10.1017/S1049096518000367

Horner, R. (2011). Culture, communication, and competence: A commentary on variables affecting social and academic behavior. *Journal of Behavioral Education, 20*(4), 306–11. http://dx.doi.org/10.1007/s10864-011-9139-4.

Horowitz, J. M., Brown, A., & Cox, K. (2019, April 9). *2. Views of racial inequality*. Pew Research Center. https://www.pewresearch.org/social-trends/2019/04/09/views-of-racial-inequality/

Hudson, T. D. (2022). Interpersonalizing cultural difference: A grounded theory of the process of interracial friendship development and sustainment among college students. *Journal of Diversity in Higher Education, 15*(3), 267–87. https://doi.org/10.1037/dhe0000287

Hughes, D. (2003). Correlates of African American and Latino parents' messages to children about ethnicity and race: A comparative study of racial socialization. *American Journal of Community Psychology, 34*, 15–33.

Hughes, D., Rodriguez, J., Smith, E. P., Johnson, D. J., Stevenson, H. C., & Spicer, P. (2006). Parents' ethnic-racial socialization practices: A review of research and directions for future study. *Developmental Psychology, 42*(5), 747–70.

Huguely, J. P., Wang, M. T., Vasquez, A. C., & Guo, J. (2019). Parental ethnic-racial socialization practices and the construction of children of color's ethnic-racial identity: A research synthesis and meta-analysis. *Psychological Bulletin, 145*(5), 437–58. https://doi.org/10.1037/bul0000187

Human Rights Watch. (2020, May 12). *Covid-19 fueling anti-Asian racism and xenophobia worldwide*. https://www.hrw.org/news/2020/05/12/covid-19-fueling-anti-asian-racism-and-xenophobia-worldwide

Hunter, L., & Elian, M. J. (2000). Interracial Friendships, multicultural sensitivity, and social competence: How are they related? *Journal of Applied Developmental Psychology, 20*(4), 551–73. https://doi.org/10.1016/S0193-3973(99)00028-3

Ilchi, O. S., & Frank, J. (2021). Supporting the message, not the messenger: The correlates of attitudes towards Black Lives Matter. *American Journal of Criminal Justice, 46*, 377–98. https://doi.org/10.1007/s12103-020-09561-1

Iyer, A. (2022). Understanding advantaged groups' opposition to diversity, equity, and inclusion (DEI) policies: The role of perceived threat. *Social and Personality Psychology Compass, 16*(5), e12666. https://doi.org/10.1111/spc3.12666

Jackson, J. B. (2021). On cultural appropriation. *Journal of Folklore Research, 58*(1), 77–122. https://www.muse.jhu.edu/article/783863

Jaros-White, G. (2021, October 8). *Teaching students to be global citizens*. Level Up Village. https://levelupvillage.com/helping-kids-become-global-citizens/#:~:text=Oxfam%20defines%20global%20citizenship%20as,can%20all%20make%20a%20difference.%E2%80%9D

Jost, J. T., & Banaji, M. R. (1994). The role of stereotyping in system-justification and the production of false consciousness. *British Journal of Social Psychology, 33*(1), 1–27. https://doi.org/10.1111/j.2044-8309.1994.tb01008.x

Kendall, F. (2006). *Understanding white privilege: Creating pathways to authentic relationships across race.* Routledge.

Killen, M., Luken Raz, K., & Graham, S. (2021). Reducing prejudice through promoting cross-group friendships. *Review of General Psychology*, 10892680211061262. https://doi.org/10.1177/10892680211061262

Kim, Y. Y. (1995). Cross-cultural adaptation: An integrative theory. In R. L. Wiseman (Ed.), *Intercultural communication theory* (pp. 170–93). Sage.

Kim, Y. Y. (2002). Adapting to an unfamiliar culture. In W. B. Gudykunst & B. Mody (Eds.), *Handbook of international and intercultural communication* (pp. 259–73). Sage.

Kim, Y., Park, J., & Koo, K. (2015). Testing self-segregation: Multiple-group structural modeling of college students' interracial friendship by race. *Research in Higher Education, 56*(1), 57–77. https://doi.org/10.1007/s11162-014-9337-8

Klausen, J. C. (2014). *Fugitive Rousseau: Slavery, primitivism, and political freedom.* Fordham University Press.

Klausen, S. M. (n.d.). *Eugenics Archives world map: South Africa.* Vivid Maps. https://vividmaps.com/eugenics-archives-world-map/

Kornbluh, M., Johnson, L., & Hart, M. (2021). Shards from the glass ceiling: Deconstructing marginalizing systems in relation to critical consciousness development. *American Journal of Community Psychology, 68*(1–2), 187–201. https://doi.org/10.1002/ajcp.12512

Kousser, J. M. (2003). Jim Crow laws. In *Dictionary of American History* (3rd ed., Vol. 4, pp. 479–80). Charles Scribner's Sons. https://resolver.caltech.edu/CaltechAUTHORS:20130909-100931915.

Kurtz, J. (2021). Sport, social justice, and the limits of dissent after George Floyd: A reply to Butterworth. *Communication & Sport, 9*(2), 171–87. https://doi.org/10.1177/2167479520976359

Ladson-Billings, G. (1995). Toward a theory of culturally relevant pedagogy. *American Educational Research Journal, 32*(3), 465–91. https://doi.org/10.2307/1163320

Lemay, E. P., Jr., & Teneva, N. (2020) Accuracy and bias in perceptions of racial attitudes: Implications for interracial relationships, *Journal of Personality and Social Psychology: Interpersonal Relations and Group Processes, 119*(6), 1380–1402. https://doi.org/10.1037/pspi0000236

Leonard, D. J. (2012, July 12). Never just a game: The language of sport on and off the court. *Journal of Multicultural Discourses, 7*(2), 137–43. https://doi.org/10.1080/17447143.2012.694449

Leonard, R., & Locke, D. C. (1993). Communication stereotypes: Is interracial communication possible? *Journal of Black Studies, 23*(3), 332–43.

Leonard, T. C. (2005). Protecting family and race: The progressive case for regulating women's work. *American Journal of Economics and Sociology, 64*(3), 757–91. https://doi.org/10.1111/j.1536-7150.2005.00391.x

Little Fenimore, W. (2021). "Freedom is everybody's job": Elizabeth Waring's rhetorical strategies to dismantle Jim Crow. *Rhetoric & Public Affairs, 24*(4), 645–83. https://www.muse.jhu.edu/article/850848

Lockhart, P. R. (2018, August 1). *Living while Black and the criminalization of Blackness*. Vox. https://www.vox.com/explainers/2018/8/1/17616528/racial-profiling-police-911-living-while-black

Loller, T., & Crary, D. (2021, June 11). *Racial tensions simmer as Southern Baptists hold key meeting*. Associated Press. https://apnews.com/article/racial-injustice-baptist-race-and-ethnicity-religion-900a3edd9

Lu, D., Huang, J., Seshagiri, A., Park, H., & Griggs, T. (2020, September 9). Faces of power: 80% are white, even as U.S. becomes more diverse. *New York Times*. https://www.nytimes.com/interactive/2020/09/09/us/powerful-people-race-us.html

Marcin, T. (2020, June 9). *Babynames.com makes a powerful statement on Black Lives Matter*. Mashable. https://mashable.com/article/baby-names-website-black-lives-matter-tribute

Maume, D. R, Jr. (1999). Glass ceilings and glass escalators: Occupational segregation and race and sex differences in managerial promotions. *Work and Occupations, 26*(4), 483–509. https://doi.org/10.1177/0730888499026004005

McCarter, M. (2020, June 14). Why the USA Today Network is capitalizing the B in black. *USA Today*. https://www.usatoday.com/story/opinion/2020/06/12/why-usa-today-gannett-capitalizing-b-black-uppercase/3178288001/

McIntosh, M. (1998). White privilege and male privilege: A personal account of coming to see correspondences through work women's studies. In M. L. Anderson & P. Hill Collins (Eds.), *Race, class, and gender* (3rd ed). Wadsworth.

McIntosh, P. (1989). *White privilege: Unpacking the invisible knapsack*. Wellesley Centers for Women. https://www.wcwonline.org/Publications-by-title/white-privilege-unpacking-the-invisible-knapsack-2

Meer, N. (2019) W.E.B. Du Bois, double consciousness and the "spirit" of recognition. *Sociological Review, 67*(1), 47–62. https://doi.org/10.1177/0038026118765370

Mele, C., Pels, J., & Polese, F. (2010). A brief review of systems theories and their managerial applications. *Service Science, 2*(1–2), 126–35. https://doi.org/10.1287/serv.2.1_2.126

Milner, A., Franz, B., & Braddock, J. H. (2020). We need to talk about racism—in all of its forms—to understand COVID-19 disparities. *Health Equity, 4*(1), 397–402. https://doi.org/10.1089/heq.2020.0069

Minniear, M., & Soliz, J. (2019). Family communication and message about race and identity in Black families in the United States. *Journal of Family Communication, 19*(4), 329–47. https://doi.org/10.1080/15267431.2019.1593170

Moody A. (2011). *Coming of age in Mississippi: The classic autobiography of growing up poor and black in the rural south*. Bantam Dell.

Moore, R., & Nash, M. (2021). Women's experiences of racial microaggressions in STEMM workplaces and the importance of white allyship. *International Journal of Gender, Science & Technology, 13*(1), 3–22.

Mor Barak, M. E. (2005). *Managing diversity: Toward a worldwide inclusive workplace*. Sage.

Morrison, A. M. (2010). Straightening up: Black women law professors, interracial relationships, and academic fit(ting) in. *Harvard Journal of Law & Gender, 33*, 85. http://dx.doi.org/10.2139/ssrn.1905156

Munn, C. W. (2018). The one friend rule: Race and social capital in an interracial network. *Social Problems, 65*(4), 473–90. https://doi.org/10.1093/socpro/spx020

National Geographic Society. (2022, July 8). *The Black codes and Jim Crow laws*. https://education.nationalgeographic.org/resource/black-codes-and-jim-crow-laws

National Human Genome Research Institute. (2022). *Eugenics and scientific racism*. https://www.genome.gov/about-genomics/fact-sheets/Eugenics-and-Scientific-Racism

National Museum of African American History and Culture. (n.d.). https://nmaahc.si.edu/learn/talking-about-race/topics/being-antiracist

Neville, H. A., Gallardo, M. E., & Sue, D. W. (2016). Introduction: Has the United States really moved beyond race? In H. A. Neville, M. E. Gallardo, & D. W. Sue (Eds.), *The myth of racial color blindness: Manifestations, dynamics, and impact* (pp. 3–21). American Psychological Association. https://doi.org/10.1037/14754-001

Nicholson, Z. (2020, June 15). *Clemson removes John C. Calhoun's name from Honors College, asks to rename Tillman Hall.* https://www.greenvilleonline.com/story/news/2020/06/12/clemson-university-removes-john-c-calhouns-name-honors-college/5341257002/#:~:text=Clemson%20removes%20John%20C.,asks%20to%20rename%20Tillman%20Hall&text=The%20Clemson%20University%20Board%20of,its%20original%20name%2C%20Old%20Main

Norander, S., & Galanes, G. (2014). "Bridging the gap": Difference, dialogue, and community organizing. *Journal of Applied Communication Research, 42*(4), 345–65. https://doi.org/10.1080/00909882.2014.911939

Orbe, M., & Harris, T. M, (2015). *Interracial communication: Theory into practice* (3rd ed.). Sage.

Orbe, M. P., & Harris, T. M (2022). *Interracial communication: Theory into practice* (4th ed). Wadsworth/Thompson Learning.

Ortiz, E. (2018, July 6). *#WhileBlack: Calling police on black people become teachable moments for law enforcement.* NBC News. https://www.nbcnews.com/news/nbcblk/whileblack-calling-police-black-people-becomes-teachable-moments-law-enforcement-n889276

Ouali, N., & Jefferys, S. (2015). Hard times for trade union anti-racism workplace strategies. *Transfer: European Review of Labour and Research, 21*(1), 99–113. https://doi.org/10.1177/1024258914561419

Oyez. (n.d.). *Loving v. Virginia.* https://www.oyez.org/cases/1966/395

Padron Eberline, A. L., & Shue, C. K. (2022). Family communication about race and culture: Do white families talk about race? *Communication Studies, 73*(2), 171–89. https://doi.org/10.1080/10510974.2022.2026427

Paleologos, D. (2021, Dec. 4). Paleologos: City polls show Black, white Americans divide in views on being treated differently due to race. *USA Today.* https://www.usatoday.com/story/news/politics/analysis/2021/12/04/city-polls-find-views-treatment-over-race-vary-black-white/8837772002/

Patel, V. (2020, June 22). *"Walk the talk" on racial diversity—Black solicitors network pens open letter to law firms.* Law.com International. https://www.law.com/international-edition/2020/06/22/walk-the-talk-on-racial-diversity-black-solicitors-network-pens-letter-to-law-firm-leaders/?slreturn=20230008235836

Patrick, H. A., & Kumar, V. R. (2012). Managing workplace diversity: Issues and challenges. *Sage Open, 2*(2), 1–15. https://doi.org/10.1177/215824401244461

Peeples, L. (2020, June 19). *What the data say about police brutality and racial bias—and which reforms might work.* Nature News. https://www.nature.com/articles/d41586-020-01846-z

Petronio, S. (2002). *Boundaries of privacy: Dialectics of disclosure.* State University of New York Press.

Petronio, S., & Caughlin, J. P. (2006). Communication privacy management theory: Understanding families. In D. O. Braithwaite & L. A. Baxter (Eds.), *Engaging theories in family communication: Multiple perspectives* (pp. 35–49). Sage.

Pinsker, J. (2021, March 30). Trump's presidency is over. So are many relationships. *Atlantic.* https://www.theatlantic.com/family/archive/2021/03/trump-friend-family-relationships/618457/

Plaut, V. C., Thomas, K. M., Hurd, K., & Romano, C. A. (2018). Do color blindness and multiculturalism remedy or foster discrimination and racism? *Current Directions in Psychological Science, 27*(3), 200–206. https://doi.org/10.1177/0963721418766068

Plummer, D. L., Stone, R. T., Powell, L., & Allison, J. (2016). Patterns of adult cross-racial friendships: A context for understanding contemporary race relations. *Cultural Diversity and Ethnic Minority Psychology, 22*(4), 479–94. https://doi.org/10.1037/cdp0000079

Policarpo, V. (2015). What is a friend? An exploratory typology of the meanings of friendship. *Social Sciences, 4*(1), 171–91. https://doi.org/10.3390/socsci4010171

Poole, S. M., Grier, S. A., Thomas, K. D., Sobande, F., Ekpo, A. E., Torres, L. T., Addington, L. A., Weekes-Laidlow, M., & Henderson, G. R. (2021). Operationalizing critical race theory in the marketplace. *Journal of Public Policy & Marketing, 40*(2), 126–42. https://doi.org/10.1177/0743915620964114

Pride, C. (2020, June 23). *5 things I want to tell my white friends.* Cup of Jo. https://cupofjo.com/2020/06/a-letter-to-my-white-friends/

Pun, R. (2020). Understanding the roles of public libraries and digital exclusion through critical race theory: An exploratory study of people of color in California affected by the digital divide and the pandemic. *Urban Library Journal, 26*(2), 1–27.

Qureshi, A., & Collazos, F. (2011). The intercultural and interracial therapeutic relationship: Challenges and recommendations. *International Review of Psychiatry, 23*(1), 10–19. https://doi.org/10.3109/09540261.2010.544643

Ramasubramanian, S., Sousa, A., & Gonlin, V. (2017). Facilitated dialogues to combat racism: A goal-based approach. *Journal of Applied Communication Research, 45*(5), 537–556. doi:10.1080/00909882.2017.138270

Race Forward. (n.d.). *What is racial equity.* https://www.raceforward.org/what-racial-equity-0

Ransom, J. (2020, July 6). Amy Cooper faces charges after calling police on Black bird-watcher. *New York Times.* https://www.nytimes.com/2020/07/06/nyregion/amy-cooper-false-report-charge.html

Ranzini, G., & Rosenbaum, J. E. (2020). It's a match (?): Tinder usage and attitudes toward interracial dating. *Communication Research Reports, 37*(1/2), 44–54. https://doi.org/10.1080/08824096.2020.1748001.

Rastogi, R., & Juvonen, J. (2019). Interminority friendships and intergroup attitudes across middle school: Quantity and stability of Black-Latino ties. *Journal of Youth & Adolescence, 48*(8), 1619–30. https://doi.org/10.1007/s10964-019-01044-9.

Reis, H. T., & Shaver, P. (1988). Intimacy as an interpersonal process. In S. W. Duck (Ed.), *Handbook of personal relationships* (pp. 367–89). Wiley.

Richardson, E., & Ragland, A. (2018). #StayWoke: The language and literacies of the #BlackLivesMatter movement. *Community Literacy Journal, 12*(2), 27–56. https://doi.org/10.25148/clj.12.2.009099

Robinson, M. A. (2017). Black bodies on the ground: Policing disparities in the African American community—an analysis of newsprint from January 1, 2015, through December 31, 2015. *Journal of Black Studies, 48*(6), 551–71. http://www.jstor.org/stable/44631324

Rodriguez, S. (2020, June 9). *Jack Dorsey says Twitter and square will honor Juneteenth—June 19—as a company holiday.* CNBC. https://www.cnbc.com/2020/06/09/jack-dorsey-twitter-square-to-honor-juneteenth-as-company-holiday.html

Rogers, R. A. (2006). From cultural exchange to transculturation: A review and reconceptualization of cultural appropriation. *Communication Theory, 16*(4), 474–503. https://doi.org/10.1111/j.1468-2885.2006.00277.x

Rosenthal, L., Deosaran, A., Young, D. L., & Starks, T. J. (2019). Relationship stigma and well-being among adults in interracial and same-sex relationships. *Journal of Social and Personal Relationships, 36*(11–12), 3408–28. https://doi.org/10.1177/0265407518822785

Rosenthal, L., Levy, S. R., & Moyer, A. (2011). Protestant work ethic's relation to intergroup and policy attitudes: A meta-analytic review. *European Journal of Social Psychology, 41*(7), 874–85. https://psycnet.apa.org/doi/10.1002/ejsp.832

Roy, R. N., James, A. G., & Brown, T. L. (2021). Racial/ethnic minority families. *Journal of Family and Economic Issues, 42*(1), 84–100. https://doi.org/10.1007/s10834-020-09712-w

Roy, R. N., James, A., Brown, T. L., Craft, A., & Mitchell, Y. (2020). Relationship satisfaction across the transition to parenthood among interracial couples: An integrative model. *Journal of Family Theory & Review, 12*(1), 41–53. https://doi.org/10.1111/jftr.12365

Rubel, F. (2020, September 11). *Racist language and origins I didn't always know.* JD Supra. https://www.jdsupra.com/legalnews/racist-language-and-origins-i-didn-t-35616/

Rubin, K., & Bowker, J. (2018). Friendships. In M. Bornstein (Ed.), *The SAGE Encyclopedia of Lifespan Human Development* (Vol. 1). SAGE. https://doi.org/10.4135/9781506307633.n339

Ruffin, A., & Lamar, L. (2022). *The world record book of racist stories.* Grand Central.

Rynes, S., & Rosen, B. (1995). A field survey of factors affecting the adoption and perceived success of diversity training. *Personnel Psychology, 48*, 247–70.

Sawyer, J., & Gampa, A. (2018). Implicit and explicit racial attitudes changed during Black Lives Matter. *Personality & Social Psychology Bulletin, 44*(7), 1039–59. https://doi.org/10.1177/0146167218757454

Scaramuzzo, P., Bartone, M. D., & Young, J. L. (2021). A conceptualization framework of allyship: Bidirectional allyship between Black heterosexual women and white gay males. *Cultural Studies ↔ Critical Methodologies, 21*(5), 381–93. https://doi.org/10.1177/15327086211035354

Shelton, J. N., Trail, T. E., West, T. V., & Bergsieker, H. B. (2010). From strangers to friends: The interpersonal process model of intimacy in developing interracial friendships. *Journal of Social and Personal Relationships, 27*(1), 71–90. https://doi.org/10.1177/0265407509346422

Shook, N. J., & Fazio, R. H. (2008). Interracial roommate relationships: An Experimental field test of the contact hypothesis. *Psychological Science, 19*(7), 717–23.

Shropshire, C. (2021, March 9). Friendships in Black & white. *Chicago Magazine.* https://www.chicagomag.com/chicago-magazine/march-2021/friendships-in-black-and-white/

Sisco, S. (2020). Race-conscious career development: Exploring self-preservation and coping strategies of Black professionals in corporate America. *Advances in Developing Human Resources, 22*(4), 419–36. https://doi.org/10.1177/1523422320948885

Smith, T. (2020, October 27). *"Dude, I'm done": When politics tears families and friendships apart.* https://www.npr.org/2020/10/27/928209548/dude-i-m-done-when-politics-tears-families-and-friendships-apart

Smith, W. A. (2004). Black faculty coping with racial battle fatigue: The campus racial climate in a post-civil rights era. In D. Cleveland (Ed.), *A long way to go: Conversations about race by African American faculty and graduate students* (pp.171–190). Peter Lang.

Smith, W. A., Yosso, T. J., & Solorzano, D. (2006). Challenging racial battle fatigue on historically white campuses: A critical race examination of race-related stress. In C. Stanley (Ed.), *Faculty of color teaching in predominantly white colleges and universities* (pp. 299–327). Anker. http://dx.doi.org/10.1163/ej.9789004203655.i-461.82

Smith-Jones, S. E., & Jones, J. (2022). Discovering your social justice gift amid the distraction of systemic racism. In S. J. Blithe & J. C. Bauer (Eds.), *Badass feminist politics: Exploring radical edges of feminist theory, communication, and activism* (pp. 82–87). Rutgers University Press.

Snyder, C. R. (2012). Racial socialization in cross-racial families. *Journal of Black Psychology, 38*(2), 228–53. https://doi.org/10.1177/0095798411416457

Sondel, B., Kretchmar, K., & Hadley Dunn, A. (2019). "Who do these people want teaching their children?" White saviorism, colorblind racism, and anti-Blackness in "no excuses" charter schools. *Urban Education, 57*(9), 1621–50. https://doi.org/10.1177/0042085919842618

Sonnemaker, T. (2020, June 13). *Facebook fired an employee who criticized a coworker on Twitter for not issuing a public statement supporting Black Lives Matter on a project they worked on.* Business Insider. https://www.businessinsider.com/facebook-fires-employee-who-protested-its-inaction-on-trump-tweets-2020-6

South African History Online. (n.d.). *Race and ethnicity in South Africa.* https://www.sahistory.org.za/article/race-and-ethnicity-south-africa

Sue, D. W., Capodilupo, C. M., Torino, G. C., Bucceri, J. M., Holder, A. M. B., Nadal, K. L., & Esquilin, M. M. (2007). Microaggressions in everyday life: Implications for clinical practice. *American Psychologist, 62*, 271–86. https://doi.org/10.1037/0003-066x.62.4.271

Sue, D. W., Alsaidi, S., Awad, M. N., Glaeser, E., Calle, X. Z., & Mendez, N. (2019). Disarming racial microaggressions: Microintervention strategies for targets, white allies, and bystanders. *American Psychologist, 74*(1), 128–42. http://dx.doi.org/10.1037/amp0000296

Sullivan, J. N., Eberhardt, J. L., & Roberts, S. O. (2021). Conversations about race in Black and white US families: Before and after George Floyd's death. *Proceedings of the National Academy of Sciences of the United States of America, 118*(38). https://doi.org/10.1073/pnas.2106366118

Terry, P. E. (2021). Allyship, antiracism and the strength of weak ties: A barber, a professor and an entrepreneur walk into a room. *American Journal of Health Promotion, 35*(2), 163–67.

Thompson, D. (2018, April 24). Oblivious person calls 911 on "suspicious" Black cop & other #LivingWhileBlack stories. *VIBE.* https://www.vibe.com/music/music-news/living-while-black-hashtag-stories-581533/

Ting-Toomey, S. (1993). Communicative resourcefulness: An identity negotiation theory. In R. L. Wiseman & J. Koester (Eds.), *Intercultural communication competence* (pp. 72–111). Sage.

Trail, T. E., Shelton, J. N., & West, T. V. (2009). Interracial roommate relationships: Negotiating daily interactions. *Personality and Social Psychology Bulletin, 35*(6), 671–84. https://doi.org/10.1177/0146167209332741

Trepany, C. (2020, June 6). "Law & Order: SVU" producer says George Floyd's death 'has to come up' in future episode. *USA Today.* https://www.usatoday.com/story/entertainment/tv/2020/06/05/law-order-svu-producer-george-floyd-has-come-up-show/3158480001/

Tropp, L. R. (2007). Perceived discrimination and interracial contact: Predicting interracial closeness among Black and white americans. *Social Psychology Quarterly, 70*(1), 70–81. https://doi.org/10.1177/019027250707000108

University of Southern California. (2021, October 26). *How to explain structural, institutional and systemic racism.* https://msw.usc.edu/mswusc-blog/how-to-explain-structural-institutional-and-systemic-racism/

Utt, J. (2013, November 8). So you call yourself an ally: 10 things all "allies" need to know. Everyday Feminism. https://everydayfeminism.com/2013/11/things-allies-need-to-know/

Vallejo, J. A. (2015). How class background affects Mexican Americans' experiences of subtle racism in the white-collar workplace. *Latino Studies, 13*(1), 69–87. https://doi.org/10.1057/lst.2014.70

van der Toorn, J., & Jost, J. T. (2014). Twenty years of system justification theory: Introduction to the special issue on "Ideology and system justification process." *Group Processes & Intergroup Relations, 17*(4), 413–19. https://doi.org/10.1177/1368430214531509

VanLear, C. A., Jr. (1987). The formation of social relationships: A longitudinal study of social penetration. *Human Communication Research, 13*(3), 299–322. https://doi.org/10.1111/j.1468-2958.1987.tb00107.x

VanLear, C. A., Koerner, A., & Allen, D. M. (2006). Relationship typologies. In A. L. Vangelisti & D. Perlman (Eds.), The Cambridge handbook of personal relationships (pp. 91–110). Cambridge University Press. https://doi.org/10.1017/CBO9780511606632.007

van Sterkenburg, J., & Knoppers, A. (2012). Sport as a contested racial/ethnic terrain: Processes of racialization in Dutch sport media and sport policy. *Journal of Multicultural Discourses, 7*(2), 119–36. https://doi.org/10.1080/17447143.2012.687001

Villarreal, D. (2020, November 16). Hate crimes under Trump surged nearly 20 percent says FBI report. *Newsweek*. https://www.newsweek.com/hate-crimes-under-trump-surged-nearly-20-percent-says-fbi-report-1547870

Vincenty, S. (2020, June 12). *Being "color blind" doesn't make you not racist—in fact, it can mean the opposite*. Oprah Daily. https://www.oprahdaily.com/life/relationships-love/a32824297/color-blind-myth-racism/

Wade, R. (2020, June 11). *Nike to recognize Juneteenth as an annual paid holiday*. Yahoo! Sports. https://sports.yahoo.com/nike-to-recognize-juneteenth-as-an-annual-paid-holiday-141219946.html

Waring, C. D. L., & Bardoloi, S. D. (2019). "I don't look like her": Race, resemblance, and relationships in multiracial families. *Sociological Perspectives, 62*(2), 149–66.

Waymer, D. (2021). Addressing disciplinary whiteness and racial justice advocacy in communication education. *Communication Education, 70*(1), 114–16. https://doi.org/10.1080/03634523.2020.1811362

Weaver, H., & Walsh, S. (2021, November 29). You can now support the Black LGBTQ+ community using your Sephora Points. *Elle*. https://www.yahoo.com/news/businesses-standing-support-black-lives-165900868.html?bcmt=1

White House. (2021). *Executive order on diversity, equity, inclusion, and accessibility in the federal workforce*. https://www.whitehouse.gov/briefing-room/presidential-actions/2021/06/25/executive-order-on-diversity-equity-inclusion-and-accessibility-in-the-federal-workforce/

Whitesides, J. (2017, February 7). *From disputes to a breakup: Wounds still raw after U.S. election*. Reuters. https://www.reuters.com/article/us-usa-trump-relationships-insight/from-disputes-to-a-breakup-wounds-still-raw-after-u-s-election-idUSKBN15M13L

Wiggins-Romesburg, C. A., & Githens, R. P. (2011). The psychology of diversity resistance: A psychological perspective for overcoming resistance to an organizational development issue. *Human Resource Development Review, 17*(2), 179–98. https://doi.org/10.1177/1534484318765843

Wiggins-Romesburg, C. A., & Githens, R. P. (2018). The psychology of diversity resistance and integration. *Development Review, 17*(2), 179–98. https://doi.org/10.1177/1534484318765843

Williams, S. (2020, June 30). PepsiCo Foods North America CEO: "In this new era, we must get comfortable being uncomfortable." *Dallas News*. https://www.dallasnews.com/fwddfw/2020/06/18/pepsico-foods-north-america-ceo-in-this-new-era-we-must-get-comfortable-being-uncomfortable/

Williamson, V., & Gelfland, I. (2019, August 14). *Trump and racism: What do the data say?* Brookings. https://www.brookings.edu/blog/fixgov/2019/08/14/trump-and-racism-what-do-the-data-say/

Willow, R. A. (2008). Lived experience of interracial dialogue on race: Proclivity to participate. *Journal of Multicultural Counseling and Development, 36*(1), 40.

Wolfe, B. (2021, February 25). Racial integrity laws (1924–1930). In *Encyclopedia Virginia*. https://encyclopediavirginia.org/entries/racial-integrity-laws-1924-1930

Wong, C., & Cho, G. E. (2005). Two-headed coins or Kandinskys: White racial identification. *Political Psychology, 26*(5), 699–720. https://doi.org/10.1111/j.1467-9221.2005.00440.x

Wood, J. T. (2005). Feminist standpoint theory and muted group theory: Commonalities and divergences. *Women and Language, 28*(2), 61–64.

Wu, C. S., Lee, S. Y., Zhou, X., Kim, J., Lee, H., & Lee, R. M. (2020). Hidden among the hidden: Transracially adopted Korean American adults raising multiracial children. *Developmental Psychology, 56*(8), 1431–45. https://doi.org/10.1037/dev0000881

Wu, M.-H. (2021). A critical examination of Asian students' interracial and interethnic friendships at a multiracial urban school. *Urban Education, 56*(3), 424–50. https://doi.org/10.1177/0042085917690206.

Wynne, K. (2020, July 25). *Black woman says white woman had police called on her family at Fort Lauderdale Pool*. NBC 6 South Florida. https://www.nbcmiami.com/news/local/black-woman-says-white-woman-called-police-on-her-family-at-fort-lauderdale-pool/2266350/

Yep, K. (2020, June 13). *Disney releases video in support of Black Lives Matter*. Inside the Magic. https://insidethemagic.net/2020/06/disney-video-black-lives-matter-ky1/

Yudell, M. (1971). A short history of the race concept. In S. Krimsky & K. Sloan (Eds.), *Race and the genetic revolution: Science, myth, and culture* (pp. 13–30). Columbia University Press.

Zhang, C. (2021). Media framing of color-blind racism: A content analysis of the Charlottesville rally. *Race Social Problems, 13*, 330–41. https://doi.org/10.1007/s12552-021-09321-8

Zhou, L. (2020, June 3). *The trope of "outside agitators" at protests, explained*. Vox. https://www.vox.com/2020/6/3/21275720/george-floyd-protests-outside-agitators-ferguson-civil-rights-movement

Index

2016 U.S. presidential election, 6, 42–43

Abbott, B., 72, 127, 130–132
activism, 3, 6, 8, 22, 119, 136; advocate-mentorship and, 35–36, 40; allyship and, 15, 18–19, 101; Black Lives Matter movement, 9, 15, 57, 99–100; microaggressions and, 133–134; online, 15, 51, 107; scholarship as, 26, 60, 67. *See also* protests
adultification, 44
advocate-mentorship, 12–13, 35–36, 40
Afifi, W. A., 45, 53, 56
Agyeman, J., 39
Ahmed, R., 38
All Lives Matter, 57
Allport, Gordon, 10
allyship, 25–26, 42, 58, 108, 112, 122; advocate-mentorship and, 12–13, 35–36, 40; essentials of, 18–19, 22. *See also* performative allyship
Andrews, Kehinde, 114
antimiscegenation laws, 62, 80–82, 89, 93–95
applied communication research (ACR), 60
Asian American and Pacific Islanders (AAPI), increase in hate crimes against, 9, 17, 25, 47–48, 101

Ayón, C., 125
Azu, Crystal, 8

Banaji, M. R., 49
Bandura, A., 71
Banks, Marc, 15
Bates, B. R., 38
Belk, Judy, 57–58
Bernier, Francis, 31
Biden, Joe, 3, 111
Black Aziz, 107
Black Lives Matter (BLM), 9, 57, 99–100; #BlackLivesMatter, 15
Blackout Tuesday campaign, 15
Blue Lives Matter, 57, 99–100
Blumenbach, Johann Friedrich, 31, 51, 61–62
Bonilla-Silva, E., 63
"bootstrap" mentality, 43, 63
Bourabain, D., 109
Brookings Institution, 6, 112
Brown, E., 12
Bryant, Carolyn, 52

Caughlin, J. P., 48
Chauvin, Derek, 1–2
Chingaipe, S., 60
Clinton, Hillary, 43
Collazos, F., 11

colonialism, 6, 31–32, 80–81, 111
colorblind mentality, 3, 10, 16, 22, 115; in families, 49, 53–55, 125; institutional racism and, 30–32; interracial friendships and, 59, 63, 66
communication in families, 19–20; anti-racist recommendations for, 56; and socialization, 12–13, 41–44, 52–55, 60, 71–72, 90, 96, 124–126; theories of, 46–49; "the talk," 44–52, 55–56, 124, 136
communication in interracial friendships, 11, 14, 21, 47–48, 63–64, 76–77; navigating ingroup communication, 28–29; "one friend rule," 13, 68–69; relational inventory and, 57–58, 60, 65–66; five steps of, 67–75; stigma and, 59–62, 82
communication in interracial romantic relationships (IRRs), 19, 21, 59, 73, 84, 97; antimiscegenation laws and, 80–82, 89, 93–95; coping strategies and, 92–94, 96; racial identity development and, 91–92; Trickle-Down Theory and, 82–83, 85–90, 95
communication in the workplace, 16–17, 21, 72, 99–101, 106–109; advocate-mentorship and, 35–36; five forms of racism and, 112–114; need for diversity and, 115–116; racial awareness in institutions and, 102–105; responses to injustice and, 110–112
communication privacy management theory (CPM), 45, 48–49
communication studies, 38–39, 45, 49, 59; interpersonal subfield of, 88; social justice and, 30, 60, 67, 74–75, 130
confirmation bias, 89–90
Confronting Racial Microaggressions Model (CRaMM), 72–73, 127–132, 136
COVID-19 pandemic, 4, 8–9, 101; racial inequity and, 14, 17–18, 57

critical race theory (CRT), 29, 72–73; definition, 26, 30
Crowley, C., 14
cultural appropriation, 29, 33
cultural competence, 38–39, 116

Dastagir, A., 15
Davies, K., 69, 75
Delgado, R., 26
Desormes, Ingrid, 16
de Souza Briggs, X., 112
difficult conversations, 27, 42–43, 64–65, 97; barriers to, 10–17, 34, 56; examples of, 28, 35, 47–48, 57–58, 127–128; initiated after murder of George Floyd, 4–5, 7–8, 55, 57; necessity of, 9, 18–20, 22, 40, 49–50, 136; race taboo among white people and, 44–46, 48–49, 52–53, 132–133; recommendations for, 56, 122–125, 128–130. *See also* "the talk"
disenfranchisement, 9, 25–26, 56, 95
diversity, equity, and inclusion (DEI) initiatives, 16–17, 21, 73, 76, 100–105, 109–116
Docan-Morgan, S., 48, 53–54
double consciousness, 29, 63, 70, 91, 117–118, 120
Du Bois, W. E. B., 63, 91, 117–118, 120

emotionality, 14, 34–35, 73, 75, 127–128
Erickson, J. S., 39
eugenics, 81, 84–85
Everyday Feminism (Utt), 19

families. *See* communication in families
Fazio, R. H., 10
Ferentz, Kirk, 15, 102
Floyd, George, 1–5, 7–8, 55, 57; racial unrest after murder of, 15, 17, 42, 49, 80, 94–95, 99, 111
Foeman, A. K., 93–94
Foucault, Michel, 108
Frazier, Darnella, 2–3

Frey, L. R., 60

Galanes, G., 20
Gampa, A., 100
gender privilege, 32, 51, 91; in the workplace, 103, 107, 109–111
Githens, R. P., 103
global citizenship, 18–19, 22, 27–28, 71–72, 95, 133; activism and, 7–8, 99, 136; cultural sensitivity and, 33–35; definition, 5
Great Awokening of 2020, 6–7, 9, 19, 22, 38–40. *See also* protests
Grothaus, T., 12
Guerrero, L. K., 45, 53, 56
Guterres, Antonio, 17
gypped (slur), 34–35

Harris, Tina M., 14, 34–36, 41, 72, 127, 130, 132; "I Can't Breathe," 1
Hasford, J., 108
hate crimes, 5–6; against Asian American and Pacific Islanders (AAPI), 9, 17, 25, 47–48, 101
Herda, D., 10–11
Hitler, Adolf, 85
Holoien, D. S., 11
Hudson, T. D., 75–76

"I Can't Breathe" (Harris), 1
institutional racism, 3–4, 8–9, 18, 22, 106, 113–114; challenges to, 36; colorblind mentality and, 31–32; considerations for BIPOC, 122; considerations for white allies, 122–124; critical race theory (CRT) and, 30; difficult conversations and, 19; enslavement ideology and, 59, 61, 79–80; societal privilege and, 32–33, 111. *See also* macroaggressions; structural racism
insurrection at U.S. Capitol (2021), 6
intentionality, 13, 39, 61, 70, 74–76, 107, 117; colorblindness and, 16, 53, 125; Confronting Racial Microaggressions Model and, 127–132; definition, 34–35; education as important for, 26–27, 30, 40; positionality and, 119–124; racial future and, 132–134; racial past and, 124–126; racial present and, 126–132; roadmap (RaIR), 22, 118–119, 121, 124–126, 132, 134–136
internalized gaze, 108
interracial friendships. *See* communication in interracial friendships
interracial romantic relationships (IRRs). *See* communication in interracial romantic relationships (IRRs)

Jackson, J., 33
Jackson, Jesse, 6
Jim Crow laws, 57, 59–62, 65–66, 69, 80–82. *See also* antimiscegenation laws; segregation
Jost, J. T., 49
Juneteenth, 58, 100
Juvonen, J., 73

Knoppers, A., 31

Lee, C. N., 35–36
Lemay, E. P., Jr., 90
#LivingWhileBlack, 107
Loving v. Virginia, 80–81, 94
Lu, D., 106

macroaggressions, 36–37, 113, 118, 120. *See also* institutional racism; structural racism; systemic racism
macroculture, 29, 31, 83, 86, 91, 106, 113, 126
Manifest Destiny, 96, 110
Maslow's hierarchy of needs, 43
McGahey, R. M., 112
McKenzie, Mia, 19
Michele, Lea, 15

microaggressions, 10–12, 15, 107, 118; definition, 36–37; responding to, 72–73, 127–132
Miller, Christie, 16
Mills, Charles, 54
Minniear, M., 124–125
Moffitt, K., 14
Munn, C. W., 13–14

NAACP, 15
Nance, T., 93–94
Norander, S., 20
n-word (slur), 28, 127–128

"one friend rule," 13, 68–69
Orbe, M. P., 34, 41
Oxfam, 5

Padron Eberline, A. L., 125
pandemics, 9, 14, 57; anti-other rhetoric and, 17–18; COVID-19, 4, 8, 17–18, 101
performative allyship, 14–15, 42; in organizations, 73, 100–102, 109–110; in personal relationships, 14–15, 40, 68, 74, 122, 124
Petronio, S., 48
Pierce, Chester M., 36
police brutality, 4, 13, 15, 58, 74, 114, 120; colorblind mentality and, 32; debates about, 57, 64; family communication about, 42, 44, 46, 50–51; heightened risk for BIPOC, 44, 50, 80, 95; murder of George Floyd and, 1–3, 7–8, 17; police departments and, 99–101; white awareness of, 39–40
police reform bill (U.S. H. 4860), 25
Population Registration Act No. 30 of 1950 (South Africa), 85
positionality, 3, 51, 71, 102, 135; intentionality and, 119–124; racial location and, 37–38
postracial society myth, 57, 83
Pride, Christine, 57–58

protests, 2–3, 17, 25, 57, 80; Great Awokening of 2020, 6–7, 9, 19, 22, 38–40; by medical professionals, 8–9; "outside agitators," 42; performative responses and, 15, 74, 100–101, 110–111. *See also* activism

Qureshi, A., 11

racial battle fatigue (RBF), 2, 122, 131–132
Racial Integrity Act of 1924 (U.S.), 81
Racial Intentionality Roadmap (RaIR), 21–22, 118–119, 121, 124–126, 132, 134–136
racial profiling, 44–47, 50, 64
racial spokesperson expectation, 15–18, 58, 105
Rastogi, R., 73
relational inventory, 21, 57–58, 60, 65–70, 126; assessing contributions to structural segregation, 72–73; assessing ideological indoctrination, 71–72; committing to racial justice through relationships, 74–75; identifying essential qualities for interracial friendships, 75–76

savior complex, 35
Sawyer, J., 100
segregation, 59, 61, 65, 67, 72–73, 96, 103
Shook, N. J., 10
Shue, C. K., 125
slavery, 28, 69, 107, 110, 117; abolition of, 59, 61, 100; forced marriage metaphor and, 79–80
slurs, racial, 28, 34–35, 113, 127–128
Smith, W. A., 131
Snyder, C. R., 53–54
social capital, 13
social learning theory, 71
social media, 4, 14, 80; activism, 15, 51, 100, 107; conversations about racism and, 6, 8, 17, 30, 43, 57, 64, 67

societal privilege, 29, 31–33, 38, 40, 135. *See also* white privilege
Soliz, J., 124–125
South Africa, 85
Stefancic, J., 26
structural racism, 31–32, 99; segregation, 59, 61, 65, 67, 72–73, 96; workplace communication and, 103–106, 111, 113–115, 117–118. *See also* institutional racism; systemic racism
Sue, Derald, 36–37
Sullivan, J. N., 49–50, 53
systemic racism, 4, 6, 8–9, 15, 18–23; family communication and, 43, 45, 48–49, 51; intentionality and, 120–121, 123–124, 126, 130, 134–135; interracial friendships and, 57, 59–60, 63–64, 76; interracial romantic relationships and, 86, 91, 94–97; shared vocabulary and, 25–29, 31–32, 36–38; workplace communication and, 100–104, 107, 110–111, 113–114. *See also* institutional racism; structural racism
system justification theory, 45, 47–49
systems theory, 45–46, 48

"the talk," 124, 136; avoidance by white families, 49, 50–51, 53, 55–56; experiences with racism and, 49–52; necessity of, 44–49; recommendations for families, 56
Taylor, Breonna, 3, 15, 42, 55, 58, 99
Teneva, N., 90
Till, Emmett, 52
Title IX Educational Amendment (U.S.), 25–26
tokenism, 12–13, 103
Trail, T. E., 12
transgender people, 32
transracial families, 46, 48, 53–54
Trickle-Down Theory (TDT), 21, 82–83, 85–90, 95
Tropp, L. R., 11

Trump, Donald J., 5–6, 26, 42, 101

U.K. Commission on Race and Ethnic Disparities (2021), 113–114
U.S. Executive Order (EO) 13985, 25, 111
U.S. House Bill 4860, 25
U.S. House Bill 5018, 111
U.S. Senate Bill 2723, 111
Utt, Jamie: Everyday Feminism, 19

van Sterkenburg, J., 31
vocabulary, shared, 20, 25–27, 29, 120; categories for understanding racism, 28; of external identity expression, 38–39; of institutional racism, 30–33; intentionality and, 39–40; of internal identity reflection, 37–38; of outgroup consciousness, 34–37

Washington, Kerry, 3
Waymer, D., 74–75
#WhileBlack, 51
white guilt, 5, 31, 48, 91, 120, 123, 130
White House Office of Management and Budget, 111
white privilege, 5–6, 22, 120, 123, 132–133; definition, 45; family communication and, 44–45, 48–51, 55–56, 125; interracial friendships and, 63–64, 70, 72, 76; interracial romantic relationships and, 80–82, 95–96; Jim Crow laws and, 61–62; in organizations, 106–107, 109–111; racial identity and, 115, 117–118; racial location and, 37–38; societal privilege and, 29, 31–32, 36, 40, 43–45, 135. *See also* colorblind mentality
white supremacism, 6, 17, 31, 81, 85, 88, 111
Wiggins-Romesburg, C. A., 103
woke mentality, 57, 102, 135; Great Awokening of 2020, 6–7, 9, 19, 22, 38–40

About the Author

Tina M. Harris is the Manship-Maynard Endowed Chair of Race, Media, and Cultural Literacy in the Manship School of Mass Communication at Louisiana State University. She is the first African American female to be named a Distinguished Scholar of the National Communication Association for "a lifetime of scholarly achievement in the study of human communication." Her primary research interest is interracial communication, with specific foci on interpersonal communication, critical communication pedagogy, race and identity, diversity and media representations, racial social justice, mentoring, and racial reconciliation, among others. She is a well-published and very active senior scholar with numerous accolades and awards for her long-standing history of making significant contributions to her discipline, university, and department in teaching, research, and service.

www.ingramcontent.com/pod-product-compliance
Lightning Source LLC
Chambersburg PA
CBHW050907300426
44111CB00010B/1425